CECIL BEATON:
Memoirs of the 40's

Drawing of Cecil Beaton, by Pavel Tchelitchew

CECIL BEATON:
Memoirs of the 40's

by Cecil Beaton

McGRAW-HILL BOOK COMPANY

New York • St. Louis • San Francisco
Düsseldorf • Mexico • Toronto

Book design by Elaine Gongora

123456789HABP79876543
This book was set in Caledo by University Graphics, Inc.

Library of Congress Cataloging in Publication Data

Beaton, Cecil Walter Hardy, date
  Cecil Beaton: memoirs of the 40's.

  London ed. (Weidenfeld & Nicholson) has title:
The happy years.
  I. Title. II. Title: Memoirs of the 40's.
TR140.B4A28 1972b 779'.092'4 [B] 72-5857
ISBN 0-07-004225-X

CONTENTS

PREFACE

Someone once said, "I always mistrust people who keep diaries." I started this literary vice just after the First World War, when I was still at Harrow School. My diary notes were mostly about expeditions with art class to paint barnyards in neighboring villages. It was at Cambridge University that I poured out my heart on paper in earnest. I had little else to do. I was a bewildered and excessively shy undergraduate. The recorded thoughts were trivial in the extreme. So it was that I began the habit of a lifetime.

Was it out of boredom, loneliness, frustration, the need for self-assertion? Or was it the same obscure motive that has impelled me to take snapshots all my life? Even as a child I felt haunted by a sense of the ephemeral. And when I grew up, *carpe diem* became my watchword. I used up thousands of rolls of film, wrote hundreds of thousands of words in a futile attempt to preserve the fleeting moment like a fly in amber.

My diaries of the twenties reveal a pathetic young man, inordinately self-conscious, snobbish and frustrated without any particular gift but an oversize desire to break away from the ranks of anonymity and be someone.

But what were my talents? Since childhood my chief interest had been the theatre, and if I possessed any measure of assurance I might have become an actor.

It was as an amateur maker of snapshots, imitating the commercial photographers of stage personalities, that I took my first steps into the world behind the stage door. By degrees my photography became more experimental—even daring—and it took me into more intellectual worlds. My pictures of the poetess Edith Sitwell lying like a figure on a medieval tomb launched me on my first career. An exhibition of my photographs and watercolors drew crowds to the opening day in Bond Street in spite of a thick London fog.

Then why, at this busy and exciting time in London when new vistas were opening for me every week, did I want to discover a whole new world? When I was a child, it had seemed to me that my father, a lumber merchant, was always in the throes of leaving for, or returning from, business trips to the United States. Always a reticent man, he related little of his experiences in this land that from his shiny sepia snapshots seemed to be all dollars and honey. He also produced souvenirs of his visits to the New York Theatre with pictures of the exquisite Marie Doro, Laurette Taylor of the surprised crescent eyebrows, and Hazel Dawn of the "Pink Lady." They first whetted my appetite to see Broadway for myself. Thus it was that as a stranger I arrived in New York armed with fifty pounds, a No. 3A pocket folding Kodak, and a portfolio of photographs and caricatures of English celebrities.

My journal of that period describes how Wall Street was at the height of the boom that was soon to deflate. Everyone seemed to be in a frenzy of delighted activity. I was a penniless foreigner. But I was lucky in my friends; they helped me to make a start. Happily, most of them are as steadfast today.

Naturally all the Fifty-seventh Street picture galleries had long since organized their season's showing, but when Elsie de Wolfe, the first woman to make a brilliant career as an interior decorator, offered me her boiseried showrooms for an exhibition, I accepted with gratitude. Even quite a few of my Harrow School sketches were sold, and Condé Nast gave me a contract to work for *Vanity Fair* and *Vogue*. I had learned to assume a certain self-confidence even though I was still full of tiresome misgivings. In spite of my "making it difficult for people to like me" (the phrase used by Lynn Fontanne), a group of delightful and witty people headed by Anita Loos and Addison Mizner, the architect, gave me the moral support I needed, and it was with them that I had my first glimpses of Florida and California.

At this stage my state of mind changed from my accustomed self-pity at not having become the successful designer I wished to be, to high elation. It seems strange to me today that Hollywood should have filled me with such euphoria. Yet no film fan can have been happier than I as I met the stars of the late twenties. Invitations were accepted to Pickfair and to the Hearst ranch. In New York the tempo did not slacken. Although seldom to bed before dawn, I managed to sustain a heavy schedule of work for Condé Nast and Frank Crowninshield.

During the war, the Ministry of Information sent me to all parts of England and to the battle fronts in Libya, Egypt, Burma, India, and China as a journalist and photographer. I was able to write about new people and new places.

The scribbled pages of my notebooks then tell of a return to peacetime existence. And at last my own career seemed to take on the life that I had always wanted, not only as a photographer but as a designer for theatre and films. These phoenix years were even more exciting for me than those that had preceded the war.

While I was writing about these early personal experiences, it never occurred to me that they would one day be published, that they might have some public interest as a piece of private period history. From a morass of largely uninteresting undergrowth I found some shoots that seemed to have survived the passage of time. These I was urged to publish.

It isn't easy to make public the private record of the years. Of all forms of writing, diaries are the most personal; their publication cannot but invoke question or criticism. There is, of course, the precedent of other diarists who have published intimate journals in their own lifetime. But they have been men of letters, adventurers, generals, or statesmen. My province is more frivolous, as my critics never cease to remind me. But my writings are honest and frank, and not doctored for publication.

When the time came for this diary to be published, I did not realize that the years would so quickly catch up with me. Although the contents were of things past, some of the passages seemed still too immediate. I delayed publication. Then I asked myself, was I waiting for my own death or the demise of certain friends before going further into print?

Doubtless some who appear in this volume may consider that these happenings of twenty-five years ago are still not appropriate for print. If I have offended any friends I hope they will believe that it was far from my wish to do so. Least of all have I wanted to cause any pain to one who occupied my thoughts (and the bulk of my diary) in the period just after the war. If I had omitted her from this present volume, it would denigrate a relationship that was, for ten years, meaningful and pertinent, and reduce it to the level of an episode. Moreover, it would not be natural or justifiable to myself—and still less to her—if I effaced my recollections of this remarkable woman.

Cecil Beaton

Cecil Beaton at Reddish House in the village of Broadchalke in Wiltshire, England

Mrs. Beaton, the author's mother, photographed during her visit to New York

Above, Cecil Beaton as Cecil Graham in the New York production of *Lady Windermere's Fan*. Below, working on the ballet *Les Sirenes* for Covent Garden. Left to right: Cecil Beaton, Frederick Ashton, and Lord Berners at the latter's house, Faringdon, in Oxfordshire, England

Above, corner of Cecil Beaton's apartment in the Plaza Hotel in New York
Left, in the British Embassy in Paris; left to right: Louise de Vilmorin,
Vivien Leigh, Cecil Beaton, Laurence Oliver

Part 1
LONDON
and PARIS
1944–45

The flying bombs and those beastly V2.s, exploding from out of nowhere, have created new havoc in London since I had left for the Far East nearly a year ago: I had been sent there by the Ministry of Information and Royal Air Force to write and to take photographs. After travelling home via the States and enjoying for a spell the glitter of New York life, I was stunned to see such wreckage to poor inoffensive streets which contain no more important a target than the pub at the crossroads. Miles of pathetic little dwellings have become nothing but black windowless façades. Old, torn posters hang from scabrous walls, the leaves on trees have changed to yellow under a thick coating of cement powder. Nothing has been given a wash or a lick of paint. Everything's so shabby and sordid. The poverty displayed in shop windows—those that still have glass in them—reminds me of Moscow in 1935 and is just as depressing.

After celebrating the liberation of Paris in New York I thought that things might be looking up a bit everywhere. But no. War in England is more total than ever, hardships are always increasing. People look terribly tired and tend to be touchy and quarrelsome about small things.

Yet, in spite of all the horror and squalor, London has added beauty. In its unaccustomed isolation above the wastes of rubble, St. Paul's is seen standing to supreme advantage, particularly splendid at full moon. The moon in the blackout, with no other light but the stars to vie with, makes an eighteenth-century engraving of our streets. St. James's Park, without its Victorian iron railings, has become positively sylvan.

Even in the center of the town there are aspects of rural life. While the buses roar along Oxford Street the gentler sounds of hens and ducks can be heard among the ruins of nearby Berners

Street. There are pigs sleeping peacefully in improvised sties in the craters where seeds that have been buried for three hundred years have propagated themselves and make a display of purple milkwort and willow herb. The vicar of St. James's, Piccadilly, counted twenty-three different varieties of wild plant behind his bombed altar.

Each evening at nine, everyone stops — as for the muezzin call to prayer in Mohammedan countries — for the evening news. It is almost an offense to telephone at the hour of the BBC bulletins, and as you walk along the pavements the announcer's voice echoes through all open windows. Every language is spoken on the pavements, and in some parts the English voice is seldom heard. Baseball crowds cheer in Hyde Park while in the long twilight of double summer time Piccadilly Circus is transformed by the khaki figures squatting along the wall of sandbags around Eros's statue into the sleepy Southland from which many of these raw recruits have come.

_____*Ministry of Information/October*

Hugh Francis of the Ministry of Information still finds me odd "propaganda" jobs. These take me to Jarrow, Nottingham or Bradford. Here my Rolleiflex is aimed at the continuing war effort: at unphotogenic scientists in laboratories, at weathermen foretelling the future or measuring the invisible sun. But now that the end of war is in sight, at any rate on the European horizon, my particular contributions to the national cause seem more ineffectual than ever. My enthusiasm on these expeditions is becoming very forced, and I notice all the more keenly the pinpricks: trains are frigid, the food unappetizing — surely even for animals — and the discomfort and tyranny inflicted on the unfortunate guest of the average English hotel are past being a wry joke.

Now, however, Francis has given me a thrilling assignment — to organize an exhibition of photographs to show the people of France what happened to England during the last four years. Under the German occupation, the French have naturally seen nothing of this. As well as the scenes from the battlefronts the pictures at home — the bombing of London, Coventry, and of so much of our heritage — will come as a revelation. My difficulty is in sifting from the hundreds of thousands of pictures only a few hundred. So many service and press photographers have produced really great historic documents.

_____ *Assignment to France*/*October 28th*

The airplane moved through the cotton-wool mist above compact country houses with formal, stiff gardens and turreted farm buildings; all the architecture appeared taller in proportion than at home. Some spidery poplars and other trees with feathery topknots passed below in rows, and rivers were winding intricately. This was unmistakably the familiar, yet almost forgotten, landscape of France.

_____ *Paris Regained*/*British Embassy, Paris*

At Le Bourget a quick glance was enough to show how much had changed: airport completely destroyed yet nearby dwellings intact; roads almost empty; no private cars, no trams; families with their belongings crowded on the tops of lorries were being given lifts by the Americans. Lucky break for me to hitch a ride into Paris with the King's Messenger. King's Messengers are men entrusted with letters and documents belonging to the Crown that are too important to be handled by public communication. These Messengers are sent throughout the world and must never allow their dispatch cases out of their sight for one instant. This most auspicious and noble title belongs to a small, querulous man whose life, to me, still unnerved as a result of that Dakota crash and hating every subsequent sortie into the air, would be a purgatory of almost unending fright. The crash was an experience that has affected me ever since, for soon after takeoff on an icy night at Land's End in Cornwall, the plane carrying us to India crashed in flames on the edge of the sea cliffs. I found myself precipitated to the far end of the burning fuselage but incapable of making any effort to save myself until told in no uncertain terms not just to lie there but to jump. I survived, but for some time my nerves were shattered. It was an ordeal to take another plane three nights later to Delhi, but I felt that since my miraculous escape the odds must, at least for a while, be in favor of my having no further mishaps in the air. This, in fact, was not to be the case, and my dislike of flying has remained.

As we neared Paris, the King's Messenger remarked on the many more signs of life than on previous visits: markets had opened which were not there a week ago. Confectioners were empty, but bakeries' shop windows were prettily dressed. Towards the heart of the city many bicycles. I looked for signs in faces of their domination by the Hun, but everyone appeared as before — the regard in eyes as clear and determined, showing no softening by suffering. In fact, people appeared just as ugly as equivalent English crowds would be.

When France was occupied Duff Cooper was the British Representative to the Free French in Algiers. He has now been made our Ambassador in Paris, and Diana, of the love-in-the-mist eyes, samite, wonderful complexion, and glorious goatish profile, is suddenly cast in the role of Ambassadress. The youngest daughter of the eighth Duke of Rutland, Lady Diana Manners, was said to have been a contender for the hand of the Prince of Wales, but her choice fell on a particularly intelligent but unknown young man, Duff Cooper, who was a friend of Winston Churchill's. Duff Cooper was to have a long and dazzling political career that included serving as First Lord of the Admiralty, as Minister of Information, and now in this most important diplomatic post. Lady Diana was for many years renowned as England's greatest beauty, and her stage appearances in aid of charity made her known to a wide public. Max Reinhardt, the Austrian impresario, prevailed upon her to become the Madonna, and alternatively the nun, in his production of *The Miracle.*

Diana, recently arrived in Paris and reluctant, especially after the Arab picnic existence that she loves, to take on the burden of a formal life, wanted me to encourage her with humanizing the grandeur of the Embassy in the Rue Faubourg St. Honoré. Hurrying after her in her old velveteen pants, cotton vest, and Algerian peasant's straw hat down the enfilades of Pauline Borghese's gilded suites, the tempo of existence accelerated. In a flash she has spread a warmth of character to these frigid rooms of state. By scattering her books and candlesticks, by hanging a favorite Victorian picture on a red cord over a mirror, by propping silhouettes, wax mask, and family photographs along a bookshelf, she has already transformed the place. And not only in matters of appearance is her love for the impromptu displayed. The rate of exchange is so crippling for the English in France that shopping is out of the question. Instead she has given enormous amusement to her staff and to herself by using the household stores for barter —exchanging soap, candles or whisky in payment for ice machines, typewriters or clothes.

This afternoon she drove me to the outskirts of Paris in her toy car. When Diana appears there is no slacking. One is galvanized into activity and sharpening one's wits. She injects life and entertainment into every situation. To go on an expedition with her is always a memorable event, and anyone she meets on the way is likely to remember it also.

Diana combines, in an unique way, a gift for using her friends, and the amenities they have to offer, with a lack of selfishness. Someone has a car at the door: "Then can't you take us round to the garage to fetch my Simca which is being repaired?" The torrential flow of interesting conversation is not interrupted by any nonsense such as: "You sit in the back—I'll be here." Her instructions are given in shorthand or semaphore. No delays brooked at the garage. As she walks down the cobbled ramp she shouts: "Hullo, hullo, hullo!" commanding immediate attention. "You've not been able to mend the car? Well, we can't wait. Here's something for the poor box. I love this car," she says as we rush off without horn or brakes. "On the bat's back I do fly. You creep in and out of all the traffic—nowhere you can't go!" We dart under the mudguards of oncoming motor buses. The cross-looking man of whom she asks the way is surprised, stimulated, then amused. Likewise the *gendarme,* who at first is outraged that anyone should have the impertinence to park in such a place, becomes a friend. Every expedition with Diana at the wheel has its own particular charm and excitement, for she makes her own rules of the road. A natural law-breaker, she experiments without a qualm and thinks nothing of squeezing past a line of traffic between curb and pavement as part of her own code of right of way. Today's excursion was to visit a suburban, but friendly, dentist who would sell a particle of his gold supply, strictly allocated for gold teeth, in order to mend a friend's ring.

Diana is a card, a flamboyant eccentric, and a professional extrovert in that the performance she gives is always her best. But one must not forget that she is fundamentally a serious and noble character whose whole reason for existing is her love of Duff. Every thought is of him. Everything she does is for his sake, her every action for his benefit.

When first she met and loved this comparatively unknown young man, and even faced the opposition of her beloved mother in order to marry him, she recognized his extraordinary qualities, and the world has proven her right. Duff is regarded by many who have a better knowledge of his potential than I do, as one of the most remarkable men of his generation; he has political foresight, courage and wisdom that are unique. Diana knows this and is all the time helping to make others see that behind Duff's shyness there is a force that could make him worthy of leading the country.

It was one of the most brilliant autumn days—a few leaves falling already, skies periwinkle blue with dazzling white clouds gladdening the spirit. I had forgotten how beautiful Paris is. The cobble streets and silvery façades, the proportions of almost every building, give an effect of consummate urban grace. Everywhere there seem to be lacy arabesques of ironwork balconies and statues luxuriously allotted in rows or in crescents. The clotted *"patisserie"* on walls and ceiling make the most modest cake shop all the more inviting: every man in a beret in the street, every woman carrying a long loaf, seems to possess a natural reverence for *"l'aesthétique."*

As we drive in the wrong direction down a one-way street Diana, oblivious to the shouts, talks about de Gaulle. In answer to Duff's congratulations on the day he was recognized as head of the French Republic the General said: *"Oh, ça finira jamais!"* Diana admits that in Algiers she found it agony to converse with the General. "After childhood—which never fails—there's nothing else."

_____ *The British Embassy's Guests*/Sunday, *October 29th*

Duff, calm and immaculate, appeared by air from London. Diana, ravaged with suspense until his arrival, was then beatified with joy—also at the arrival of the Aubusson carpets from her old home. They look well in these ornate, loftily gilded rooms.

At drinks time a few old cronies assembled in *le salon vert* to reforge severed links of friendship. Although Diana takes her own unconventionality with her wherever she goes, awe of the British Embassy is obviously paramount in the minds of the Parisians. As they mounted the imposing staircase the men, in black coats and striped trousers, were excessively formal, bowing from the waist and kissing hands. All seemed to have a conservative, even ceremonial, attitude that made one realize how much more relaxed and at ease would be their equivalents in London. Little wonder that an elderly Frenchman, arriving unexpectedly early, was surprised when Diana, unbuttoning her trousers to change into a skirt, asked him point blank: "And what can I do for you?"

The women were a curiously dressed bunch in a fashion that struck the unaccustomed eye as strangely ugly—wide, baseball players' shoulders, Düreresque headgear, suspiciously like domestic plumbing, made of felt and velvet, and heavy sandal-clogs which gave the wearers an added six inches in height but an ungainly, plodding walk. Unlike their austerity-abiding counterparts in England these women moved in an aura of perfume. Women and men alike were all avid for the unaccustomed bounty, now presented on a marble-topped table, of chippolata sausages, *petits fours* and cheese biscuits garnered from the NAAFI stores. "What we have suffered!" they exclaimed, prodding their sausages with little picks.

Sad were the ravages of time on some that I had known before. Countess Jean de Polignac, the fair and fortunate Marie-Blanche, a famed musical hostess, had turned into a tearful little old lady. Her mother, Madame Lanvin, the great dressmaker, whose picture dresses had made her a fortune, had today designed for her daughter a Salvation Army bonnet and widow's weeds. Baba Lucinge, daughter of the wonderfully eccentric and scarlet-haired Baroness d'Erlanger, now married to the noble and handsome Prince Jean-Louis (Johnnie) Lucinge, was the first to bring into fashion the exotic, simian grace of the jungle and thereby created an astonishing effect of originality and allure. Today, however, she had changed her type and appeared as a conventionally well-dressed, middle-aged mother. Baba nervously told of the petty humiliations that the Germans invented in an increasing determination to show themselves masters—how the French were made to walk in the streets while the sidewalks were roped off exclusively for the Krauts. The soldiers billeted next door to her enraged her so much that, at various times, she threw twenty of her Staffordshire china poodles at them. I noticed with chagrin an habitual shrugging of her head and a *tic nerveuse,* the result of a recent motor-bicycle accident.[1] However, Drian, the painter of elegance, whether of women, flowers or the Prince of Wales — whose etchings and drawings epitomized for me as a child the fashions of the period before the First World War — seemed as critical, caustic and mundane as ever. The years have not sweetened him, neither have they aged him. As for darling old Marie-Louise Bousquet, the merry widow of a dramatic critic and one of the few people in Paris of the last fifty years to preside over a salon, with guests from every walk of life, she does not seem a day older than when I first met her twenty years ago. Like a marionette of *La Fée Carabosse* she hobbles bravely on a stick, her hip out of joint and her back hunched, but her complexion is as sweetly pink as a dog rose and her large eyes have all the pathos of a young hare. In a guttural croak she expresses the vitality and heart of France.

It has been said of the French that a higher percentage were willing to collaborate with the enemy than in any other Occupied country. Marie-Louise was saddened to discover that certain friends had fallen for the blandishments of the Germans, that they could not resist the opportunity of reappearing in the limelight and exhibiting themselves again as stars no matter under whose management.

Marie-Laure de Noailles, the wife of Vicomte Charles, whose house is regularly filled with artists, described the Occupation under the Nazis as being like a warm bath: soothing to begin with, but the bath became hotter and hotter so that eventually one was scalded. She described how, early one morning, a German and two French accomplices arrived in her room to search her apartment. She remained in bed, combed her hair and called for her breakfast. After studying her family papers for two hours, in an effort to discover if she were one-quarter Jewish, the strangers quit.

---

[1] From the effects of which, a short time later, she died.

Each guest gave us his snippet about the appalling prices on the black market and about the *"collabos"*: Johnnie Lucinge, so highly cultivated and kind, told, in his rich plummy accent, how one never knew if the ringing of a doorbell portended the last moment of liberty. Most people placed a ladder against their window in case it was needed for flight. Every day brought with it the possibility that one might be carried off, without a word of explanation, to camp and torture. They told us a saga of torture chambers, hot walls and electric baths, and all the other diabolical means whereby the Gestapo tried to extract secrets. A pianist had his hands chopped off. A cellist had his fingers pared as though they were pencils being sharpened. Many friends had faced their appalling deaths with incredible bravery.

Return to Paris with Diana

The M. of I. Exhibition of war photographs again takes me to Paris. The difficulties of finding a suitably large gallery, and then competing with the intrigues, prevarications and rank dishonesty of the owners, have now been overcome; a contract has been duly signed for a showroom off the Champs Elysées to be hung with dark red velvet (hired). With a large crate of photographs I cross the Channel with Diana, who has been to London to collect provender for the Embassy. Merely to accompany an ambassadress is enough to give anyone *"folie de grandeur"*: first off the ship at Dieppe—a fleet of cars waiting on the *quai*—but Diana is the last person who could ever become spoiled. She hates fuss. Arriving to spend the night in a strange town she never seeks the best hotel; rather she says: "Charm is what we're after, not revolving doors." With Diana at the wheel of the van, motoring takes an insignificant place beside her conversation. Talk is never allowed to flag: "Who knows about toads? They're fascinating: they fall from the sky." "What is the most squalid thing you know?" "What is an incubus or a succubus?"

We bowl towards Paris with the tires making a greasy hot noise as they whirl over stones. Flying at our approach are geese, women and children. We fly so fast that there is hardly time to notice the passing scene, but from the corner of a terrified eye I note that the trees have turned orange prematurely because of the drought. It is causing a disastrous dearth of potatoes. In fact food prices are astronomic. Black marketeers, of all sorts, have become so plutocratic that they have not yet returned from their summer holidays. Many shops and theatres are still shuttered: even the Louvre is only partly opened, and the pictures that are exhibited, with the kipper veneer of years upon their surface, are scarcely visible without any electric light.

_____ *Cartier Bresson*

Henri Cartier Bresson, who has taken some of the best photographs in existence, has escaped after three years in Germany (he had become a prisoner of war while serving in the French army). In appearance he has become more rugged, with russet, shining cheeks. But his cherubic, almost simpleton, appearance is most disconcerting, for it gives no indication of the far from simple character of this somewhat twisted artist of the secret, prying lens. Henri told me how the farmer on whose property he was working always took the largest slice of meat. He, the prisoner, was allowed the second biggest — so that he could work hard; the children were next; and the mother, who nevertheless did most of the work on the place, received the pauper's share.

Henri now finds it difficult to pick up the threads in Paris where there is no unity of spirit, where everyone is suspicious of one another and denunciations are still going on all the time. And according to him there are too many political factions — all of them wrong.

_____ *Bérard and Kochno*

It has been a great experience to meet old friends long separated, but perhaps the supreme moment of all was when, having climbed the endless flights of stairs in Number 22, Rue Casimir la Vigne, I was greeted at the summit by Bébé and Boris. Bébé [Christian Bérard], a pupil of the painter Vuillard's, was not only a fine painter of serious canvases, but also the most inventive of all theatre designers since Diaghilev. He had an enormous influence on the taste of Paris for many years and was sought after by society to such an extent that he found it difficult to ward off offers that would keep him from his more important work. Boris Kochno, a Russian of intrinsic taste, was a great friend of Diaghilev's, an inventor of ballets, and a collector. Amazingly, neither of them seemed to have changed in any detail: Bébé's henna beard as long, dirty and untidy, Boris's bullet head as closely shaven. Dressed in shirtsleeves like any happy workmen they laughed, thumped my back, and vied with each other with exclamations of disbelief and joy at seeing someone straight from England. Bébé became theatrical and allowed his imagination to run away with him when describing their recent experiences. Laughingly he said the last days of the Occupation were like a de Mille production of the 1840 revolution. "We were imprisoned for one whole week in this apartment, and the entire neighborhood was posted with 'Attention! Ne vas être tuè' while wild citizens rushed out with bottles filled with alcohol trying to set tanks on fire—very 'Victor Hugo of the Barricades.'" When the "great festivity" had taken place around the Arc de Triomphe they had overlooked the fact that there were still German machine-gun men on the top.

Bébé described the terror of living under the Gestapo. Boris's bag had been packed for prison lest at any moment, and for no known reason, he should be taken away. Yet, in spite of rules to the contrary, they had both listened to the radio and done everything they were told not to do. The French went out to watch the RAF raids while the Germans remained under shelter. Bébé also told me about the swinish Hun practices that made the cruelty of the Borgias pale into insignificance. It became quite usual to hear screams issuing from buildings in the center of the city. Max Jacob, the surrealist painter, Marcel Khill, writer and protégé of Cocteau's, Jean Desbordes, a promising young poet, and so many other friends had been tortured or had died in camps. Of course the Germans had also wished to appear "correct," and had made a great play of offering seats to women in the Métro and chucking babies under the chin, but they tried too hard to make anti-British propaganda about Oran, where we were forced to destroy the French fleet harbored there so that it should not fall into German hands.

The war created favorable circumstances for Bébé to abandon his more frivolous work for theatre and magazines, the better to devote his great talent solely to the purpose of painting pictures.

But the volume of output of painting seems disappointing, although, of course, Bébé has the excuse that most of the canvases are sold, and therefore he is not able to exhibit them to us. However, he showed me enchanting and tender illustrations for Colette and half a dozen other books, all beautifully produced; these were a revelation of printing after the restrictions and poor quality paper at home. He showed also some sensitive lithographs of young girls and village children done with gutsy grace and an almost Chinese offhand understanding of draftmanship.

Later, when I took Bébé and Boris out to dinner, the people at neighboring tables all joined in talk about the Occupation and gave lurid details of German cruelty. The waitress said that the French working-class man would never forgive the Boches, for they had got him by the *bec* and made him hungry. The Germans had taken wine and used it for petrol in their cars. Bébé named with shame the friends who had fraternized with the Germans, but they were very few—maybe one percent of the population. Coco Chanel[1] was cited as an arch-offender, also a Russian ballet dancer and three American women.

Dinner in this cold and poor little bistro cost £2.10. a head.

_____ *Jean Cocteau*/*October 31st*

Jean Cocteau telephoned. Knowing I am at the Embassy he is particularly anxious to see me, because he has been accused of many crimes and wishes to be freed of guilt by being accepted by the Ambassador. When someone suggested he had not taken a strong enough line about non-cooperation with the Germans, another answered: *"Ce n'est qu'une danseuse!"*

I hurried to see Jean. We sat in his small, wine-red velvet room with blackboards for chalked memoranda notes, dates and telephone numbers and Christian names. ("Verlaine" was for some unknown reason crossed out.)

Jean called himself a phantom, trapped in Paris ("Paris is now 'occupied' by the French"), despising the gossip, the bitchy wit, cynical epigrams, and enforced leisure. Inactivity—"the occupa-

---

[1] It is said that when Chanel was brought to court after the liberation and asked if it were true that she had consorted with a German she replied, "Really, sir, a woman of my age cannot be expected to look at his passport if she has the chance of a lover."

tional disease of the defeated Parisians"—had encouraged them to backbite and bicker but he had been fortunate to be busy writing plays and films. Now, with his friend Jean Marais at the front, he was too worried to write.

Jean boasted to me that the Germans had attacked him daily in the newspapers and for some time he had remained hiding in his apartment. The young sculptor Arno Brecker, he said, had saved his life, though quite how I did not understand. It is no business of mine to judge Jean's behavior during the war, but I can imagine how difficult it must have been for him, of all aging vedettes, to feel forgotten, and that he, more than most, found it hard to resist appearing on lecture platforms even when the auspices were highly suspect.

With his wiry, biscuit-colored hands stabbing the air, he droned on in his deep nasal voice, his lips in a pursed smile. "Paris life today is clandestine—the reality is only whispered. The papers never give any impression of the way things are. There is still so much *politique* in Paris. Even the artists are exerting themselves too much with things outside their milieu. Picasso's being a Communist is typical. Paris provides too many disruptive distractions." Jean considered that "everything artistic" was dead here—one exception being Genet's pornographic novel *Notre Dame des Fleurs.* He envied my having been in India and China and living "through different epochs." England was united with one object— to carry on the war. He longed for England: to make films with Alexander Korda, to work in London, and to have his new play put on there before anywhere else.

We now sat at the little bistro near the cloistered Palais Royal where night after night writers, poets and painters—Colette, Balthus, the Polish painter of haunting pictures of young girls and aged crones, and others—had forgathered for their clandestine evening meal. In my honor as an Englishman, the proprietor opened a bottle of champagne tonight and a toast was drunk to the Allies.

Jean, with his metallic violence, still possesses a fantastic youthfulness of spirit, and as an artist he manages to overrule technique by mastering it instinctively. If he has not developed his early promise as a serious poet he has surely become a poet in life. As for his powers of seduction—he is a real virtuoso. What wit, what manners, what brilliance! Jean excelled himself in charm for me, and put on his best performance in order to justify himself.

_____ *November 2nd*

Yesterday there was an alert, and in the distance a great explosion. The evening paper appeared with a poem by Aragon on the crimes of the Germans against civilization, inveighing against the bombing of women and children, above all on All Saints' Day. It appears his muse was an ammunition train that went up by mistake.

_____ **Picasso**

Lost somewhere under the debris accumulated in my bedroom were the odd bits of paper scrawled with addresses and telephone numbers. Who would know where I could find Picasso at his secret, unlisted address? Another search brought me near panic before the missing scrap was found. I rushed off in torrential rain to cope with transport difficulties. But on arrival at the Picasso apartment, 7 Rue des Grands-Augustins, a sad and rather sinister-looking man, perhaps a secretary or an agent, received me enigmatically. I realized that no one was conscious of my being an hour late. No one seemed to know of my appointment: "But don't bother: there are others upstairs already." I went up a small, winding, dun-colored Cinderella staircase. The first room I went into was filled with huge bronze heads and squat, naked men holding animals sculptured by the painter. In the studio next door dozens of vast abstract canvases were stacked back to back. Further upstairs was a group of visitors, among them Balthus, the Polish painter, here for a morsel of shop talk, an American soldier, and two dealers. Conversation was spasmodic and cursory while they awaited the master.

Picasso quietly slipped into the room. His whole ambience was calm and peaceful, but his smile was gay. He was as pleased to see me as if I had been a close friend. The fact that Hitler had been the reason for our enforced separation now made us fall into each other's arms.

"You've not changed—except for gray-white hair!" He pointed at me; he, too, had gone white. He said that he hadn't reconciled himself to his appearance. "Have you?" he asked. "No," I replied, "but there's nothing to do about it except barge on." "It's so unfair! It isn't as if one changed and became something else"—he screwed up his face into a childlike grin showing small teeth—"as if a chair became a piano, for instance. No, it is merely a *dégraingolade* [deterioration]—horrible!" But since he was not a movie actor it didn't matter a lot. But nowadays he confessed a hatred of mirrors.

Picasso has recently shown his latest paintings at the Salon d'Autonne and his fame has become worldwide. At every newsstand his face stares from the covers of magazines from every country. Perhaps I am foolish to regret the passing of the blue and rose periods, the cubist, and the neo-Greek, but I find the newest works of boss-eyed women with three noses and electric light bulbs or fishes for hats have an almost appalling violence. They are doubtless diabolically clever, bad-mannered and brutal with the effect of making every other picture pale in comparison. However, these newest Picassos have caught the imagination of the people, and Picasso said he'd heard the crowds arriving to see them were like those which file past Lenin's tomb—"and what a strong smell those people have!"

A further posse of visitors appeared and the host talked to them in grand seigneurial manner. In fact, he is quietly delighted and amused with his success, which is of film-star proportions.

When the visitors departed, I asked how on earth he could find time to paint with such an influx of people. "Oh, it's the victory! It's terrible! I can't do any work since the victory—it's been too big, and all of a sudden the floods have started." He doubted if he'd ever be able to work again. Perhaps only another war would make him work.

Later I took photographs of the master. For changes of scene we moved from one room to another, ending in the attics with sloping red tile floor, sparsely furnished with a few zebra and other animal skins thrown around—the whole of a monochrome tonality. Here he sat in his small bedroom, and also posed sitting on the edge of his bath.

Picasso again. Shock to find at least sixty American soldiers and WAACs making a pilgrimage—_homage au maître_—the _maître_ being revered like Buddha. Picasso seems to take his popularity in his stride, and the gloomy Sabarthes, his well-known secretary and "gray eminence," an unsmiling Cerberus who together with some ambiguous servants, like muses in attendance, take charge of the telephone and welcome the pilgrims. A blonde Frenchwoman with a dashing hat over one eye, acting as interpreter, cornered Picasso in the bathroom (the warmest room in the house) and the GIs started asking questions. "Mister Picasso, how come you see a woman with three eyes—one down on her chin?" Picasso laughed. "Why do you change your style so often?" He was amused to answer: "It's like experimenting in chemistry. I'm always carrying out my experiments on certain subjects in this laboratory. Sometimes I succeed—then it's time to do something different. I'm always trying to make new discoveries."

He did not excuse himself for speaking no English, and told the story of two lovers, one French, one Spanish, who lived together happily loving one another until she learned to speak his language: when he discovered how stupid she was, the romance was at an end. Many GIs brought cameras, also books for signing. Picasso said they were like a bunch of college boys—so _naïf_.

Perhaps partly in order to get rid of them, he escorted the soldiers down the street to the neighboring studio of Adam, a sculptor and engraver. When he returned alone to his place he discovered that some of the GIs had left anonymous gifts: a package of cigarettes by the bed, a cake of soap on the rim of the bath. "They often do that," he said, smiling.

Picasso seemed far removed from the war and spoke of it in fairy-tale simplifications. But when I showed him M. of I. photographs of the destruction in London he was obviously moved. "_C'est épouvantable!_ And that is happening all over the world?"

I asked if I might do some sketches of him. He sat in profile and laughed that I should not make him look like Whistler's mother. Then a Hindu silence fell between us. He said: "How refreshing not to talk! It is like a glass of water."

André Gide

At one time Gide's scorn of convention, together with his sexual proclivities, was too much for society. But unconcerned, perhaps even unconscious of the opinions of others, he continued to do just what he wanted. Now that he has become venerable, he is given the highest acclaim as a man of great culture and, although some still find it difficult to understand how this strict Protestant can reconcile his church with his life, general approbation is fully granted.

The elderly Gide has acquired the grand manner. Nothing remarkable about the swept and garnished, orange-varnished apartment, with its rows of bookcases, other than that it is permeated by the leisurely omniscience of its occupant.

It was a lesson to me to watch how Gide is able to preserve a climate of calm throughout a morning which might have been nothing but a succession of interruptions. As I arrived at his Rue Vaneau rooftop apartment an enthusiastic and somewhat over-encouraged literary disciple was saying: "We'll meet again very soon." Gide put a chair between the young lady and himself and leaning on it, said: "Perhaps." He received the laundry like a god accepting an offering. He was in no way irritated by the ring of telephone and doorbell, for he now had no further intention of answering either of them. He rolled his cigarettes, and while I did my drawing of him he sat impassive as a Chinese deity. I peered at the small tadpole eyes, white vellum skin, and hard-boiled-egg pate. I could smell parched lizard, dry new tweed, and reams of acrid stationery. The sudden quiet in his apartment was only broken by his stertorous breathing. For a while he read a paragraph or two from Plutarch, but most of the time he sat staring into the distance. He, more than any other that I have met, has the writer's essential gift of leisure. Big business tycoons, theatrical impresarios and film directors do not seem to need time in which to digest their thoughts. Even actors must on occasions sit back and watch their fellow human beings, but reading and contemplation are essential to writer, philosopher, and poet. How could I tell that possibly, with so many threads of ideas weaving exciting patterns in his mind, Gide was enjoying a quiet morning?

Stocking the Cellar

Diana, wearing trousers, yachting cap, and biscuit-colored fox coat, is to have two days picnicking with "Bloggs" (what a name!) Baldwin[1] en route to Beaune to buy wine for the Embassy entertainments. Thrilled at the prospect of escaping from the bonds of diplomatic life, again she shows herself to be a real gypsy, a rebel. In the turnip-white-faced, ginger-topped Bloggs she has found the ideal companion for such a trip. In company Bloggs is reticent, shy, and even gauche. Often silent, he sits back blinking myopically through large glasses. But when he is with one or two old friends he can become funnier than anyone. He has the liveliest and most original mind, and his point of view is completely fresh. He is a master of the anecdote and delights in turning the joke against himself. "There - I'd said it! I was jolly windy—for people were as shocked as if I'd made a smell." He tells of how his grandmother suffered acutely from boredom: once she was so bored that she fainted. He described how his sister had "a battery of boils going off in her mouth, and she couldn't let her upper lip touch them for fear of fretting them."

Diana returned exhausted from what she admitted was a rather pointless expedition, although reporting that Bloggs had never been in better comic vein. But they had arrived at Beaune on a Saturday to find all wine shops shut. At the last minute a wine merchant said: "You can buy what I have, but you will have to decant it and help bring it from the cellars." She had enjoyed this running down long corridors with tin perambulators and seeing where the best wine had been walled up to hide it from the Germans.

Conversation in le salon vert

Colette (like an old chinchilla marmoset sitting deep in a sofa): "There are few people with whom I want to spend enough time even to go to bed with them, and no one with whom I want to sleep the night."

---

[1] Now Lord Baldwin of Bewdley, son of Mr. Stanley Baldwin, Prime Minister, later ennobled.

Louise de Vilmorin (the poetess and writer of fantasies): "Oh, I'm always so alone, I adore to have someone to spend the night in my bed. And the more remote from my life and interests he is, the better I like it. During the day I want excitements; during the night, mystery. With the warmth of an unknown head on my shoulder I can pass an exquisite night."

Diana: "Listen to her embroidering upon the thought of a moment. She hasn't thought this all out before. She has all the ingenuity, flexibility and lack of plan of the Conservative party!"

_____ *M. of I. Exhibition and* Vogue *Studio Sitting*

The M. of I. Exhibition was opened formally this morning by Duff, very important and solemn. Quite a crowd and many friends turned up, mostly on bicycles. I felt very proud.

Then a great contrast: to the *Vogue* studio for my first shot at Paris fashion photographs for many years. Here again was Madame Dilé to give one a big hug of welcome. Madame Dilé, a small birdlike woman with raven's-wing hair and huge thrush's eyes, has managed the Paris *Vogue* studio and its often difficult "star" photographers through untold phases of fashion. When I first came to Paris on assignments for the magazine I was unable to understand the language and proved inadequate in dealing with both technicians and my illustrious sitters.

But Madame Dilé at once became my friend, and no matter how difficult an editor might be to please she always had an encouraging word. As the years progressed, and my knowledge of French improved and my style of photography became ever more elaborate, Madame Dilé's task increased in difficulties. Yet at a moment's notice, and on a last-minute whim of mine, she would produce fishnets, statues, waxwork figures, cemetery wreaths, and any imaginable assortment of objects as part of my neo-romantic or surrealistic compositions. She did not quail at the thought of going out at midnight to bring back to the studio an old seller of violets from the Madeleine or lobster in pots from the market. Nothing ever surprised or daunted her.

Then came the war—and silence. Of course there was no fashion and no magazine; the studio was empty. But here, once more, was Madame Dilé. Today she was wrapped up against the cold in

woolen shawls over woolen cardigans over woolen sweaters, a
muffler covering her slightly shrunken mouth. Her hair was now
gray and her dark eyes told of unspoken tragedy. But, more interested in what others are doing than in personal misfortune, she has
no use for self-pity. With her deep crackling notes of sympathy and
nods of wide-eyed recognition, she is one of those rare human
beings who spread throughout one's adult life the feeling of comfort that has been missing since the night nursery.

_____ *Diana's Reverie*/Monday

The reveille of Diana is like a chapter out of Evelyn Waugh,
which, of course, is putting the cart before the horse. Diana has
awakened at 7:15 A.M. after a late night. Before the crimson curtains are pulled and her tea is brought to the vast crimson and gold
bed in Pauline Borghese's crimson-walled bedroom, she has
already written an eight-page letter to Conrad Russell, an addition
to a remarkable correspondence that has continued a lifetime.
Conrad Russell is a most learned member of the Russell family
—the head of which is the Duke of Bedford—who had eschewed
the glitter of London life for the solace of farming on the west
coast. A highly literate man, many years senior to Diana, his
letters inspired her to exercise her own remarkable epistolary
talents. Diana, alabaster white, is wearing, tied under her chin,
a tight nightcap that might have come out of a medieval German
engraving. Arrival of mail: packages and parcels unfolded; envelopes and unwanted paper thrown on the floor. There follows a
careful—not too careful—reading of the newspapers. The bed is
soon a litter of work baskets and trays of correspondence. Then
she dials a telephone number. She is trying to get an old English
governess into the already over-crowded English hospital here.
She makes another call: "Have you heard the latest? This will
blow your ear off. That beautiful little Laura Finch Berkeley has
married an Indian snake charmer—no, don't gasp—nothing wrong
with that, I'm also charming to snakes—but listen to this. He's as
tall as Emerald Cunard and completely circular—so fat that he
falls over. He's twice married and has four children. . . ." Now a
call to the secretary: she gives instructions. . . . "That one was a

brute—now I've got a nice one for you. Will you tell Sergeant
Spurgeon to go to Madame Taquiere and fetch a poodle—it's got
long legs like arms—and take it to have its hair cut at the coiffeur
and then bring it back here for life." The telephone from the
porter's lodge. "She wants to be paid, does she? How much? Oh,
she does! Well, don't let her have a penny. Ask her if she'll take a
bottle of whisky and some soap." From now on the telephone is
never silent. How to find a job for her son, John Julius, which will
prevent his being sent by the Foreign Office to Outer Mongolia?
Who could bring over from Jackson's in Piccadilly some kippers
for Duff's breakfast? The house guests, clad in night or dressing
gowns, come into the room to hear and spread news. A black-
coated man (very important in his line of antique business) arrives
to help one of the guests sell a watch for ready cash; another
comes in to supply bobble fringe for re-doing Josephine's bed
canopy (the Empress Josephine Borghese had not only lived in
this house but had also decorated her bedroom with these furnishings); a workman appears with a ladder to mend a chandelier
and is asked his advice about new lamp shades. An unexpected
visitor places a pug dog on the bed. Madame Porthault ("the sheet
woman") is announced: two girls accompany her. Soon the floors,
chairs, and bed are covered with finely embroidered sheets. "This
is a 'Roi Soleil' design." Everyone is exclaiming rapturously: "It's
too lovely—too lovely!"

All the while Bloggs Baldwin, waiting to take Diana out in his
car, is sewing buttons on his khaki tunic. "Don't look at me now,"
says Diana, wrapped in a bath towel at the dressing table as she
paints her face with her back to us. This is about the only privacy
she demands.

When, at last, Diana is ready Bloggs says: "I'm sorry, but I
can't come yet as I'm doing something that I don't think has ever
been done before. I'm sewing on a back trouser button without
taking off the trousers."

The grave butler bows and shows a typewritten list. "Coming
to lunch? Sir David Keith. What can he be?" The chef comes in
with his book of menus and suggestions for dinner—"*Idéal*"—and
is dismissed. Finally the Ambassador appears.

Diana hands him a list of tonight's dinner guests. Duff feels in his pockets. "What are you looking for, your glasses?" "I can read this just as well without my glasses as you can hear without your ear trumpet."

Bloggs drove Diana and me to Rambouillet to see an eighteenth-century pavilion made of shells. En route we passed St. Cyr Training College and noted the precision of the RAF bombing. The destruction was entirely confined to this important military target.

Rambouillet park was in a haze of mist. A child with long thin legs and long black cape walked like a character in a Grimm fairy story. Diana asked her:

"Où sommes nous?"

"C'est la laiterie de la reine Marie Antionette."

A gray stone mausoleum greeted us, the interior of marble and gold. The child unlocked another door and lo! a vast rockery with Venus among the artificial rocks and fountains for cooling the milk.

The child, quiet and silent and grown-up in manner, then led us down an avenue of flaming trees to a thatched rustic house. With large keys more doors unlocked and behold!—a wonderful shell house. After exclamations of delight had echoed from shell to shell, the child pulled aside a hidden door. We were now in another small room exquisitely painted with flowers and birds. Here the serious child opened some secret cupboards and some revolving dolls appeared. An atmosphere of magic.

Diana decided that this should be the place to bring Churchill for a picnic when he arrives in a few days' time.

Harold Acton[1] and I went to *Huis Clos,* a short existential play by Sartre about hell, the premise being that we make our own hell. Three characters are shown in an empty bricked-up room, here to remain intriguing and fighting with each other. The com-

---

[1] The novelist and historian of the Bourbons—half-English, half-American—formerly living in Florence, whose job in connection with the Royal Air Force had now brought him from India to Paris.

plications are infinite: misery of all sorts—including unrequited Lesbianism—and there is no conclusion. Depressing and brilliant.

Churchill's Arrival/*November 10th*

The household this morning was in quite a flap preparing for Churchill's visit tonight. Candles were put in all the candlesticks, furniture rearranged once more. Diana, in pants and bandanna, delivering strange orders to the servants. "Give that light a wash— it's got too much London on it, but it's useful: it may help us all to look a bit better." "Would you, what is known as, 'bring this up' – it'll 'come up' beautifully." "Place that sofa kitty-wise. No, no— that isn't even pure-kitty!"

Saturday, November 11th: Armistice Day

Churchill and de Gaulle are to lay a wreath on the Unknown Warrior's grave and watch the march past of France's war effort— including the Moroccans, Algerians, Fire Services, Post Office men, etc.

In the Embassy courtyard below bands are playing and the guard is changed. Diana calls up on the house telephone very early, for she is leaving for the procession and may never be seen again. There has been great anxiety lest some of the Germans— still in hiding—might throw a bomb or bring out a machine gun.

The whole of Paris seemed to be turning out. I had no place, was without plans, but had a great stroke of luck when I got a lift from a young American officer in the bullet-proof, landmine-proof car that once belonged to Eisenhower, and we drove through the crowds, up the Champs Élysées into the very jaw of the oncoming pageant. Thus we had a ringside view of Churchill, de Gaulle and Eden laying wreaths on Clemenceau's tomb.

Almost unbelievable that, after those long, interminable years of suffering, France was once again freed. Today was a landmark in all our lives. The weight of emotion robbed one of all individuality; one became just a minute spectator of history.

The crowds, red-nosed with cold and crying, were quiet in their gratitude; some who had climbed up trees looked like black rag dolls perched without moving. When the leaders passed the crowds shouted in unison: "Chour-cheel!" and during the playing of "God Save The King" they "sh-shussed" for silence and the men removed their berets. The sky was filled with airplanes; a number of Spitfire squadrons were being utilized to keep any German bombers away. Even so, it was remarkable that this great mass of humanity should gather within a few miles of an enemy that was now in retreat, but, until only a short while ago, all-conquering.

Lunch at the Embassy. Mrs. Churchill, feeling very cold and looking rather severe, with her daughter Mary in the blush of English, Pre-Raphaelite perfection, in attendance, described how a Dakota had brought them from England yesterday with an escort of Spitfires. When Mrs. Churchill had passed over France she wept. On arrival they had bundled into a car, which at once had conked out. They changed cars and had the terror of passing others at breakneck speed in order to keep their place in the procession. On arrival at the Quai d'Orsay Mrs. C. was amazed at the luxury, the grandeur of the salons, and her bedroom and sitting room had been filled with white lilac! The hot baths in such elaborately appointed bathrooms had been a great event, and dinner, too, with such delicious food and so much of it: soup, scrambled eggs with truffles, followed by chicken—and as much cream and butter as you wished. Every member of the Churchill family possesses an unspoiled quality of *naïveté* that is always delightful.

Mrs. Churchill told of the effort it had been to make conversation with de Gaulle at yesterday's great banquet. While sitting on the General's right, and seeking desperately for conversational gambits, she reflected to herself on the difficulties of the lot of Madame de Gaulle. Suddenly, the General broke the silence by remarking: "I have often thought it must be very difficult for you being the wife of Winston Churchill."

After lunch Mrs. Eden asked if I'd go with her to see the rooms at the Quai d'Orsay, and Mrs. Churchill said she'd like to join us. It was an interesting experience walking through the crowds—none of whom recognized Mrs. Churchill, who was buffeted by *gendarmes*, bystanders, jeeps, etc. But she was thrilled to be in Paris again and, like most women, could not resist taking an interest in the shop windows. She thought the Düreresque hats hideous.

Outside the Quai d'Orsay the *gendarmes* challenged our approach and told us to go to a side entrance, but Mrs. Churchill pleaded: "My name is Churchill"—at which moment a jeepful of American GIs drove up: "Say, if you're English can you tell us the way to . . .?"

We toured these grand but monstrous apartments of the Quai d'Orsay with their oceans of Savonnerie carpet and mountains of ormulu and boule. Baskets of red, white and blue flowers had come from the most expensive florists and were in great contrast to the way in which these illustrious guests lead their lives. Nothing could have been less pretentious than the collection of toilet articles belonging to Mrs. Churchill; Churchill's toothbrushes, hot-water bottle, sponge and shoddy bedroom slippers looked as if they belonged to a public-school boy. By Eden's bedside was an Everyman edition of the classics and the rubber dummy hands with which he does his exercises each morning to prepare him for endless hand-shaking.

One does not realize, when the cheers are resounding in one's ears, that the hero, acclaimed at one moment by the world, is for most of his life just like any other quiet, possibly somewhat solitary, individual.

_____*Churchill and de Gaulle Visit the Front Lines/November 13th*

Already I am becoming soft. The day-to-day life at the Embassy is too fascinating to me. I know full well that after a four years' absence Paris offers so much, and I should be investigating every street and corner. There are still so many questions to ask, and old friends to track down. But it is hard to leave these precincts, knowing that Duff is always in the center of some excitement, while things are never dull around Diana. Whoever comes down the long enfilade, it is bound to be a person of the greatest interest: Petchkov, the son of Maxim Gorki who has just somehow escaped from Poland, or a member of the British Cabinet whom I would never be likely to run across at home. I have only to remain in the *salon vert* for the poets Eluard or Aragon to appear.

Therefore it came as quite an upheaval when someone from de Gaulle's office suggested I should go, with my camera, on a trip to the Vosges front and watch Churchill and the General inspecting the French troops pursuing the Germans in retreat.

By now it is a foregone conclusion that the war in France is over, and here in Paris it is already everyone's wish to try and forget so terrible a subject: even the papers can find it of little news value. But Diana, never one to miss any event, spurred me on to uproot myself. There was no time to organize any rough or warm clothing to be sent from home so, wearing everyday clothes, thin shoes, a dark blue overcoat and black Homburg hat, I went off in a blizzard to the railway station.

The temperature was falling hourly. In the front part of the train were the two leaders with their entourage. The bulk of the long caterpillar was filled with troops while at the back I was herded in with a hundred journalists of many nationalities. It was a gloomy picture that I stared at in the semidarkness: the snow falling fast, every few yards a soldier stood at the salute, all along the railway track towards Strasbourg. It was difficult to sleep, and I was haunted by the sight of these young men standing like dummies in their solitary watch all through the night.

By dawn the snow had covered everything with a pall of silence. Here even sounds of battle were muted. A distant gun was muffled; a single airplane droned in the sky; just an occasional clattering arrival of two or three tanks, the purring of a large limousine bringing an important general, and the raucous, throaty commands of some officer and the ensuing clank of steel and stamp of boot.

I can never understand how it is that decisive battles are so often fought in areas far from the countries at war. Who would have guessed that Germany and England should fight it out in the torrid heat of the Egyptian desert? It took quite an effort of the imagination to realize that the fetid jungle skirmishes that I saw a year ago in Burma were part of this same war being conducted under gray skies, with frozen mud and snow underfoot.

It is doubtful if during this whole day more than a handful of the visitors understood the maneuvers at the edge of these black, leafless woods: certainly no journalist was able to give me any indication of the mysterious comings and goings. We waited in groups; we bundled into buses and jeeps; we arrived at a small, bomb-damaged town to wait again. Scowling Churchill and disdainful de Gaulle, sitting silently in their automobile, appeared at the head of a cavalcade and soon disappeared. Again in another village we waited. The motorcade appeared again. Churchill and de Gaulle still silent.

By lunchtime not only my thinly-shod feet, but my legs and entire body had turned to ice. We were now taken to an evacuated château of gray stone and gaunt proportions turned into a sort of boarding school in which we were all reduced to the rank of new boys: none of us seemed to know quite where to go, what to do, who to speak to, or if it would be all right to go to the lavatory. De Gaulle arrived with his distinguished visitor. As they passed into their private dining room the pair still appeared not to be on speaking terms. De Gaulle has *par excellence* the imperviable face of a self-satisfied schoolmaster: without a word, but with swollen nose and bloodhound eyes, he surveys the world around him with utter contempt. The rest of us, almost three hundred soldiers and men, were now taken to our quarters where long trestle tables were laid. Never before has the French art of cooking been better employed. The *cassoulet* kindled warmth in our veins and gave us the courage and tenacity to continue through to the end of the program.

The round continued. Churchill, with stout cigar jutting from his clenched jowl, grimly inspected more troops. Mostly young boys, they were disguised in American-sent steel helmets and grayish khaki coats as soldiers. The snowflakes fell gently onto these boys, onto Churchill, onto de Gaulle, and onto the smiling, excited villagers: to them this was a red-letter day. That Churchill himself was among them meant that, after all, they had survived: this seemed a miracle. Children in Balaclava helmets, with adenoids, stood and stared. Aged, fang-toothed old women jumped and laughed and cried in the snow. Then they saw the opportunity to sell their provisions. With transportation at a standstill, many French villages are suffering from a surplus of home produce. Now the villagers ran out with eggs, butter, pots of jam, and all manner of cheeses. The journalists were their most avid customers. Was it believable that such things could be bought without coupons? I bought a Brie cheese the size of a farm cartwheel. It became my most important possession. I nursed it with more care than my films and Rolleiflex; I would not let it out of my sight on the journey back to Paris. (Again those ghostly figures every few yards, lining the railway lines all through the night.) No matter who objected to the aroma I would jettison it out of the window only with my life.

On my return to the Embassy, having thrown off my wet clothes and thawed out in a bath, I dressed and went out with my high-smelling cartwheel to give it to my long-loyal friend at the *Vogue* photography studio, Madame Dilé. At the sight of this cheese tears welled up into her large, brown eyes. I don't think I have ever enjoyed giving a present as much.

_____ ***Diana on Her Childhood in the Late Nineties***

Flying weather bad: "Report back in an hour." My delayed return to London was agreeably spent talking to Diana who was having a day in bed without lunch, pottering about barefoot, sorting scraps, and wondering why the Embassy ran itself so badly.

Back in Pauline Borghese's huge crimson and gold bed, Diana exclaimed: "To me, it's always a shock to hear you all saying 'Bébé' to Bébé Bérard because I was always 'Baby'—the baby of the family. I was terribly spoilt, because it was found that I had some sort of paralysis. The paralysis was discovered when some-one came from Sweden and showed us all new exercises, and Baby couldn't raise her arms above her head, or turn the pages of music in front of her. But Baby had never known anything was wrong. Baby had fallen on her face whenever Baby tripped up and was always covered with scabs, unable to raise her arms to save her-self, but it didn't worry her. English doctors all said the paralysis would creep; my mother was told I had only a certain time to live so I must be denied nothing. A big ground floor room in Arlington Street was given to me as my bedroom (I wasn't to walk upstairs). I liked the theatre. That was easy because Mother was such a friend of Sir Herbert and Lady Tree, who managed and put on the great Shakespearean productions at His Majesty's Theatre, but I wouldn't go to matinées; I disapproved—I liked the waiting up late. I sat in the box, not allowed to clap. (Lady Tree said I mustn't clap from the box.) I went to dinner in a hansom. Very dangerous. If the horse slipped in the rain you went through the window sure as fate.

"I was always eccentrically dressed—in black satin with won-

derful Van Dyke aprons and collars of lace. I didn't mind that, but
I was terribly embarrassed at being made to show off, at having
to recite, and play the piano, and come downstairs in my 'pinnie.'
(Mother liked the reflected lights from the pinafore on the face.
We, in the nursery, thought a pinafore was meant only to preserve
the dark dress beneath and must be taken off when going in to the
grown-ups.) There was always a lot of photography: at Belvoir
Castle, the ancestral home of my father, the Duke of Rutland, it
was dressing up for pictures from a huge chest with old Thespian
robes in it — kings and queens. We took photographs as the five
senses — smelling, hearing, et cetera, or being very medieval pray-
ing in a Gothic chapel, or admiring a hollyhock. We burnt magnesi-
um wire for lighting and did the magic of developing and printing
on P.O.P. (daylight paper). The smell of the developing dishes —
the thrill of the hypo — the printing frames that fell out of the window! And then we sculpted hands. We put the guests to work and
covered their hands with grease and plaster, and then the panic
of the moment when the plaster dried quickly — then the breaking
— would it set? It never set! The dipping in water . . . then the
greased plate . . . Oh, the greased plate for toffee!

"Mother never stopped finding new doctors. Eventually the
paralysis was cured by galvanization — electric jerks. The muscles
gradually strengthened, and then Baby had to be educated. But
Baby dictated: Baby wouldn't do mathematics or German. That's
why Baby's mind — not that it's been too much of a drawback — is
so undisciplined today. . . . How can it be that now silly, paralyzed
Baby is a character, a wit — that she is carrying on this conversation in this particular room?"

_____ *Gertrude Stein and Alice Toklas*

Gertrude Stein and Alice Toklas have returned to Paris from their
refuge in the mountains near Aix. Gertrude is much thinner and
shrunken, Toklas fatter and more hirsute. Alice Toklas said, about
the difficulties of buying food and other scarce essentials: "Nowadays one doesn't buy with money but with one's personality." She described a scene in the Rue St. Augustin when she and
Gertrude went to buy vegetables, and suddenly some GIs shout-

ed: "Miss Stein, Mister Picasso wants you," and Pablo appeared, laughing, and they all got together with the butcher in the street and he gave them extra bits of meats as a celebration.

Gertrude talks about the hordes of GIs who come to see her and Picasso. "Why do they come to us?" She explains that for some reason she and Pablo stand for humanity: the two of them have always had the courage to fight for, and uphold, the things that they think are important. The problems of contemporary life have got out of hand; that is why so many GIs turn up to seek advice. They want to discuss their difficulties with these two people, not because they are celebrities, but because they are pioneers. One GI, however, was an exception for he ended his conversation with Gertrude by saying: "I think I'll go off and do a lot of hard work to become a celebrity; it seems so damned practical to be a celebrity."

I had heard rumors that Gertrude had become anti-British in her views, and even in front of me she said: "The English are so stubborn and haven't shown enough democratic spirit. The English are always too determined to be governesses. You must internationalize the Ruhr." Gertrude has become too much of an authority with an unfailing conviction of her own greatness ("When I say something I speak with maturity and you think something."), but when she starts telling me that we are too fond of "putting kings on thrones" I realize she is talking a lot of cock. However, one must admit the old girl believes in her own cock!

Gertrude is still convinced that Francis Rose is today's greatest English painter, and it is high praise when she says: "He paints in the great English tradition!" I recoiled when she produced his latest offering, a large Le Nainesque peasant. "This is a study of violence — that's why people hate it so. Of course the English critics turn away in dread, but a good picture should take as much courage on the part of the spectator to appreciate it as on the part of the painter to paint it."

During the years of cold and shortages, Gertrude and Alice became friends with a neighbor at Aix, a simple young man named Pierre Balmain, who had a taste for antiques and a natural bent for designing women's clothes. In fact he made with his own hands

heavy tweeds and warm garments for Gertrude and Alice to wear
during the hard winters. Now he has opened a shop in Paris. At
his first showing to the press Gertrude and Alice arrived with their
huge dog, Basket. Gertrude in a tweed skirt, an old cinnamon-
colored sack, and Panama hat, looked like Corot's self-portrait.
Alice, in a long Chinese garment of bright colors with a funny
flowered toque, had overtones of the "Widow Twankey," a comic
transvestite from the vaudeville stage. Gertrude, seeing the world
of fashion assembled, whispered: "Little do they know that we are
the only people here dressed by Balmain, and it's just as well for
him that they don't!"

_____ *A Tariff for Guests?*/*February 3rd*

Sitting next to Louise de Vilmorin at dinner tonight I was saying
how extraordinarily infallible people are. Diana plans this party
over a week ahead. Notes are sent out, and as a result, fourteen
people, seven women and an equal number of men, are sitting
around a big formal table. Very few chuck or fall out at the last
minute. Even more extraordinary is the fact that in the theatre the
same forty people assemble backstage for every performance probably for a year on end. (It is rarely that one reads a program slip:
"Owing to indisposition the part of . . . will be played at tonight's
performance by. . . .") The only difference is that the actors are
paid to turn up. "That," said Louise, "is how it should be! We
should all be paid for coming to dinner—and we should each have
a separate price. The most important guests would receive the
highest salary: people would receive their cheques at the *'place-
ment.'*" "Would you make me a *prix d'amis?*" I asked her. "Some
people, of course, would cheat by pretending they could command
a greater fee than that they received. But some guests could
be paid by barter instead of cash: the dentist would be invited
instead of having to pay his bill, and the dressmaker too. It would,
of course, lead to tragedy. Certain lovers wouldn't be able to meet:
he too poor and unimportant, she prohibitively expensive." Louise
embroidered the variations on this theme in an amusing way and
said: "Don't tell Jean Cocteau—he will be on to the idea in a
minute and make a play out of it."

Bébé Bérard and the Jackals/ British Embassy, Paris

How the Parisians do enjoy destroying their favorites! With what relish is a reputation undermined overnight! It seems that Bébé Bérard is the latest martyr of parasites who, without talent of their own, give themselves spurious importance by living off those whom they will reject the moment they can discover a new face on the horizon. Forgotten is the fact that Bébé's imagination has been an inspiration to hordes of admirers who ran after him, feeding avidly on the crumbs he threw in their path. Bébé, fat, his buttons bursting, untidy, with his long shaggy beard, opium-dirty fingernails, and dirtier white dog, has for many years now been poised on the highest and most precarious pinnacle of fashionable acclaim. A pupil of Vuillard, and with Degas his master, he has painted some extraordinarily beautiful canvases of peasants, urchins, circus performers, and people far removed from the grand world. But much of his time has been taken by the theatre, where his work has been about the only original contribution to stage design since Diaghilev ballet. In addition Bébé has worked for magazines, done book illustrations, posters, scarves, materials and advertisements. In matters relating to the decorative arts he has become the oracle. Gertrude Stein, while reprimanding him for his frivolities, praised him for being the quintessence of French taste.

Now the jackals spread the word: "Bébé has done no serious painting." "Bébé's place in the theatre is being taken by Beaurepaire."[1] "Bébé is slipping!" "Bébé has slipped!" Bébé was drowning in their crocodile tears.

My own faith in Bérard could never be shaken. His potentials as an artist are without bounds, his qualities as a human being unique. Bébé enlarges one's powers of appreciation: he always provides one with something new to ponder upon. An evening in his company is food for thought and inspiration for a year. He tells one so much of architecture, history, of paintings to discover, authors to read, and such strange and different people to know.

Before I had time to call him Bébé telephoned me. He must see

[1] A young architect who recently had had enormous success with his etchings of fanciful Piranesilike settings.

me immediately. He was sad—in fact, suicidal. No one, even "Lady Diana" (with whom I was again staying), liked him any more—he was sure of it. Anyhow, I know Diana, the most loyal of friends, loves and admires him.

When I broached the subject to Diana she admitted that, for his own benefit, she had given him a dressing down for not painting more seriously and for scattering his talents on Christmas cards and decorations for shops. "He does too much that fritters his talent." When I asked Diana if Bébé might be invited to discuss the subject again, she at once asked him to dinner.

There were six of us. Bébé appeared with his aquamarine eyes as clear as stars: he seemed much less pudgy, his cheeks pinker. His suit was pressed, and he even wore a neat bow tie under his trimmed beard. When Duff talked about English lore—country houses, Thackeray, Trollope—Bébé showed that he knew as much about England as any of us. In English literature he is as well-versed as Duff.

Bébé, inspired, proceeded to illustrate with his pencil the fashions of the new dressmaker Dior. These, he says, have the same new sense of sex appeal as Chanel created after the First World War. A theory was put forward that fashion was anti-art, that "chic" was to art the same as sex appeal is to love.

When the guests dispersed Bébé came upstairs to my room. He told me that after being a month in a *maison de santé*, where he suffered the tortures of purgatory, he is now disintoxicated and cured of his opium addiction. He lives afresh, he says: at last he can smell everything as if for the first time. But the torture of the cure has left him very weak, and he becomes easily tired. Already he regrets that he has to return straightaway to a job that he dislikes (designing for a play) for he says the theatre has no further interest for him. He only wants to be allowed to paint. He finds his first freshness being squandered on a job which he could almost do with shut eyes.

We talked as frankly as only best friends can: there is nothing I keep secret from Bébé or he from me. He told me how he had had to tell the Galerie Charpentier this morning that the painting he had promised them by twelve o'clock was not finished, how he must convince his new agent that the rumors that Bébé is now quite incapable of finishing a picture are again false.

We talked of our work and projects, and Bébé remarked that the people he painted were not those who attracted him sexually. He knew my type from watching me. He knew I liked a certain mouth formation: he had seen me at various times in my life.

Suddenly Bébé clutched his chest with a violence that was terrifying. Was this a heart attack? He became panic-stricken, for he had lost his wallet. "It has my passport in it!" he moaned. His eyes blazed, his fingers trembled. He was in a frenzy.[2] Jacinth, his small dirty dog (of the same breed as Marie Antoinette's) smelled alarm and yapped hysterically. Bébé suddenly rushed to the telephone. The wallet was found *chez* Marie-Laure [de Noailles]. Bébé and the dog calmed down. Bébé explained that the dog understands everything in his life.

Echoes of the Gestapo

Paris was cold, gray, and wet today. It was a leaden day that will haunt me for the rest of my life.

A member of the police took me on a tour of the Headquarters of the Gestapo and the prisons where the Germans, until recently, had subjected their victims to atrocities more terrible than any conceived before in history. The chief centers of torture were right in the heart of the city in the Rue Saussaies, the Rue Mallet Stevens, and the Rue Laurestan. At Mont Valérien, suspected members of the Resistance were punished beyond human endurance to compel them to give away the names of others in the movement; at least four thousand people were done away with. The cries of the sadists' victims were bloodcurdling, yet those who heard them dared not say or do anything for fear of bringing the same fate on themselves.

The French by now have become almost accustomed to stories of sons being tortured in front of fathers, of fathers killed by slow and diabolic degrees in front of their families, of eyes put out, of ice-cold baths with electric currents turned on, of rooms heated like ovens, flame jets. For me the horror was new. I heard two women relating how the *concierge* had had to clean up the mess

---

[2] For a Frenchman who had been under the thumb of the Germans for four years, a passport was the most valuable of possessions; without it he would have found himself in terrible trouble.

after Jean Desbordes's[1] screams had ended in a death that left blood everywhere.

On the walls of the chapel at Mont Valérien some of those awaiting their doom had scribbled a last tragic message: *"George Maliard mort le 26 octobre 1943."* "My last thoughts are of Suzan, France, and tomorrow." Other scrawls were terrible and bitter. *"Si jamais je crève ici Maxya, ma fiancée, habitant 119 Rue de la Convention, sera responsable de ma mort."*

In the Avenue Foch, in the garrets on the top of the Gestapo HQ, people were herded together for days on end awaiting further torture or the unknown in its most terrifying forms. Here again are pencilled last desperate messages and testaments: "Courage! *Méfiez-vous des moutons!*" "All is well in the best of worlds." *"Vive le Communisme! Vive la France!"* Terrible indictments of the way the Germans treated their prisoners were manifest in the names of RAF pilots and WAAF who had gone through these rooms to their deaths. Yes, here they were, their names: "Shelley RAF," "D.A. Ronden WAAF." These scrawled, desperate messages, written possibly in the hope that they would come to the ears of one person, are now a writing on the wall for all the world. They ought to be preserved for future generations to read them and know that Germans are capable of perpetrating such brutality.

For a visitor like myself, these rooms today were so haunting that even to imagine the feelings of those whom fate had arranged should be trapped here—that escape could never be—was something that would wake one with horror for nights on end.

On my way home I tried to feel thankful that such a destiny had not come my way, but my heart and whole frame were crushed that such things could exist. I crawled into my bed and hoped that the pictures that insisted on asserting themselves in front of my closed eyes would one day fade.

— *Charles Beistegui*

While others in their own various ways have been fighting a hideous war, Charlie Beistegui, a rich Spanish—Mexican bachelor who before the war became famous for his circle of beautiful

[1] The poet, a great friend of Cocteau.

women and his luxuriant entertainments, has been busy trans-
forming a large house outside Paris to look like an eighteenth-
century Russian palace. Word has it that by employing these
draftsmen and artisans, the best in France, cabinet masters, stucco
workers, and silk weavers from Lyons, Beistegui prevented them
from being sent to Germany.

Beistegui's adolescence is something he has never been willing
to leave in the past. Here at Groussay he has reproduced his night
nursery with white furniture, a model train on the mantelpiece,
and a *pot de chambre* under the stark bed. Stained wood is much
in evidence, and the baths and lavatory seats are boxed around
with mahogany. Beistegui has never forgotten that he was at Oxford, where he came into contact with the English aristocracy. His
first glimpse of country houses — with studded green baize doors
leading from the butler's pantry to the silver room, and with halls
hung with souvenirs of the hunt — made so lasting an impression
upon him that he had to re-create them today.

Although he is nothing of an "outdoors" type himself, the entrance to his fantasy world is dotted with antlers' heads and the
corridors are lined with sporting prints while stuffed fish hang in
glass cases. Guest bedrooms are hung with tartan silk, old Paisley
cashmere, yellow damask, or Victorian chintzes of bunches of
violets. In the silk drawing room Edwardian *jardinières* are filled
with everlasting sea-lavender and topped with potted palms, and
turn-of-the-century photographs of royalty are grouped on the
draped piano that is seldom opened. A vast electrolier shines onto
the cumbrous billiard table in the dark green room where no one
will ever pocket the white off the red. The lofty library comprises
three floors and is splendid with mahogany and gilded bronze
Louis XVI furniture. The bookcases are filled with effectively
bound books bought en bloc, but few people notice that they are
quite unreadable. Besides, who would take a volume out of these
shelves? Certainly no one has ever seen Beistegui reading a book.
Yet he is versed in the knowledge of most works of art and on certain aspects of history could be considered an expert.

Groussay is the most elaborate *pastiche* of something that no
longer exists: a re-creation created against, and to spite, the
present times. Here, inside a Russian façade, is a long-discarded
Victorian England peopled with Beistegui's French, Spanish-

Mexican, and South American weekend guests. They wear English tweeds, English cashmere jerseys, English brogues. They skim through *The Illustrated London News* and walk on lawns until it is nearly lunchtime when tasselled footmen serve marrow on toast with a glass of Madeira. (Perhaps because of my nationality he has always shown a tolerance to me and has been lavish with invitations.) Conversation is mainly about those who do, or do not, possess great taste—or great furniture. The host does not encourage political argument or controversial or inflammatory subjects. Unfashionable pursuits or unpopular personalities are distasteful. Here is one place where, at whatever cost—and the cost must be astronomical—the outer world is determinedly kept at bay. Beistegui is utterly ruthless: such qualities as sympathy, pity, or even gratitude, are sadly lacking. He has become the most self-engrossed and pleasure-seeking person I have met.

Comparisons/ Paris, 1945

Many people in Paris still appear stunned from the effect of Occupation. Their recent suffering caused them to close their eyes to reality, and they are not yet fully awake. It is hard for those who have been taught during four years to defy the enemy by breaking laws to realize suddenly that rules and regulations must be respected. But the negative habits of Occupation are by degrees being discarded for the more positive techniques of resuscitation, and those who have been idle must start to work again in real earnest. Although an incentive has sprung into being, the organization to put the wheels in motion is not evolved. The rich produce of Normandy is rotting for lack of transportation. The black market, encouraged by the Germans, continues to flourish. Those with money enough are able to live on velvet, but when others are starving this does not make for contentment.

Some people appear to have lots to spend. For a thousand francs you can eat a superb dinner. Luxury trades are flourishing. Queues of GIs outside dressmakers' shops buy scent and silk scarves. The antique shops are filled with porcelain and rare objects that, in England, are still entombed against bombs. Florists display leafless lilac, long-stemmed roses, and the sort of hothouse blooms we have not seen for years. Fashionable women look extremely strange to English eyes in their billowy clothes and clumsy velvet and cocks' feather hats—but then English women have worn only that ubiquitous handkerchief over their heads for five years. Most surprising to an Englishman is to find that in private apartments menservants answer the bells, while a middle-aged butler, assisted by young liveried footmen in white gloves, waits at table.

But soon one realizes that, though Paris may still purvey her luxuries to the privileged, only a small proportion of people have any heating in their rooms, and many have not enough to eat.

In England today, travel is uncomfortable enough, but here you cannot travel at all. In England people are poor, taxes are still mounting, and no luxuries are encouraged. There is still not a sign of the spoils of victory, but in England people are united; they share and share alike. The tension, stress, irritating and often seemingly unnecessary restrictions, the coupons and the queues, the petty tyrannies disguised as safeguards of liberty, and the lack of freedom—these are all endured in preference to the paralysis that overcomes a people whose whole life has become clandestine.

In Paris one is aware of the aftermath of bitter feuds, of private enmities which made even more unendurable these years of humiliation. Denouncements were made for no apparent reason, everyone was suspect, even friends and lovers accused one another.

Behind the lofty façades of Paris there is still bitterness, resentment, mortification, and unrest.

England and France have both suffered. There is, in my mind, no doubt as to which country has suffered the more deeply.

_____ *War's Ending*/May 4th, 1945: Ashcombe, Tollard Royal, Wiltshire

During these long years of war the one o'clock news has so often brought disappointment or dread that we have learned to brace ourselves for almost any kind of shock. Yesterday we were caught off guard and could hardly grasp what had happened when we learned of the utter and complete collapse of Germany.

Perhaps we are too exhausted to retain any strong emotions. We can just manage to give a hungry gasp of relief from perpetual queasiness in the pit of the stomach—and a sigh of gratitude.

The winter this year seemed bleaker, colder, and grimmer than ever before. Then, prematurely and all of a sudden, spring arrived and was immediately followed by a freak fortnight of summer heat. Out came—all at once—the lilac, the tulips, and honeysuckle. It's been almost too much to believe in. Now, with the avalanche of summer, good news, like the blossom and flowers, is pouring from every source. "Berlin falling!" "Goebbels dead." "Germans surrender to Montgomery." Now, any moment, we expect the full, unconditional surrender. The worst of the nightmare is past: the terrible casualty lists, the ghastly deaths of so many unquestioning young people fighting in all the elements, the gassing of Jews, the torturing of prisoners, the butcheries in German-occupied territories, the children soaked in petrol and set alight, the rows of naked women hung upside down from windows. . . . Yet one is conscious of so much continuing suffering throughout the world that it is hard to celebrate. . . .

V.E. Day/ *May 8th, 1945: Pelham Place*

In Kensington it is as quiet as a Sunday. Flags are hanging from the balconies of the houses opposite. Some young people have gone to the West End to let off steam, but there is no general feeling of rejoicing. Victory does not bring with it a sense of triumph, rather a dull numbness of relief that the bloodletting is over. Hitler's reign of terror has left behind it a ruined and exhausted Europe and throughout the world a desperate uncertainty about the future.

The spontaneous joy of deliverance from war is missing. We are told that if we wait patiently some important news may be given to us in the near future. One more restraint: it is the Russians who will give the word when to celebrate with a triumphal march in Berlin. We are having no marches ourselves.

V.E. Night

By twilight the crowds have poured into the West End of London. St. Martin's-in-the-Fields and the National Gallery are already floodlit in cold greenish light, looking like Regency engravings. In Pall Mall the flaming torches cast a golden glow on the façades of huge Venetian-palace clubs. Small separate groups are celebrating in the ruins outside the pubs. Much strutting and capering in strange hats. Someone sacrifices a front door as a bonfire and around the burning glow, Merchant Navy stewards, Wrens, old hags, American GIs, young boys, and anyone you can think of join in the hula dance. Someone shouts at a passing brigadier: "Come on, Colonel, join the fun!"—and he does. A sailor in command of a large mug of beer sings "Have You Ever Been To Ireland?" Then a jig is struck up. A small tired woman embodies a wiry toughness as she knifes her way through the concourse. In spite of years of poor food and a hard life she could still drive a dynamo with her strength and vitality. A handkerchief on her head, her tight nutcracker jaw working avariciously, she puffs violently at one cigarette butt after another. This is her way of celebrating the moment for which she has so intensely waited.

By now they are ten thousand strong outside Buckingham Palace. Lancelot Gobbo, the delightful clown and servant to Shakespeare's Shylock, high on the railings, waves a wand and shouts: "We want the King!"

Then the crowd in unison cries, "We want the King. We want the King!" A hush, the tall windows giving on to the long stone balcony above the front courtyard of the Palace are being opened. Then we can see minute figures like specks in the distance. They are the King and Queen with their children. They are receiving that traditional acclamation of the crowds reserved for very special occasions—an anniversary, a marriage, or a coronation. But now the head of the country is the symbol of all that we have considered worth fighting for: the freedom and liberty of the individual. And the enemy of these things has been defeated.

The roar that comes up from the people is like thunder. The tiny figures on the balcony can be seen to wave. Then, when they retire from view, the cheering continues. Again the waving dots appear and are greeted with an even greater expression of joy and thankfulness.

Something remarkable happens. The diminutive personages bring forward another figure, clad in black and white. It is none other than Winston Churchill. That he, a commoner, is here on the balcony with the reigning family is a break with tradition, but no one denies him this honor since he is the man who, perhaps more than anyone else, has brought us to victory. He is now waving at the loving grateful crowds who are in a state of frenzied euphoria.

Lady Alexander, widow of actor and theatrical manager Sir George Alexander

Above, Pablo Picasso in the bathroom of his apartment at 7 Rue des Grands-Augustins in Paris. Left, Sir Laurence Olivier, with dyed hair for film role of Hamlet, photographed at Notley Priory, his country house in England

Below, Adele Astaire (Mrs. Kingsman Douglas), always vivacious and
enthusiastic, after her retirement as partner to her brother Fred
Left, Sir Alexander Korda directing a scene in the film of Oscar Wilde's
An Ideal Husband, featuring Michael Wilding and Diana Wynyard

Lady Diana Cooper in the Yellow Drawing Room of the British Embassy in Paris

Paulette Goddard as Mrs. Cheveley in Alexander Korda's film *An Ideal Husband*, in orchid satin evening dress designed by Cecil Beaton

Anita Loos (*Gentlemen Prefer Blondes*), one of the author's first friends
in America and always a devoted companion

Christian Bérard, on scaffolding, decorating the ceiling of the Paris house of Comtesse Marie-Blanche de Polignac

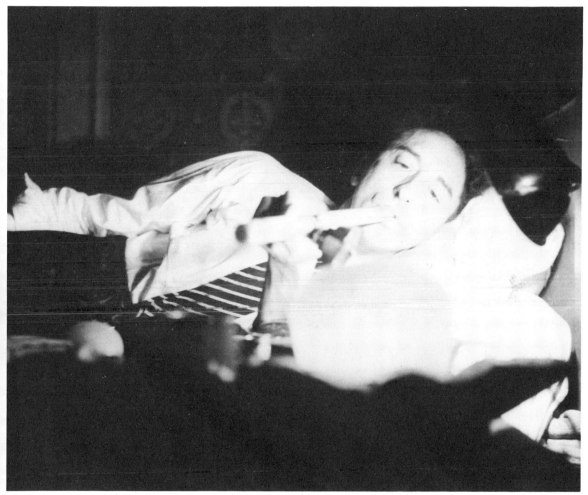

Above, Jean Cocteau smoking opium in his apartment in Paris
Left, Gertrude Stein, seen with Alice B. Toklas and dog, Basket, in
their apartment in the Rue Christine in Paris

Right, General de Gaulle and Winston Churchill inspecting French troops behind the front lines in France. Below, Pavel Tchelitchew, Russian artist, working on drawings of Alice Astor Obolensky von Hofmannsthal

Part 2
ENGLAND
1945

A group of us were having what should have been a quite uneventful little supper party at Prunier's. It was given by Ti Cholmondeley, whose claim to theatrical fame was that she had originated the role of Water in Maeterlinck's *Blue Bird.* After years of being happily married into the aristocracy she still enjoys the feeling that she has connections with the stage, and, indeed, she has recently appeared in a club production of a Strindberg play directed by an unknown young man of promise named Peter Brook. To-night her star guests were Binkie Beaumont of H.M. Tennant who, for years now, has had the monopoly of London's theatrical management, and John Gielgud. The talk was of recent play productions, and we all praised the revival of Oscar Wilde's *The Ideal Husband.* Particularly delightful were Rex Whistler's last designs, which he had done while he was under canvas in the army. Later, in Normandy, an enemy shell picked him off, robbing us of one of the greatest scenic talents the English theatre has known since Inigo Jones.

Binkie vaguely discussed the possibility of reviving some other Oscar Wilde comedy; John suggested that Isabel Jeans would be excellent as Mrs. Erlynne in *Lady Windermere's Fan.* As if we were playing a country-house writing game, we all jotted down on menus the names for other members of the cast. "Who would direct?" asked Binkie. John said that if he was wanted he'd like to take on the job. I summoned enormous courage and spurted out: "And I will do the *décor.*" "Right!" concurred Binkie. It was as easy as that.

This was the great, glorious, golden moment for which I had been waiting all my life! As a child my chief enthusiasm was my toy theatre. On that small stage the sets of *Oh, Oh, Delphine!* and *The Whip* had been re-created on cartridge paper by my water

colors. The filigree of the wisteria and the rambler rose borders
had been carefully cut out with nail scissors, and the two-inch-
high performers, pillaged from *The Play Pictorial* and painted
with heavy make-up, were propelled on tin rods from the wings.
At Cambridge I had ignored lectures and the end-of-term exami-
nations in favor of climbing up ladders with buckets of size and
paint to do the *décors* for the undergraduate productions of the
Marlowe Society and Amateur Dramatic Society.

But I had been waiting a long time now for a big breakthrough
into the real live London theatre with human actors to clothe and
ornament. So far I had had only the opportunity to design one or
two ballets, a much-too-literary play, and an odd costume here
and there. Whenever a job was going that would be an important
opportunity for a designer, it was offered first to Oliver Messel,
and if he were unavailable, then to Rex Whistler. For a long while
I had been gathering up feelings of frustration that my chance to
materialize as an important designer would never come.

All at once, I felt confident that a whole new vista was opened
to me. This was a play I knew I could do well. As I walked upon
air with Gielgud up the Haymarket late that night, I kept pumping
him with a stream of suggestions as to how the production should
look: overcharged, richly stuffed and upholstered, with a great
use of *trompe l'oeil* and enfilades, in false perspectives, of Victorian stucco and heavy chandeliers. Lots of parma violets,
maidenhair fern and smilax, and Lady W. in apricot. He seemed
a bit overwhelmed, and laughed nervously, but made no objec-
tions.

"Then can I really start tomorrow?"

"Why not?"

I got into my small Ford and drove immediately home to Ashcombe, there, quietly, to put my ideas on paper. For nights sleep
was impossible, for my brain was working overtime and would
not quiet down. Too many ideas of decoration that had been kept
in cold storage came flooding out into the glow of my enthusiasm.
Things that I had remembered in childhood: the candy-striped
silk of Elfie Perry, the first actress who ever came to our house;
and my Aunt Cada's love of japonica pink. Then more recent im-
pressions: the green silk walls, covered with engravings, in some
London club; and the gilded garlands framing the plaques in the

Bow Room at Buckingham Palace. All the ideas, like the pieces of a large, complicated jigsaw puzzle, eventually fell into place. My hands could not wield the crayons, chalks, and paint brushes quickly enough. A week later my designs were accepted.

——————————————————————————— *Vyvyan Holland*

Oscar Wilde's son is still receiving royalties from his father's plays, but it was not for this reason that Vyvyan Holland was so helpful and interesting a collaborator on our exciting project. He at once invited me to dine with him in his flat, filled with mahogany and rare books, in Sloane Street. V.H. has now become somewhat hard of hearing and his manner of speech has never been spontaneous. Age has made his mouth twitch and his eyes sag. But the more one knows him, the more gentle and delightful a person he becomes.

After an excellent post-war meal with Château Yquem, *marrons glacés*, pineapple, etc. (his wife, Thelma, is as great a gourmet as he is), he reminisced about the original production of *Lady Windermere*. Later in the evening V.H. had relaxed sufficiently to talk about his father. "He was very good with us as children: he was great fun. I remember his saying to me he'd give me ten shillings when I grew to be as tall as his stick. One evening I stood on a footstool behind the curtains and said: 'Look! I'm as tall as your stick,' and he gave me a ten-bob note. But it was an appalling shock to find what complete pariahs we became after 'the period.' My mother and I went to Montreux, and when they discovered who we were we had to leave the hotel. I was seven at the time and it has made a terrible impression on me ever since. I can't bear even to see my name in print: it gives me the horrors. We had to change our name because everywhere we went we were hounded: people even changed the names of their dogs if they happened to be called Oscar, and in my aunt's house I came across a copy of *The Happy Prince* with the name of the author covered with sticky paper."

Thelma disclosed that talk about Oscar Wilde was a rare occurrence and that for years this had been a forbidden subject in the household. She had just recently discovered the whereabouts of Oscar's valet. He had come to tea with her and spoken affectionately of his erstwhile master whom he had accompanied in the carriage on his last journey of freedom: When he had passed his usual tie shop, Oscar had decided to stop the carriage; he got out and bought a new cravat.

Even the valet found it hard to find employment when it became known that he had worked for Oscar Wilde. It was the world's scorn that had killed his father, said V.H.

Hiroshima

Lady Windermere has opened to excellent notices on its trial trip to the provinces. All portends well: it has been a comparatively smooth undertaking. Few major alterations have had to be made although John Gielgud went on changing his direction until the last minute. The most important and painful necessity and upheaval was the eleventh-hour substitution for Mabel Terry-Lewis of a younger, more forceful actress. That the frail, forgetful, and irascible old lady doomed to the axe happened to be Gielgud's real-life aunt only made the situation more fraught with tension.

Another major change: they needed an entirely new setting for Act I. For economy's sake we had ignored Wilde's directions and played Lady W.'s boudoir scene in the ballroom of Act II. But Wilde was right; the first scene calls for a more intimate atmosphere.

When a designer has used a certain chart for his colors, it is difficult to juggle them around. Gielgud and the management agreed that if Lady W.'s small gilded cage of a boudoir should be of yellow silk — very fussy and overcharged — her last-act blue dress would be more suitable than the red and white "Elfie Perry" candy stripes intended to be seen against the dark red walls of the ballroom. But we all reckoned without the actresses involved. Lady W. would not switch, and she was aided and abetted by Mrs. Erlynne in Aunt Cada's japonica pink. Binkie shrugged: "After all, it is the actress who has to wear the clothes for the run of the play." I was upset out of all proportion.

I did not intend to give in to defeat without a struggle, which might have to continue with Binkie the entire length of the return journey to London. But as the early morning train pulled out of Manchester station Binkie and I opened the morning papers. It was impossible to discuss theatrical trivialities after reading of the magnitude and horror of the devastation caused by the bomb dropped the day before over Hiroshima—far greater than any that has been known since the beginning of time.

Lady Alexander

The management gave me some seats for the first performance in London of *Lady Windermere's Fan.* I thought it would be kind to invite Lady Alexander to accompany my mother. Lady Alexander, the widow of George Alexander, an actor-manager of earlier days, had been involved in the original production of the play, and she had befriended my brother and myself when we knew few sparkling people. Reggie and I were always vastly amused in her somewhat grotesque company. Although of an alarming vintage she took Reggie and me to benefit performances, charity balls, first nights, and all sorts of public places. When we first saw her she presented a strange spectacle with her pig's snout, dog's mouth and bird's eyes, wearing the most exaggerated clothes and feathered headgear. Even in broad daylight she appeared to be in full fancy rig, yet we dared not laugh at her for she was a kind, good soul with a golden heart. Someone said she looked like a caricature of an old marquise, but she always reminded us of some circus dog dressed up—a white poodle covered in frills and diamanté.

"Everyone" in London knew Lady A. by sight, and she enjoyed being stared at in a friendly way. However, when she went to Paris where no one knew her (although she was said to be half-French), crowds gathered as she tottered along in her jerky, mechanical fashion carrying a high cane, her bosoms almost popping out, her bottom proffered, and her face covered with flour and Hogarthian beauty spots. Some bystanders were so elated by the display that they applauded.

In ordinary conversation Lady A. never made much sense, but she perfected for all and sundry a confidential manner which worked for her as real friendliness. Once when Boy Le Bas, a painter and close friend since we were schoolboys together at Harrow, and at the time an undergraduate at Pembroke College, had motored from Cambridge and told her how, in his car, he'd nearly run over a dog, she whispered to him with great import: "You know, these dogs don't realize how quickly one comes upon them!"

Lady A. herself was always surrounded by old Pekineses. Two years ago, the favorite dog of the moment died. The leading florists in London sent miniature wreaths and sheaves, and the corpse was taken down to Chorley Wood to be buried beside Sir George. Lady Alexander was so upset at the dog's death that she nearly made a trinity. One afternoon about six months later, she met a Mrs. Tate in a hat shop. Mrs. Tate was in deep mourning for her husband and son who had both been killed in a tragic accident. Lady A. said: "I'm so sorry to see you all in black. I do hope you haven't lost someone?" Mrs. Tate shed a tear and replied: "Yes, my poor dear husband and son." Lady Alexander turned a sympathetic eye upon her: "I, too, have had a great sorrow. My little Pekinese, Mimosa. . . ."

Every summer Lady Alexander sent out "At Home" cards to hundreds of friends who would throng her red brick house in Pont Street for a gala bun fight. It took determination and patience to mount the white marble steps of the porch, ease into the Wedgwood-medallioned hallway, then slowly scale the stairs jammed with humanity in morning coats and flowered chiffon. But there was much to beguile one's attention as one waited, squashed in line. Older-than-time actors and never-say-die actresses would appear with the aura of the footlights still about them. Sir Squire Bancroft, an eminent actor of an early vintage, one of the first to give respectability to the London stage, could be seen adjusting his monocle; Dame Madge Kendal, a stage dowager going back as far as the Victorian era, would appear still wearing her inevitable bonnet and bustle; Mary Wyndham, wife of well-known actor-manager Sir Charles Wyndham and a drawing-room-comedy actress of great charm who retired in the nineties, now terribly deformed by illness, would be enveloped in embraces by loving friends; and—of a younger generation—Lilian Braithwaite would float in, moon-colored and with eyes as startled as if she were seeing ghosts, hobbling on bad feet. Miss Braithwaite was for many years beloved by the hostess's much mourned husband, and her daughter Joyce Carey referred to the theatrical knight as Uncle George. It would be interesting now to watch the hostess's greeting.

An old-fashioned string band played lazily in a corner; smilax was hung in festoons from curtains. An aged stage butler stertorously pronounced the names of guests: "Sir Trehawks and Lady Kekewich. Lady Hicks and Miss Betty Hicks. Sir Bindon and Lady Blood. Miss Mieville. Cherry, Lady Poynter. Sir Cunningham Graham and Mrs. Dummet." Then came the long-awaited reward. Lady A. would be discovered standing in a bower of rambler-rose trees. Above her hung the over-life-sized portrait of Sir George wearing the white satin breeches and cotton-wool wig of *The Prisoner of Zenda.* Our hostess looked like a wound-up fairy doll as she bowed to left and right, croaking in a barely audible whisper. Her snout seemed more turned up than ever, her huge gash of a mouth like a torn pocket, her eyes small, unseeing currants. She wore a daring *décolletage,* a sheath of silver and old lace trimmed with pink rosebuds, and tulle frills encircled her head and wrists. She exuded a strong pharmaceutical odor, possibly that of calomine lotion with which she was whitewashed. How enjoyable it would have been to stand by and watch the flow of this pageant and to note all the gyrations of this specter receiving her friends. But the crush was too great. One had to move on and push, with a lot of greedy geezers, for iced coffee, mustard-and-cress sandwiches, éclairs and rose-pink ices.

On quieter occasions I used to ask Lady A. about the St. James's Theatre in the days of Sir George's management, when she used to help with the choosing of dresses and effects (all very casual in comparison with today's *décors*). But she was always deliciously vague and appeared not to remember Oscar Wilde—perhaps because her husband eventually came to disapprove of him. Alexander was playing in *The Importance of Being Earnest* at the time of the trial and behaved disgustingly by continuing to make money from the play while taking the author's name off the billboards and turning his head away when eventually they again met. Lady A. *did* tell me, however, that at the dress rehearsal of *Lady Windermere,* Wilde leaned out of a box and gave the order that at the ball Lady W. must wear opals. Everyone concerned was aghast: "They are such unlucky stones!" But Wilde insisted, so Lady Alexander was sent off to supply the *parure.*

Since the war I had not seen Lady Alexander, but I gathered that her physical condition has deteriorated sadly. My mother told me about Lady Alexander's arrival to see our revival. As she hobbled into the lobby, resplendent in crimson velvet, one of the more elderly of the Haymarket Theatre staff recognized her and came forward to conduct her through the crowd. She was steered to her berth, leaning heavily on his arm, and kept muttering, sotto voce: "Oh, you know things are so different these days. The times we knew are over forever, and it's difficult to get accustomed to these new ones." Then she apologized: "I'm such a nuisance to everyone nowadays. I don't see properly and I'm so old, and I can't move since I had that nasty tumble. I really shouldn't have come." Whereupon the theatre manager, who had joined them, remarked: "You're just as charming as ever you were, you don't look any older, and we're all very proud and honored to have you here again."

_____ *Exit from Ashcombe/Ashcombe*

Surely Mr. Borley wouldn't turn me out of Ashcombe after all these happy years—it can't be possible! And yet now I see that it is just what he has been planning eventually to do ever since I appeared before him as a foolish young man willing to make a derelict ruin habitable.

When I first discovered Ashcombe it looked like an illustration from a romantic fairy story. The beautiful little lilac-colored box of a house with the long stable building like an orangery opposite was placed in a remote valley in vast wooded downlands. It seemed as if no one had been near it for two hundred years. A hugh ilex tree poured itself over the courtyard of cobblestones; the diamond-patterned windows were elegantly proportioned and from all of them the views were of unimaginable beauty. Originally there had been a fine and grand mansion, but it had disappeared and only the outhouses and the remains of an ornamental grotto were still to be seen. The owner was a Mr. Borley, formerly the successful publican who owned the Grosvenor Arms in Shaftesbury. He had become a great enthusiast of the gentlemanly sport of shooting and used these dilapidated buildings as storehouses and to rear his pheasants. Even his gamekeeper declined to live in such discomfort as these presented and was ensconced in a modernized dwelling further down the valley. When I told the landlord that I would like to convert the property into a place of retreat for myself ("Strange it appears who so'er could build a seat in so an inaccessible retreat") he saw the advantages to himself and eventually condescended to give me a seven-year lease. He smiled as he saw the arrival of the builder, plumber, gardener and electrician.

At the end of that lease his ferret eyes glistened and he smiled again as he made his tour of inspection and asked: "What other improvements have you in mind?" I did not suspect his interest. "Oh, we are going to terrace this part of the garden and make an orchard." "But what are you going to do about the tiles on that roof?" he asked. "Those walls need re-pointing," he observed, "and the private roadway must have a new surface." On eliciting certain promises from me, he agreed to another seven years.

Now I have been to Shaftesbury to drink a glass of South African sherry in a pitch-pine panelled room and have been served with an ultimatum. My lease will not be renewed, and the landlord's son will benefit by my plumbing system.

I have come away reeling from that claustrophobic Victorian villa as if galloping cancer had been diagnosed. I can scarcely swallow. I dare not be left alone with my thoughts . . . .

I was twenty-six years old when I came to live at Ashcombe, the first piece of property I felt I could call my own. With the money that I had made with my photography, illustrations, and designs I was able to plant trees and fill the flower beds and, in an impromptu fashion, to decorate the house. No matter that I could not afford to furnish the house in the conventional way: my theatrical sense and ingenuity came to the rescue. Soon my hide-out was discovered by a flow of young friends. We played; we laughed a lot; we fell in love. Ashcombe became a place where time stood still and care was a stranger.

At first, the studio was mostly used for parties and charades, and only in fits and starts did I go across the courtyard to paint. As the years passed more time was spent at the easel, and I began to wonder how I had once managed to work with such confidence and so little application. With my writing, too, I hid myself for longer periods in order to give full concentration to some forthcoming book.

Then there were alarms in the world and rumors of war were coming nearer. Eventually the dread became a reality.

Would Ashcombe, once used for little more than a peace-time idyll, be able to change its character? Could it even be maintained in the bad times to come? Within a week of war being declared so much of life in England had changed radically. With the fear of bombing, and with troops in transit, half the population seemed to be on the move. Hundreds of refugee children from Kentish Town arrived in the neighborhood.

Almost immediately the married couple who looked after us at Ashcombe left with their cat. Would our beloved gardener, Dove, a victim of chronic asthma, be strong enough to forge through the winter mists?

Ashcombe changes but it never disappoints; as usual it lived up to expectations. It became more than ever a refuge, a place to work in, a place to come back to. When the bombing of London became unbearable to my mother and sister Jessie, they left, with shattered nerves, to recuperate in the country at Ashcombe. Here they remained "for the duration."

In spite of flooding, oceans of mud, and trees being blown across the valley, throughout the worst winter weathers Dove continued to battle his way up from Tollard Royal. Sometimes on arrival his face would be blue: he could not breathe: we thought he would die on the minute. But, helped by my mother's ministrations, Dove survived yet one more attack.

Tom Curd, the postman, was another stoic: come tempest or sleet, he walked the four miles from Ashmore to Tollard Royal to collect mail, thence over the downs, past Wingreen eight hundred feet up where he could be seen — a minute speck — in the distance coming down Ann's Path to bring, from the sack slung on his back, friendly words and presents from New York.[1] When snowdrifts eight feet deep blocked him from his usual route he trudged through the fields. He never complained, though he would some-times admit that the expedition "pulled his legs a bit."

But remote, hidden, and inaccessible as Ashcombe is, it was not immune from the effects of war. A searchlight was set up by the archway to the studio and a dozen soldiers arrived to man the site. Not only did they give a feeling of protection to my mother but

---

[1] From 1919 to the time Tom Curd retired thirty-eight years later, it was estimated that in mileage he had walked sixty thousand miles, the equivalent of more than twice round the world.

they were also generous with gifts of tinned plum jam and margarine. More astonishingly still, in the dead of night a German bomb was jettisoned in the valley. It blew out our windows and caused a ceiling to come down on my aunt, who remained unscathed and unperturbed, but the explosion completely obliterated the gamekeeper's cottage.

It was at Ashcombe that, early one morning, my mother rushed into my room with the first decisively good war news: "Great victory in the desert! Rommel on the run!" It was also here that the bulletin came through that the war was over. When I ran out to tell Dove what had been announced on the radio, he said with his foot poised on a spade: "That's a good job done." After a minute he started to dig up the potatoes. He died all too soon thereafter.

Unlike Dove, I have been fortunate enough to survive the war, but I will not be able to enjoy at Ashcombe the return to peace.

_____ ***Weekend in London*** / *September: Pelham Place*

Now that I have no place of my own to go to at weekends I must take other trains to other places. Of course, I pack in my luggage a certain amount of work to do during the visit to friends, but I find that if one is absorbed in one's subject, there is no greater frustration than having to break off to help entertain neighbors. Notwithstanding, it was enjoyable at first to see how others lived: the plot of their existence would unfold like a play. Like many plays, however, the last act was often the weakest, and I would return to London somewhat disappointed. I have all too soon come to realize that it is quite an effort to organize an escape from London at the end of each week. Even if people want you under their roof, there aren't that many friends with whom one wishes to remain, even for the short length of a Saturday to a Monday. And often it is not convenient for them to have a guest just when it would suit me.

But should I complain? After all, the majority of people spend their lives in one place. Most townspeople prefer to remain at home after a tiring week, without taking a train or motoring for hours. The empty, quiet city on a Sunday has charm for many, particularly in winter. For the first quarter century of my life I spent almost every weekend in London. It was not then necessary for me to smell the downland air in order to set to work painting, designing, or taking a photograph.

But the habit of fifteen years is hard to break. As a young man I was never bored in London during the weekends but, suddenly, it lowers the spirit. The air seems to have been used up. I am acutely aware of the untidiness, the discarded bus tickets, the greasy pavements, the look of aimlessness on the faces of those with nothing to do. I felt slightly ghost-ridden by the scarcity of traffic, the deserted Underground with a pile of *News of the Worlds* sprinkled with pennies thrown while the seller has gone off to commit suicide.

A friend rented me a cottage near her house, but the cottage soon became too near her house. I wonder if I shall ever find another retreat of my own.

Dining in Churchill's Company/*December, 1945: Pelham Place*

How *can* one curb the day's activity and say "no" when interesting, unexpected, additional jobs suddenly fall within one's reach? Now that I have no longer a retreat in the country to retire to, the pace seldom slackens. Today it has reached a great impetus and it was in a condition of over-fatigue, and in a mood of self-pity, that I set off to dine with Sybil Cholmondeley.[1] Sybil, a dear friend of many years whom I generally see in the intimacy of her immediate family, had explained that tonight's dinner would be just a quiet and small affair of eight people. . . . Too bad that no taxi could be found at the last moment. Harrassed and self-absorbed, I asked the parlormaid at Kensington Palace Gardens if I were the last to arrive. I was. My dismay was increased to find a most distinguished group consisting of Field Marshal Alexander, one of Britain's great war leaders, Lady Wimborne[2] and Brendan Bracken[3] standing in the center of the drawing room listening to Winston Churchill. A few moments later I pulled myself together enough to gather that the great man was telling the company that

[1] The wife of the Marquess of Cholmondeley, the Lord Chamberlain, an exceptionally beautiful and intelligent woman of unusual wit and taste, born Sassoon.

[2] Wife of Viscount Wimborne, a former Lord Lieutenant of Ireland, and a hostess whose musical parties at Wimborne House were on a grand scale.

[3] Formerly Minister of Information, a red-headed protégé of Sir Winston Churchill.

he had been invited to go to New York to "drive through the streets," but that he couldn't do it nowadays in winter: without a hat he would catch a cold. "I'll drive through the city later," he promised. This offhand reference to being afforded a ticker-tape triumphal reception from City Hall to Fifth Avenue struck me suddenly as resembling an excerpt from *Alice.*

It was difficult to accept as part of everyday conversation such understatements as: "The last time I was in this street was when I drove to call at the French Embassy, a few houses along, and there were crowds outside."[1]

In silence I watched Churchill holding, in his feminine hands with their pointed nails and fingers, a glass of champagne too near his face so that the exploding bubbles tickled him; like a baby, he screwed up his nose and eyes, displaying an almost toothless mouth. He wore cracked patent leather shoes, his stomach was high-pitched over an immaculate shirt, and his heavy gold watch chain was like my father's. Churchill, of course, was very much the star of the evening. He has much of the show-off about him and does not brook with equanimity rival attractions or interruption. Several times during dinner he growled: "Allow me to continue this discussion," or: "Please don't interrupt, Clemmie," and indeed he knew his performance warranted rapt attention. I realized to what a degree all in his family circle must pay him due deference. But, in all fairness, he was strictly truthful, well-balanced, and impartial. At one point he interrupted himself by asking Alexander: "Am I right, Field Marshal?" "No, you're wrong, sir," said Alexander in a voice like a gun shot. Churchill was neither fazed nor angry. He "huh-huhed"—then continued. Later he claimed that he was not a bitter political loser, and although the shock of having lost the recent election to Labour's Clem Attlee must have been overwhelming, he said that in politics you must expect everything you get ("At least they haven't been rude to me!"). During the evening several topics were discussed which showed that he was altogether somewhat disgruntled— British cultural institutions and modern abstract painters were particular irritants.

---

[1] There were crowds for the good reason that it was "V" Day and Churchill went to congratulate the French.

He was appalled by the publicity about the Nuremberg trials: "Bump 'em off but don't prolong the agony."

He complained of photographers snapping him when he was putting a piece of meat in his mouth, and regretted the way the world is going. "Nowadays no one is allowed his fine house. People do not want what they are given, and they are not given what they want."

When the ladies left the dining room Churchill began talking about the Potsdam Conference. He recalled the reaction to news of the atom bomb that was let off in Los Alamos, New Mexico. Word had come through that it was a baby thing. Stalin had not been impressed. Churchill was harsh in his criticism of Sir Stafford Cripps ("that parlour Trotskyite") whom he quoted as being only one person who didn't enjoy all the things he said about them. "He resented being called 'Sir Stifford Crapps.' But I didn't know that that word had a connection with the rears. I don't have to descend to four-letter words to be abusive." Brendan demurred. Churchill replied: "Come off it, Brendan, you've also had bad luck with that word. You once called someone 'crapular' and he resented it."

But although an occasional plaintive note could be detected from the great hero dethroned, Churchill entertained no self-pity.

The evening had upon me the salutary effect of making my own troubles seem unimportant. But it also made me realize with quite a shock of humiliation the limitations of my specialized existence. Here was a group of men who are uncommonly varied in their wide range of interests, yet with none of them was I able to converse with authority or ease. I realized how remote I have become from politics and government, from history and social problems. I found myself tongue-tied and with no opinions to voice.

Churchill has never been one to put people at their ease. He is known to have an alarming effect on many. Tonight I admired him as always, relishing his turn of phrase and his wit, but I felt rather like Eve in *Howard's End*: "She was a rubbishy little creature and she knew it." It was only when, at a comparatively early hour, and wrapped in scarves and heavy clothing, Churchill was bundled off to bed by his attentive wife, that I felt able to assume even a modicum of social poise.

Scenes of London following World War II bombing, photographed by Beaton

Part 3
NEW YORK
1946

The Haymarket success of *Lady Windermere* had rekindled an interest in Wilde plays in New York, and the magnet of designing *An Ideal Husband* for Leonora Corbett, who wished to play Mrs. Cheveley, the fascinating adventuress, drew me across the Atlantic. Leonora was a dazzling personality and her performance in Coward's *Blithe Spirit* had entranced New York. This project failed to materialize, but there were other tentative suggestions, including a duplication of the London *Fan.* At any rate, there seemed to be in the air the possibility of at last breaking through the, to me, impregnable barriers of Broadway.

It was the dour, gray month of February when I eventually arrived, via a bleak and frozen Canada, in the twinkling and warm comfort of the Plaza Hotel. After the awful Atlantic crossing on a troopship filled with GI brides and their seasick children, I wallowed in my old luxurious rooms. My friend Serge Obolensky, a director of this hotel, has arranged for me to live at a greatly reduced rate in a suite I had decorated.

Although the theatrical enterprises were all, in turn, postponed or remained undecided, almost directly after my arrival so many jobs were offered to me that it was difficult to keep an equilibrium. My photographs were said to have acquired a different quality from my fanciful pre-war concoctions; I was kept on the hop with sittings, debutantes, fashion, Mary Martin, and Celeste Holm, among others.

At last I begin to feel that the war really is over. Anxiety and nervous dread are things of the past. Rationing is forgotten. The future is roseate. Of course here, as at home, the first year of peace is a period of readjustment. Here, too, it is a time of frustration, and also of fear, the bogey being Russia. Everyone is scared of spies. Economically everything is in a state of flux, with continual talk of inflation or deflation or threats of further strikes. John L. Lewis has defied Truman and can boast of having put a million men out of work with a loss of ninety million tons of coal. Vice-President Wallace, who has backed the wrong horse in Chiang Kai-chek, has been inveighing against the "British imperialist policy in the Near East" and, having done great general and lasting harm, is mercifully now in retirement. Mr. Rockefeller, on the good side, has given eight million dollars towards an East River home for a United Nations building.

My door bell rings with the printers arriving with a ballet program layout for Lincoln Kirstein. At the same time a would-be producer arrives with notes for suggestions for rewrites on a play I am working on, and messengers go back and forth with manilla envelopes containing proofs of articles, typescripts, or the latest color transparencies. Now, at last, it seems that the theatre is open to me as a designer on a big scale: it is all most invigorating. My earlier visits to New York have always seemed too fleeting. Now, with nothing specific to keep me in England, there is time to settle down and relish to the full the infinite delights that New York has to offer.

_____ *Mrs. Wellman: A Continuation*

When I first arrived in New York in the late twenties, Frances Wellman, a middle-aged woman of singular ugliness and persistence, had become quite well-known for giving parties in her hotel suite in which members of "café society" mingled with Broadway celebrities. Of all her pet guests, Noël Coward was perhaps the most cherished. The hostess, who had quite surprisingly distinguished hands, would "ssh" her guests, with her long index finger to her pouting mouth, to signal the coup of the evening: "darling Noël" at the piano. Noel is not only a brilliant, but also an indefatigable, performer. Neysa McMein, a most delightful person but a very bad painter, and a group of fans and friends, close and otherwise, would sit on or around the piano in ecstasies, while lesser devotees were "sshed" in the background.

Twenty years later the same lady was tonight giving a party to honor Noël Coward. Anita Loos said: "It's awful—no one seems to be going. Neither Madeleine [Sherwood, wife of Robert Sherwood, playwright] nor Tilly [Losch, the Viennese dancer]—they just can't bear to face Noël after the notices for his recent play [which was said to be poorly cast and without the usual Coward bite]." Noël, of course, loyal to the old hostess, was in dazzling form. So professional is he that he would never concede that he was anything but thrilled with the reception of his latest production. He appeared to be on the crest, and in spite of all that had been said, the friends had clocked in. Neysa McMein, of course, as she is the most friendly and loyal of all; Adele Astaire, too. And the rest of the guests—the nonprofessionals—were the same set that, throughout the twenties and thirties, used to stay up all night and, if no party was to be found, would sit in nightclubs till dawn.

In the meanwhile there had been a world war. I had not seen these people for so long that they now seemed to me to be caricatures of their former selves: mouths wider, eyebags lower, hair brighter, laughter louder, and Scotches stronger. Frances Wellman, even more restless than she was twenty years ago, had become a galvanized zombie and was shushing everybody while Noël sang a song he had written for Beatrice Lillie called "A Marvelous Party," a very intimate joke listing the names of friends who were unknown to the general public such as Momo,[1] John-John,[2] and Figgi.[3] The song satirized the foibles and idiocies of this particular group. Noses screwed up, teeth bared, foreheads wrinkled, everyone shrieked with laughter because they knew how damnably exclusive and smart they were. By the time everyone had joined in the old twenties songs I felt the low ceilings of the Waldorf must surely crack.

I was being a boor; however much I drank I couldn't get the "party spirit." I found this group of older people, insistent on still behaving like the bright young things they have long since ceased to be, really rather offensive. Surely they were now too old to be quite so silly.

I left early, feeling unhappy at being so censorious of these friends who were only a bit past my own age. Maybe I have changed more than I realize. This was not my evening. I prefer

---

[1] Daughter of Otto Kahn, wife of General Sir John Marriott.

[2] Son of Lady Marriott.

[3] Madame Jean Ralli, a Greek lady living in Paris.

the company of those who are still full of promise with their careers in front of them, those who have no bank balance and probably live in a cold-water walk-up in the Village, yet who, by facing failure as part of reality, create a vitality that is, to me, more invigorating.

_____ *Dinner in the Village*

Cyril Connolly, when describing New York, used the provocative phrase "the luxury of poverty." I think I know what he means: comfort and all that money can buy has become *de rigeur,* and the effort to impress the Joneses the chief incentive. In the apartments of the excessively rich, one finds *boiseries, parquet de Versailles* and Renoirs galore; imagination, originality, or vitality do not exist in them. It is more likely to be among those struggling for survival—the overcrowded families, the Italians, the Jews, and the younger writers and painters or theatre folk—that one finds people who are expressing themselves with too much vigor, ambition, or even desperation, to think of the effect they are creating. It is only when no standards of comparison have to be maintained that freedom—that greatest of all luxuries—is found.

But when I repeated Connolly's phrase to an abstract painter friend named Chuck, he was furious. "That's just damn perversity," he said, and Chuck should know because he is dog-poor. Yet Chuck himself illustrates the point, for in spite of not possessing—to use his own phrase—"a pot to piss in," he manages to do everything he wants, has a lively, lovely time somehow managing to see everything that is going on, and even creates a stimulating, congenial atmosphere in whatever overcrowded, faceless, little apartment he shares with Joseph, a poet, equally "pot-less." On my way downtown to dine with these two friends I was glowing with anticipation of an unusual evening.

In a dank, mushroom-smelling hallway I could not see the names of my friends pencilled among the others of the building: the light bulb had been filched. I started to mount the sagging stairs to 5C. I noticed that refuse from other apartments had been dumped outside each scabrous door, and some occupants had allowed their dogs to make messes on the impoverished landings.

Due to a misunderstanding about the time I should arrive, a

soufflé which, I was told, had resembled the Himalayas was now flat and of the consistency of chamois leather. However, Chuck and Joseph were pleased to see me and seemed somewhat over-excited—for they both spoke in high-pitched voices above the clattering of kitchen utensils, the decibels of radio turned on full volume, and a hysterical neighbor outside calling from her window: "Mary! Mary! Mary! Mary!"

While I wondered how much more junk and jumble could be piled into one room they exclaimed: "We just love this apartment! It's so much more sympathetic than the other which had the elevated railway running through the windows." "And, my dear, it's cheaper!" "At least by two or three dollars."

I asked if the music and the heat could be turned lower, and if the boys could please talk one at a time; neither of them seemed to resent my behavior.

In spite of their enthusiasms, I could read between the lines a story of failure and disillusion. Chuck managed to make a joke of the wicked way his dealer had treated him, and was still convinced that he himself, as well as everyone he admires and likes, is on the verge of success. But it soon became obvious that his saga was one of hopes unfulfilled and faith undermined. It was also easy to see that Joseph was in a pretty cynical state, even near to despondency, having been taken out of his humble surroundings by a rich protector and shown the bright lights of Europe, only recently to be most cruelly dropped back where he came from.

A third young man lurched in. He was also their roommate, but where space could be found for him to doss down I was unable to imagine. Ken turned out to be a prospective playwright, recently out of the army. He has not yet received acclaim though he has written a dozen plays and done much spade work for the Schuberts. (He wrote from the French a new version of a popular musical comedy which has been touring the country for three years with separate companies, and for which he was paid in full by Mr. Schubert the princely sum of $300.)

Chuck and Jo had prepared the dinner in a kitchen the size of a boothole, yet the ragoût, with savory rice and mushroom in cream, was delicious, and the sauce showed particular imagination. But with so much attention paid to pots, pans, plates, and cutlery, the talk was in jerks. Jo confessed: "I'm afraid our dessert is going to be rather skimpy," and produced about seven wizened strawberries on a blue and white saucer. The would-be playwright protested: "Oh, you can't offer those—there aren't enough of them. Keep them for tomorrow and let's have some cheese." Jo said: "But they won't last until tomorrow! Already I've had to throw away four that were mildewed, and you know fresh strawberries are terribly expensive." The playwright agreed that he would never buy fresh strawberries.

We sat back to enjoy coffee and after-dinner conversation, but somehow the temperature of the flat could not be regulated; throughout the evening the room was either suffocatingly hot or fiendishly drafty. The neighbor still kept up her wail for Mary, floorboards exploded with pops and bangs when anyone walked across them, and a number of strange characters came to tread over them. These people obviously had a quite different code of manners from those I see in my limited circle. They appeared to have a truer relationship with each other, indulging in no pretenses and saying just what was on their canny, alert minds even to the extent of exhibiting their own nakedness as well as that of others.

This was a group of *avant-garde* intellectuals who had come to hear a young Italian with long black hair read one of his short stories. The Italian began by protesting that he had a headache, had been ill all day, and didn't really want to read his story because he didn't like it or think it good. However, as everyone had come to hear him he would not disappoint them, and he would welcome criticisms afterwards. He spoke without any shyness or self-consciousness.

The short story was about a long-haired Italian being offered by a series of would-be helpful friends a succession of most unsuitable jobs. Naturally he turned each one down. But, after a while, the self-satisfied hero became so antipathetic that, contrary to the author's intention, one felt more sympathy for the friends who were being made fools of for trying to help him. One would have liked the story to have ended with the "hero's" being drafted into the army, made to accept rigorous discipline, or in some way forbidden to seek his own destruction.

When, at last, the reading was over the author was given a gruelling by everyone in the room. He was spared nothing: people were plain damn offensive to him. I had to admire his pluck in standing up against so many devastating onslaughts. Eventually everyone, including its creator, agreed that the story was of no interest whatsoever. Then everyone left—without even a "thank you." All very collegiate and casual.

Chuck gave his verdict: the evening had been a failure. But he did not apologize; failure was just something that happened every once and again—it was a natural phenomenon. In professional life too many people, especially in New York, are afraid of failure. But failure can sometimes teach one more than success—it is not something to be ignored. Too much emphasis is put on success.

I admitted to Chuck that often I felt embarrassed by failure. I told him of a calamitous evening I had spent recently with a married couple who fought all during dinner in front of their glamorous débutante daughter. The girl was so upset at my being present that she started picking off her red enamel nail varnish at the table. I, too, was chagrined. "Wouldn't I have preferred a quiet, uneventful, agreeable evening?" I asked Chuck.

"Oh, but why? It was so much more exciting! Think how much less interesting an easy, convivial evening would have been; you'd have forgotten all about it by the time you got home. But you'll never forget that evening, will you?"

On my way back to my "luxury-hotel" I realized that, in spite of everything, this too had not been just another evening to forget. But I had not completely decided in my own mind whether or not Connolly's phrase had been discounted or strengthened in this instance.

John Jacob Astor

The Museum of Modern Art must raise more funds. Alice Astor, a great lover of the arts and a most generous friend, arranges for a meeting between her step-brother, John Jacob Astor, and Monroe Wheeler, a Museum curator. John Jacob possesses millions of dollars. He is inveigled to the Museum. He does not appear to see anything. He does not appreciate most modern paintings. Conversation is extremely hard to sustain and time goes slowly for all. John Jacob remains, exhausting the various members of the Museum staff who are told to entertain him in relays.

At last John Jacob sees a painting that galvanizes him to life: "That's a Hopper, isn't it!" He explains that he too possesses a Hopper. "It's a railroad scene." John Jacob knows all about railroads. "Oh, Hopper's fine! But mine is a better Hopper than this!" "Have you seen the Hopper show that's on now?" asks Monroe. "No. There's a whole show of Hopper, is there? Oh, I'd like to see that! And I'd like to meet Hopper, and tell him how much I like my Hopper, and find out if my Hopper's as much a favorite of his as it is of mine." At last John Jacob had thawed. "It's nice to meet the people whose work you admire," he said. "Now, for instance, I've always admired Bing Crosby, and I once had occasion to meet him, and I said: 'Now, Mister Crosby, which of the songs you sing is your favorite?' He looked blank for a minute, and then I said to him: 'Mine is "Love In Bloom,"' then Bing Crosby said: 'That's strange—that's my favorite also.'"

"Well," said Monroe, "we'll arrange for Hopper to come to his show any day you can make it. He's an old man, but he lives in New York and will be available." At last the multi-millionaire left. Two days later a check for two hundred dollars arrived—"A small contribution towards the Museum."

Monroe arranged the meeting with Hopper. He schooled the elderly painter and told him the Bing Crosby story. "If you get on well with him he may possibly buy another picture of yours."

John Jacob arrived at the Hopper show. "This is Mister Hopper." "Glad to know you. I've got one of your pictures." "Oh, yes?" says Hopper vaguely. "Now tell me, of all the pictures you've painted, which is your favorite?" "Oh, I don't know," says the bored Hopper. "But what subjects do you like best? The ones you do of railroads?" "Not specially," said Hopper lugubriously. "Well, now I think I've got your best picture," continued John Jacob determinedly. "Oh, yes?" queries Hopper. John Jacob, undaunted, describes the picture: "Do you remember a painting with a view you see from the railroad on 126th Street between Lexington and Third?" "No, can't say I do," says Hopper.

The tour of the exhibition is made in silence. In front of one picture John Jacob halts. "Oh, yes, I recognize that scene. That's the railroad just before you get to Rhinecliffe. But that house—is that there? No, there's no house like that on the line!" cries John Jacob. "No," says Hopper, "I never paint from life. I do all my work in the studio; I just make up the picture in my mind!" "But the picture of yours that I have is absolutely correct. You must have painted that one on the spot." "No, in my studio," says Hopper stubbornly.

John Jacob leaves Hopper to go behind the scenes, and in a small room off the gallery he asks: "Would Hopper paint the street where I live—81st Street? At one end is the Metropolitan Museum and the other the funeral parlor." "Let's ask him." In reply Hopper shrugs his shoulders. "I never go out and paint what I see. Maybe if I look at your street I could get some sort of impression—maybe of the funeral parlor?" "I only want you to paint my house," continued John Jacob, "if you feel inspired. But 81st's a street with an atmosphere. Now I'll tell you, I love New York City and I love it all the year round. I like it even in summer, even in great heat. Except last summer—that was too much for me. Last July I went out of my house and walked up the street and there was no one about. I went as far as Fifth Avenue. There was still not a living soul to be seen. It was peculiar; I felt strange. I said to myself: 'You're in a completely deserted city. You'd better get out!' Believe me, that evening I quit! Now that just shows 81st Street has some sort of an atmosphere! So if you feel like painting a picture of 81st Street for me, I'd be very pleased."

Monroe thanked him on the part of Hopper, and thanked him on the part of the Museum for the contribution. "We're all thrilled by your generosity," Monroe said. John Jacob said: "It should have been more, and I know it."

_____ *Edward James*

Edward James[1] has been in New York for the past week sporting an extraordinary beard. Every day he is leaving for his home in Mexico on the morrow, but he goes on borrowing days and thereby enjoying a sense of holiday. When, eventually, he arrives on his remote mountaintop it will be only for a moment, for he is due back here at a certain date to continue his almost unceasing fight with lawyers. He is perhaps not the poet, writer, painter, or connoisseur of art he would like to be, but he is a great profes-

[1] Expatriate Englishman, patron of the arts, son of Edwardian hostess Mrs. Willie James.

sional fighter. Wherever Edward goes there is trouble, yet he never seems to be unnerved. On his recent return to West Dean, the family seat in Sussex, having been away all the war, he accused his father's servants of having mislaid the stamp collection, and of generally behaving badly.

But Edward knows his own failings more intimately than anyone else. The intricate complications of his mind and his startling eccentricities give him enormous enjoyment; he laughs with a high cackle at them. There is no hope for him.

Edward arranges to buy another drawing from Dali in order to induce Dali to repaint the sky of one of his earliest oil paintings, which has since become ruined by mold or blisters. Edward then discovers in Mexico City the fantastic pictures of the Englishwoman Leonora Carrington. His loyalties switch. He will tell the Dalis that his lawyers have refused to allow him to buy the very expensive Dali drawing, but in order to keep the Dalis sweet he buys a piece of costume jewelry for Dali's wife Gala. It was reduced from sixty dollars to thirty dollars at Saks. Edward roars with delight. "Gala will take it to be 'expertized,' and when she finds out it is false she will be furious, but I will be back in Mexico City. And if Dali refuses to repaint the sky I shall get my lawyers to sue him, because it is really too bad!"

Next day Edward forgets he has told me about the costume jewelry. "How do you like this brooch for Gala? Pretty, isn't it? It cost sixty dollars." "Thirty dollars, Edward." Edward claps his hands together, gives a leap in the air, and rushes round the room like a cat on hot bricks, yelling with fiendish laughter.

_____ *Audrey Bouverie*

Audrey James Marshall Field Bouverie[1] is a good friend, tough and courageous. After a varied career she has now achieved francs in France, pounds in England, and dollars in America. She manages always to overcome war-restriction difficulties: she has the best of all worlds. While in New York she has had a face lift and a new jaw and dentures. She buys like a mad sailor: Impressionist

_____
[1] Sister of Edward James

paintings, Meissen porcelain, furs, Fulco jewelry, anything that strikes her fancy. She does not know how to retrench.

A journalist interviews her. "Mrs. Bouverie, what do you think of 'the new look'? What are you going to wear to Miss Elsa Maxwell's party tonight?"

Audrey, vexed, and unable to compete with this sort of pre-war bright young thing attitude, answers: "My new teeth."

Overheard on Central Park South: Two ladies airing a dog. One says: "Well, I read the *Sure Hand of God* and it is the dirtiest thing!"

_____ *Adele Astaire*

Adele was having a whisky and soda between trills from the latest hit song, and conversing with the waiter when I arrived in her hotel suite to have lunch with her. The waiter was giving Adele fascinating titbits of information: he had once found one of the richest men in the world on his knees in the bathroom cooking a can of soup over an improvised stove in order to avoid the room-service charges. Adele's drink was ordered because she had just spent $595 on an evening dress and needed sustenance. She was aghast at the price she had paid but could not resist the beauty of the confection. "It's all right to wear ready-made clothes outside New York, but you just can't have everyone know you had only spent $25. But if you go to a party and find several other people wearing the same expensive dress, you're pleased to know how rich you are. Besides, I think it does you good to get something you've been hankering after for a long time."

"When did you first start hankering for your new dress?"

"This morning."

Adele couldn't decide whether she would ask her new husband to pay for it or whether she would stump up herself. Her husband had promised to pay for the mink cape she'd just bought. Adele's doing a lot of shopping now.

It is quite staggering to realize that Adele is almost fifty. The skinny little waif of *Stop Flirting* has put on a bit of weight (seven pounds, she says), and she admits that her neck has become "crepy." But she is still youthful, with amused, bright eyes. It is no wonder that she recently remarried. She was lonely at Lismore[1] after Charlie died, and she got sick of going to bed at nine o'clock at night. Although the castle was left to her for life, she did not feel the place belonged to her and decided, instead of becoming an old Irish vegetable, to start again in New York. If her children had lived instead of dying prematurely they would have been fifteen and twelve years old now. But Adele said: "I suppose it was meant that way," and she confessed that she really had no maternal instinct. Her husband's three sons "embarrass" her, she admitted.

The Devonshire family had been very generous to her and, thanks to Charlie's secret business transactions, she is now left well off.

Her husband, Kingsie,[2] divorced a rich wife to marry Adele, who is now boosting him to become rich in his own right. He works in Wall Street all day and often goes off on business trips. The result is that she does not feel fully married—which is just how she wishes it for, she says, she does not want to look, or to feel, married.

She accepts her age gracefully and gives genuine encouragement to new people coming up into the limelight—which is remarkable, for rarely does it happen in the theatre that those who have been stars in their youth, with all the adulation it entails, are able to adjust themselves to retirement. In her own kooky way Adele has much wisdom.

When I left her she was off to Bergdorf Goodman to buy a silk dressing gown for Kingsie, he hadn't one she liked. While she was about it, she might pop into Tiffany's.

_____ *Photographers and Photographing*

The bath water was running when Louise Dahl-Wolfe, the photographer whose work is so gentle and whose antennae are so sharp, telephoned. She thanked me for sending *My Royal Past*, which she had never seen before. She was very appreciative—even fulsome—and asked me who had posed for the pictures in the book.

She was speaking from her New York studio, but had cancelled

---

[1] Lismore Castle in Ireland where she had lived with her husband, Lord Charles Cavendish

[2] Mr. Kingsman Douglas.

the sitting for which she had specially come in from the country ("Where we live it's where all the cows and things are—oh, it's quite rural.") because she felt a cold coming on. She didn't feel like taking pictures: she had to look after herself. It gave me the thought that over here people know better than those in my country how to take care of themselves: that old heroine Gertrude Pidout in the London *Vogue* office continued to hold the fort even while suffering from 'flu till eventually she fainted in a bus trying to reach home one night. I also drag myself out to work when I'm virtually a hospital case, for I don't like the idea of cancelling other people's arrangements unless my situation is really grave.

Louise told me of the aftermath of the dinner given by Carmel Snow, chief editor of *Harper's Bazaar,* at which Frances McFadden, another *Bazaar* editor, had asked me in what direction I thought fashions in photography were going. It seems I had answered that it was time to give up all this "piss elegance" and to get more reality into the pictures. Two days later the "Editorial Beauty Conference" took place. The suggestion for the next cover came from Frances McFadden, who wanted a woman to be photographed with her hair all wet and set with pins before going under the dryer. Louise did not think that would be photogenic. Mrs. Snow said: "Oh, no!" And McFadden said wistfully: "Well, after all it *is* reality we're after!"

Louise then talked with much admiration of Charlie James's clothes and said how sad it was Diana Vreeland[1] seldom gave her his things to be photographed for the magazine. "Can't you get it right between them, Cecil? If you just explain to Diana that you think he's the one person with a grain of inspiration and originality in this country?"

We had talked so long that my bath was cold and already it was lunchtime. Thinking there's no time like the present, I telephoned Charlie to know if he were free for lunch; but I warned him not to be late because I would have to leave for a photography sitting. I explained I had a plan to discuss. The plan was how best to bring Diana and him together. She is an appreciative, sensitive person and I know she would respond to such an interesting type as Charlie. But if I arranged a lunch would Charlie give his word

---

[1] Then working on the fashion staff of *Harper's Bazaar,* later editor of *Vogue.*

not to be insulting — not to create a scene? He can be relied upon to do much harm to himself; but for his own waspish character he would have succeeded long before this. If he had decided to use his extraordinary brain as a philosopher or a writer, the world could have benefited by his originality and few individuals would have known how tricky and unhappy an individual he is. However, there are not enough women in New York who realize he has genius.

Charlie said he would come around immediately, but of course he was late. When at last he materialized my mood had changed to exasperation.

"I've been waiting nearly an hour for you, Charlie, and there's so little time left to talk."

"Oh, I stopped and had a hamburger on the way."

Is it to be wondered at that my wish to help turned sour? The more Charlie's voice droned on like a road drill about his workroom difficulties, his latest unrequited love affair, and his hatred of Elizabeth Arden, the more expert he proved himself at showing his natural instinct for saying the wrong thing. "The plan" was delayed.

Charles is in many ways like his namesake, Edward, who is less embittered as a person, for he knows his own faults and admits his guilt. Charles James fumes and foams without ever seeing that it might be he who is in the wrong.

Naturally I was late for my appointment. New York was under a heavy pall of muddy snow like fudge, and the traffic was almost at a standstill. I got into a bus, but it would have been better to walk. When I arrived at the studio my sitter hadn't appeared. I had no idea in what manner I would photograph Mrs. Vincent Astor.

Anita Loos and John Emerson

Anita Loos and I were discussing the strange, lifelong relationship of an eminent American dressmaker and his companion. Anita suggested that the basis of their link was one of mutual hatred. At meals they have nothing to talk about; the elder does not encourage the younger to speak in front of others, nor does she give him credit for any contribution to the designing business, which, in fact, should proclaim both names on the bill heads.

"It's just like John and me," Anita continued in her quavery, high-pitched voice. "All these years I've been married to him, he's hated me. He's been so jealous of my success that he could hardly bear it. Admittedly he liked the money I made for him, but he would have preferred it to have been anonymously. When my first chapters of *Gentlemen Prefer Blondes* caught on in *Bazaar* so that the circulation went up ten times, and, for the first time, men began reading a woman's magazine, John begged me not to have the series published in book form. The publishers were offering me wild sums, but John knew best, and said: 'Everyone that's going to read them has already done so.' When he at last realized that I couldn't give up the publisher's fees, he brought in a slip of paper, nipped me on the chin and said: 'Well, little bug, I want you to dedicate your book to me. I've written this out—just as it should be,' and he handed me the slip: 'To John Emerson, without whose help and encouragement this book would never have been published.' When *Blondes* had the success that it did, John had a nervous breakdown. His health never really completely recovered."

Anita made a fortune, which John invested. In 1929 most of it was lost in the stock market crash. Since then, by painful degrees, Anita has refilled the coffers in spite of the difficulties put in her way. John insisted on collaborating, but his contribution consisted solely of criticising in the afternoon Anita's morning work. "Well, bug, I'm sorry but this isn't good enough. Your punctuation is appalling: it just won't do!" and John would relapse into a hoarse cough that left him speechless and breathless.

Vast sums of Anita's money were spent travelling across Europe in search of new doctors who could do some good to John's throat. One after the other the doctors confided to Anita that they could find nothing wrong with the larynx. They considered that the illness was due to frustration and lack of personal success—so the search for other doctors went on. No matter where she was, Anita continued to work; she would start at five in the morning, and until noon she would be filling notebook after notebook with the latest longhand rewrite of new scripts, plays and novels. By signing film contracts that were like jail sentences—although her childhood was spent in Hollywood she now hated the place—once more she found herself in California churning out endless scenarios. Many of these were such successes that again she accumulated a great deal of money, which John again took control of. When Anita made her greatest success with a film for Jean Harlow, John became so wild with rage that he chased Anita with a knife. He was taken away to a sanatorium.

It was later discovered that John had, without her realizing it, gotten Anita to sign an annuity for his life. An old doctor friend was called in, told of what had happened, and asked for advice. He roared with laughter. General consternation! When his amusement subsided he explained: "John'll get the best of the insurance company!" It transpired that their financial gamble was worked out on the premise that John was now in such poor shape, and that he would not long survive. "I bet," roared the doctor, "that John lives another twenty years—just to spite the insurance guys."

This is just what is happening. Anita continued: "When John discovered that we had all found out the trick he'd played, he shook all over. He nearly went off his rocker, for, you see, he isn't really a bad man. He's a schizophrenic—a split personality—and the good man becomes appalled at the actions of the bad. John knew he had behaved in an underhand way, but he needed his independence; that was the only way he could get it.

"As it has turned out, it's all been for the best, as John's been living on less than it would have cost me if I'd had to go on maintaining him. The insurance people are the losers."

The old doctor summed up: "I knew John at school. I've never in my life come across such unbounded ambition as he had. Alas, it's never been fulfilled, and that's why he hates everyone who has the place in the sun that he could never attain."

_____ *Dining at Le Pavillon*

Last night I dined with the Garson Kanins at Le Pavillon. Margaret Case had brought Terence Rattigan, who had just scored a palpable hit with *The Winslow Boy*.

The ecstatically married Kanins (she is the redoubtable actress, Ruth Gordon) make a splendid team—both so bright, quick and humorous, they seem to spark off each other. In conversation they know to dispense with all unnecessary impedimenta, driving right to the point, sticking to it, and brooking no interruptions.

Talk consisted mainly of the various techniques writers employ in doing their work. The Kanins start at eight in the morning (Ruth, in an aside: "This, for an actress of many years' standing, is still quite an effort!"), and their creative work is done with the first flush of energy. After lunch comes the retouching and polishing of former days' efforts. They are like a couple of athletes; their training is rigorous. When on a job they do not allow themselves one drink; even a whisky and soda the night before calls for its dividend of energy the next day, they say.

Terry prefers to while away an evening with small talk and a little whisky. But tonight he was challenged; he was on his mettle to talk. It was fascinating to hear him, like a business man, assess his talent. Artistic construction is of the greatest interest to him and even *The New Statesman* admits he knows all about the well-knit play. He studies Ibsen, Shaw, and Pinero for the way in which they create their effects, but he had learned most from Shakespeare.

Terry is attuned to work only after long preliminaries and skirmishes. At eleven o'clock in the morning he starts, fully dressed, lying on a bed with his papers and sharpened pencils carefully adjusted around him. He retouches and buffs his play as he goes along, sometimes crossing out a line dozens of times before he feels he has the right one. But this decision then becomes final; he does not alter it afterwards. However, his most creative hours are nocturnal.

The intensity of expression on Ruth's face as she listens is so great that one can almost see the energy and dynamic force which drive her. It is typical of her and her husband that they both have much work in hand while there is much already ready for production: Garson with a couple of film scripts and a play, Ruth with three plays. They know the hazards of the entertainment world.

Neither of them is now in the first flush of youth, but they are completely contemporary in their outlook and bored by nostalgic revivals in the theatre. It is the immediate future that absorbs and stimulates them. Their huge success is fully enjoyed by both. They are living at a fantastic rate; their extravagances (according to their great friend, Anita Loos — but then Anita has learned to be on the careful side) are such that if both of them have a successful play running each year for the next six years, they will still be behind with their taxes.

Their leanings politically are liberal, but they live like royalty. They do not care to see films in the company of "all those crowds" and prefer to wait until someone arranges for them to be shown in a private preview room. They have their own chauffeur (a rarity in New York), and take their meals at the most expensive restaurants. Ruth buys whole hog from Mainbocher, likewise the most expensive dressmaker. Garson showers her with presents so that she resembles a little Burmese idol studded with bulbous jewelry. They consider money is of no use unless spent.

I hated the hands of the clock for revolving so quickly. The bill for tonight's "boiled dinner," followed by a *Bombe Pavillon* (an ice cream with hot prunes, pineapple, nuts, etc., etc.), with the best wines available and liqueurs, must have made inroads into many a Kanin dividend.

_____ *Reunion with Garbo*/Friday, March 15th, 1946: Plaza Hotel*

Because of the continued tugboat strike the Mayor has officially "closed the city." With the shortage of fuel there is only a small quota for heating or lighting large meeting places: banks, offices, theatres, cinemas and bars are therefore shut. New York has become a village.

The most gregarious of people are the worst hit if they are suddenly faced with the reality of relying upon their own company: they do not relish the unaccustomed opportunity of remaining at home with a book. By six o'clock the solitude becomes unbearable: SOS's are sent to anyone who will come around to share the fast diminishing supply of drink.

However, the meeting at Margaret Case's on this bitter antarctic evening had been specifically arranged—a day or two in advance—in order to bring about my first reunion with Garbo.

Ten years had passed since our first meeting in Hollywood. On that extraordinary evening, having quaffed large quantities of Bellinis (peach juice laced with champagne), we had improvised wild dances, done impersonations, acted charades, and altogether behaved as if we had known each other forever. We had been like two elemental creatures, loving and laughing with none of the usual barriers of shyness or modesty that strangers must over-come. But when, eventually, dawn broke over Beverly Hills and Garbo drove away in her ramshackle old car, she gave no in-dication that she would allow me to continue this so violent and intimate a friendship. In fact she refused my suggestion that I should eat a spinach lunch with her later that day at the studio and the following afternoon I left Hollywood. I did not write to her for I knew that was how she would have preferred it. I would certainly have received no reply.

Then with the war Hollywood lost its European film market and, since Garbo had never been considered a commercial propo-sition in America, the MGM studio allowed her career to grind to a halt.

During the years of war I never discovered Garbo's where-abouts, yet the spell that she had worked upon me had never been cast off. Each snippet of news about her intrigued me, and any little snapshot that appeared in a newspaper corroborated my belief that she was the most mysterious and alluring phenomenon in the wide world. Would I ever be fortunate enough to meet for a second time this most elusive of creatures?

I hadn't been at the Plaza more than a few days when Margaret Case informed me that Garbo was in the city. Although Garbo was no longer on the screen, her myth was as alive as ever and her secretiveness as tantalizing to the public. Yet, it was said, on occa-sions she did abandon her hermit's life to go out into the world of café society—in fact, to the most unsuitable places where she met those very people who would be most willing to exploit her and disregard her dislike of publicity. We referred to her constant companion on these occasions as "the little man," well known in New York circles for his gentle charm, business acumen, and sophisticated manner of living. Recently "the little man" had discovered a delicatessen that imported caviar straight from Rus-sia, so Garbo and her companion had invited themselves to the houses of mutual friends to drink vodka, bringing with them a pot of "the real thing."

Few people have done more good turns for me in my lifetime than my old friend Margaret Case, who had been one of the first to welcome me as a stranger during my initial trip to New York. By enticing "the little man" to bring Garbo back into my existence she was performing one more—probably the greatest—coup on my behalf.

When I came through the hallway of Margaret's apartment three people were sitting around a small circular table set with glasses and plates. At the sight of Garbo I felt knocked back, as if suddenly someone had opened a furnace door onto me: I had almost to gasp for the next breath. The warmth of her regard, her radiance, her smile—robbed me of equilibrium; I held onto the back of a chair. Garbo made no definite sign of recognition but seemed to glean amusement from the mere sight of me. She took it for granted that once again I had immediately fallen in love with her. She was kindness itself, and I was flattered beyond belief to be the object of her attentions as she spread a piece of caviar on a biscuit and offered it to me pronouncing the word "kahr-vee-yeyarr" with histrionic flamboyance. Margaret and "the little man" sat talking quietly in the middle distance while I gazed at the apparition in front of me as it laughed and jabbered and waved in a frontal attack upon me.

She had changed in appearance since our first meeting. Then she had been like a large apricot in the fullness of its perfection: she was rounded, of a smooth surface. Now the apricot quality had given place to vellum. Her eyes were still like an eagle's—blue-mauve and brilliant, the lids the color of a mushroom—but there were a few delicate lines at the corners. The face having become thinner, the nose appeared spikier, which made the modelling of its tip and the nostrils more sensitive. The hair, that had appeared golden in the Californian sun, was now an uncompromising, but beautiful, cinder-mouse. I noticed that the bold, workmanlike hands were a little weatherbeaten, and her ankles and legs had the uneven, somewhat scrawny look of a waif's or of certain poor, older people: they were at odds with the grandeur of her aura but made her seem terribly vulnerable. No shadow of the conventional New York woman of fashion hovered near her: the hat could have belonged to a tinker engraved by Callot, and her shirt was that of a highwayman. In her all-gray grays she looked like a Mantegna. Although she exuded no impression of luxury one knew her to be a person of the most sifted quality.

She did the honors of the occasion in what one imagines was the theatrical style of Bernhardt: every gesture was bold and big.

Conversing in a somewhat heightened social manner, the content of her phrases was less important than her presence and charm, which made the small gathering into a gala. She conveyed innate sweetness and delicacy of feeling as the topics changed from circus clowns to the Paris Flea Market and undergarments. She confided how much she disliked being restricted by her clothes in any way, even by garters or brassière. When she used the word *brassière* she put her hands up to her mouth in shocked surprise at what she had said. Her voice was caressing while evoking a heartbreaking pathos. Her laugh was mellow, kindly. More caviar, and more vodka. General conversation and congeniality. The companion was in good humor, making jokes and telling funny stories.

Almost imperceptibly, Garbo let drop the fact that she remembered our first charming meeting. She remarked with a smile: "I didn't wear lipstick when you knew me before." I noticed now that her mouth was slightly too generously daubed with carmine, but the effect was charming — as if a child had been at the jam jar. With her smile so incredibly spontaneous and ever-changing expressions running across her eyes, her head thrown back to look at one from under lowered lids, it was clear that nature had endowed her. She had all the arts of enticement.

Abruptly, after she had smoked five Old Golds, it was time to leave. Panic struck me. Perhaps this was the end. Or would another ten years pass before we again met? We had had no opportunity to speak to one another in private. In desperation, and on an inspiration of the second, I implored her to come out onto the roof garden and look at the extraordinary effect — like sticks of Elizabethan jewelry — of the lit-up skyscrapers around us.

The sudden cold outside went through the body like a succession of knives, but I was determined that she should remain there until I struck a chord of intimacy. She talked, talked, talked, gabbled ever harder, like an excited child, in order to cover her embarrassment at the things I was blurting out to her while discovering the knobbles of her spine and smelling the new-mown hay freshness of her cheeks, ear and hair. Before joining the others, panic-stricken and frozen, she promised she would telephone me.

Several days elapsed without her calling. I was not permitted to telephone her, so nothing to do but wait in patience and hope. I was beginning to think she would never make the initial move. One afternoon, when least expected, she inquired without explaining who it was on the telephone: "What are you doing?" I gulped: "Not a thing in the world." Of course anything I was doing, or should have been doing, was shelved forthwith, for a miracle was about to happen and she was coming to see me right away.

She arrived, somewhat out of breath, dressed entirely in darkest blue, looking pale but even more incandescent than before. A crowd of bobby-sox autograph hunters had run after her on her way to my hotel shouting her name; when she paid them no attention they jeered and laughed devishly. They had upset her. But now she would enjoy a cigarette, calmly. We sat side by side on a long red sofa. She had not telephoned before because she had been ill. She had caught cold, doubtless by going onto that roof top. I felt great guilt. But she explained she is an easy victim of colds, and it was foolish of her to be tempted out into the icy night winds. "But if you had not come out on the roof with me you wouldn't be here this afternoon." She smoked more Old Golds and drank a cup of tea remarking that cows' milk tastes so much better if it is not pasteurized, and when she pronounced a biscuit to be *"deliciosa"* I remarked: "Then this is a festival," to which she chirped: "Is zat so?" She talked with the excited vivacity of a child just home for the holidays and did not look around her at my room or show surprise or curiosity at what might be considered its somewhat startling decoration. But she did compliment me on keeping the rooms at a reasonable temperature: in fact, the steam heat was never turned on. "Ah, fresh air!" then saluting, she cried: "British Empire!" This was funny and somehow made sense, and I suppose I was flattered by, even in a fantasy, personifying the Empire.[1] Garbo employed many "service" terms and, in reply to

_____

[1] I later discovered the origin of her having purloined this phrase. When looking for a house in Hollywood she and a friend had been surprised to find a little old woman who answered the door speaking in an extremely refined manner. Garbo had asked "You are not American, are you?" to which the little woman proudly gulped; "Oh no—English. British Empire."

my question as to where she lived most of the year, said: "Oh, I follow the Fleet." She elaborated: "I don't quite know what that means, but I often say things like that, that only signify if you scratch beneath the surface." But I discovered quickly that it displeased her to be asked any direct question, and she would invariably answer with some evasion.

We continued with a game of badinage that made little sense and yet was light and fantastic and to me, her abject victim, devastatingly entertaining. "Are you a cobbler?" she suddenly asked apropos of nothing, "or are you a cutter?" "No, I don't think I am," I answered lamely, not yet on to the game. She certainly did not consider herself as an actress. "Being stared at by all those people is a pretty shabby business," she said, and went on to tell how once in Sweden she had gone to a theatre alone. The audience was well-dressed and they were watching an actor play "a well-dressed part," but he had a tear in his coat. "That was so poignant! But then things can so often be so dismal, uncongenial, and obnoxious." About a man with a goiter: "How can you laugh at a human being who is having trouble with his glands!" Albinos: "They have such uneasiness with their eyes— they can hardly see. They are so pained and humiliated! Poor creatures of the world! Poor human beings!"

The whole conversation had a rather wacky, inconsequential quality, but because the creature sitting by my side was so ineffably strange and beautiful, one automatically and willingly accepted the idiom imposed by her. This wackiness took the place of wit and would change erratically from gay to sad. "A doctor once looked at me very carefully and asked: 'Why are you unhappy? Is it because you imagine you're ill?' Another doctor asked: 'Are you bored?' I don't know why he used so violent a word!"

Another reason for my delight in her talk was that I was savoring, with a certain surprise, the still quite strong "arckscentte" with which she spoke the English language. The tongue seemed to strike the back of the upper teeth with greater force than when a native slurs over his sentences. It gave added point to words: "like fleet" ("likke-fleatte"), "luck" ("luckke"), "kid" ("kidde"), and "ring" ("wringge"). Certain vowels were invested with unusual importance. ("Valuable" became "vuargh-luobbhle," "natural" = "nahr-turrell"; while *o* and *a* became *u*—"hospital" = "huspitulle," "standard" = "stundadtt.") The Swedish version of "known" sounds strangely Cockney ("knewgnne"), and "cooler" and "cutter" assumed quite an American blurring of the *r*'s. *D* at the end of a word became a *t* ("wohrt" or "bohrt"). These variations on what had become the usual to me were all wrapped in a mellifluous sweetness of sound.

Apropos I know not what, she said: "My bed is very small and chaste. I hate it. I've never thought of any particular person in connection with marriage; but, just lately, I have been thinking that as age advances we all become more lonely, and perhaps I have made rather a mistake—been on the wrong lines—and should settle down to some permanent companionship."

This gave me the opportunity for which, subconsciously, I had been waiting. During the last few minutes I had known that—as the phrase has it—we were made for each other. Of this I was now quite certain. Not as a pleasantry, but to be taken very seriously, I asked: "Why don't you marry me?"

I had never before asked anyone to marry me, and yet to make this proposal now seemed the most natural and easy thing to do. I was not even surprised at myself. But Garbo looked completely astounded. "Good heavens, but this is so sudden!" She went on to soften her reaction. "I once said to a friend of mine who invited me out to lunch: 'Why, this is so sudden,' and he looked so hurt. But really, this is very frivolous of you. I don't think you should speak slightingly of marriage."

"But I mean it. I've never been more serious."

"But you hardly know me."

"I know all about you, and I want to tame you and teach you to be much happier."

"But we would never be able to get along together and, besides, you wouldn't like to see me in the morning in an old man's pajamas."

"I would be wearing an old man's pajamas, too. And I think we *would* get along well together—unless my whistling in the bathroom got on your nerves?"

"You're being very superficial: one doesn't plan one's life on other people's bathroom habits. Besides, you'd worry about my being so gloomy and sad."

"Oh no—you'd have to worry about why I was so happy, and you'd be the reason."

"It's a funny thing, but I don't let anyone except you touch my vertebrae—they so easily get out of place."

When it was time for her to leave, I took her down to the street. Returning to my room I wondered if she had really been here. Or had I, by some extraordinary wish fulfillment, dreamt into actuality the scene that had passed?

I looked around to see the proof that my imagination had not played a trick on me. Here was the reality: the tea cup with the lipstick, the ash tray with the Old Gold cigarette stubs, and the used matches—and the cushions against which she had leaned. I would have liked to ask the hotel maid not to tidy the room. I did not want her to puff out the cushions, but to preserve them just as they were now, or to cast them in bronze for always.

Next day was a typically busy working one with my delightful and tactful secretary, Miss Cleghorn, helping me to answer the succession of telephone calls which consisted mainly of appointments being rearranged or switched. Suddenly I was impatient for all this activity to close down and for nice Miss Cleghorn to leave, for an appointment had been made that was not to be rearranged or switched: Greta was to come in to see me at five thirty. I put a "Do Not Disturb" signal on the telephone, and a few minutes later there was an impatient woodpecker at the door.

Greta's mood was as inconsequential as yesterday's. She had no information to impart, made no reference to my outburst of a proposal, and gave a spontaneous performance of sheer gaiety and nonsense. In no apparent context she recited little pieces of Goethe in an excellent German accent, used a few French words as if to the manner born, then came down to earth with American slang: "By heck!"—"Shucks!"—"Darn it!" etc. She told me of any little oddment that had amused her: a woman wrote her a fan letter saying: "You have the character of a man, but the body of a woman—blast it!" She could not help being amused at the brutal finality of the disbelieving New York cop who interrupted a long-winded bum by telling him to beat it. Her friend Molnar, the Hungarian playwright, tells comic stories wonderfully well and has one in particular that amuses her, but it contains the use of a very crude word without which this story would not be funny.

Therefore, although she objects to the use of coarse language in her presence, Greta excuses the word and whenever she sees Molnar she begs him to repeat the story; each time he does so, Greta turns her face away and laughs.

Greta jumped from one conversational orbit to another and we talked about ourselves only in oblique terms. I tried, somewhat tentatively, to bind her down to plans that would necessitate our meeting one another continually in the near future. Would she not like to see a certain play, or go to see the Grecos in the Hispanic Museum, or to eat soft-shell crabs in a downtown restaurant? But her answers were deliciously vague, as if she never went to theatres, picture shows, or restaurants. I must be satisfied with the present and not bank upon any future dividends.

When she came to take her leave, she gathered her belongings together saying: "I never wear white gloves. I simplify life like mad!" I notice that when she puts on a hat she never looks to see how it is placed on her head. She is completely without feminine vanity, although at times she is interested in clothes—the sort that she likes: she peers a lot at shoes in shop windows, and at leather coats and sweaters. Suddenly she turned and said: "I don't know you from Adam (pronounced "Ardhum") and yet I was quite willing to stay here until breakfast time. That is, if you had remained with your head on the pillow beside me like a brother." Of course she did not mean this—it was part of a fantasy she was building. Then very sweetly and humbly she asked: "May I be permitted to make a telephone call?" and, when she lifted the receiver, doubtless to call "the little man," the operator asked: "Are you now taking your calls, Mister Beaton?" "Yes," Garbo replied. As G. was leaving the telephone rang. "Ah, there's life!" she said, but for me life was leaving.

We have started going out for walks together in Central Park. We "steppe outte" for miles very fast, around the reservoir, then all the way home from Ninety-Sixth Street to Fifty-Ninth. During these walks over the grass, under the early springtime trees, her mood becomes euphoric. To be part of nature gives her the same elation as champagne to a novice drinker. She strides, leaps, laughs, becomes as lithe as a gazelle. She takes deep quaffs of water at the public fountains.

Sometimes photographs are more like people than they are themselves. Occasionally, when I am walking along with Greta, I suddenly see her as she appeared in a prized photograph cut out from an old movie magazine. Today there were many such flashes; and once, when she stopped to turn and look at the new moon, I could see something that I knew intimately before I had ever met her. I watched her face in the varying lights of afternoon, and I could not help revealing to her that I had seen that particular effect before in *Queen Christina.* This sort of observation she considers unnecessary; she does not relish allusion to her film career, and I must try to avoid the subject. It was typically humble and unassuming that she remarked: "Once in Hollywood—to mention such a distant place. . . ."

This afternoon the park air was so cold, but bracing, that we had almost to gallop in order to stay warm. On the spur of the moment we ran up the steps of the Metropolitan Museum to thaw and to look at the fourteenth-century Angers tapestries of the Apocalypse, the terrible preface to the Last Judgment as related by St. John. They were based on the traditions of early French miniature painting, but the weavers gave a stylized rendering of nature to the backgrounds with butterflies' wings decorated with the heraldic bearings of Anjou and Brittany. Greta became so carried away that she was completely unself-conscious, as she whistled and sighed in admiration while other visitors stared at her. She made noises of delight at the birds and animals woven into the floral undergrowth of the fifteenth-century Cluny tapestries "The Hunt of the Unicorn." Pointing to some draperies done in reds and rose and dull pink: "Those are now my most beloved colors." "It's incredible that human beings can do such things!" she said. "Think of it—it's of an overwhelming elegance!" "*Quelle flamboyance!*" was her reaction to more formal Louis XIV designs. Although she may not speak any tongue grammatically, she has such an appreciation for words and sounds of words that she picks them from many different countries to use on the spur of the moment. "*Ah, le petit chien!*" she said of a little white tapestry dog that was much more a *chien* than a dog. She often uses archaic words and, for example, talks about somebody's "dwelling," and she describes her own looks as "poor and beggarly." On seeing a downtrodden bum, she would remark he was a "*verfluchter mench.*"

Her voice possesses a remarkable range of expressiveness; its warmth and sympathy are major elements in her towering personality. She imagines she now has very little Swedish accent; it is only when people do imitations of her to her face that she understands she may be wrong. When I asked her to repeat a word that began with a *j* ("jolly" she pronounces "yolly") she said: "No, won't do it! You're trying to find out if I have a Swedish accent."

I was impressed by her spontaneous appreciation of the best. Perhaps it is that, being of such a fine quality herself, she has an affinity with works of art. She does not seem even to notice the second-rate.

Soon we wandered among the plaster casts of the Michelangelo sculpture. Greta remembered from a sonnet that Michelangelo had said he liked only the things that would destroy lesser people. From this, and other scraps of odd information, she built up in vivid imagination a picture of an ugly little man, remote from sex and the ordinary contacts of life, who became to her as real as if she had known him. Her imagination is highly inflammable: given one spark she ignites into wild dreams and imaginings which can consume her completely. She said she often used to come to this sculpture room and stand for hours in front of these heads; if she stared at them long enough they became so utterly alive she was almost mesmerized.

When we looked at huge, over-life-size nudes, I realized how little the human body means to me in comparison to her. She was positively ravenous in admiration of the physical perfection of some of these figures, which she judged as if they were fruit or succulent sweets. She flicked out her tongue as if to taste them.

On the way back she quoted snatches of poetry, professing not to know the author of the poems she recites in many languages: "It's something I picked up years ago, and I've always been impressed by." In fact it is by Heine, or Michelangelo, or Sappho. Modestly she claimed that nowadays she seldom reads even newspapers—though she keeps them "for future use." "I always have a pile of three-month-old papers. I don't read them, but I collect them." However, she did admit that for a short while in the mornings now she is absorbed by the biography of a Swedish poet. "A young woman who died of tuberculosis, who wrote such adorable poetry, and whenever she referred to herself, or drew

pictures of herself, saw herself as a man. Her name was Harriet."
This is no doubt the reason why, when Greta travels incognito,
she uses the name Harriet Brown.

Today she tried to quote a paragraph from Joseph Conrad, but
she had forgotten most of it. It came, she said, from the story
called *Youth*. I later found what I thought was the quotation and
read it over the telephone: "The strength of it! And the faith of
it! And the imagination of it!" But no—that was not it. I gave
her several other quotes. "No." She said: "It's the feeling that
youth dies before you know it." Later I found the passage: "The
glow in the heart that with every year grows dim, grows cold,
grows small and expires too soon—too soon before life itself."

Each and every outing is an adventure for me. It is as if I am
learning a new language or discovering a foreign country. Each
day I feel I am able to understand more clearly how this remarkable person differs from the rest of humanity. By degrees a few
pieces of the jigsaw puzzle fall into place. Yet I have always the
feeling of her elusiveness, that perhaps inadvertently I may let
drop a remark that might create fear and cause this rare bird to
fly away forever. Thus danger is always present: one is always
keyed to a pitch of high tension. Conversation is seldom direct
and most often conducted on a children's fable level. This gives
rein to Greta's flights of fantasy. I have also discovered that she
is one of the fairest people, never indulges in prejudices, always
sees the obstacles besetting her enemies, and therefore feels
compassion.

We walked to the museum and saw the exhibition of Near
Eastern costumes. The individuality of Greta's taste has been
developed so that she can spot in a flash something that is part of
her idiom. "Oh, that's got such chic," she said about a garment
which, although of a design of many hundred years back, might
have been created for her. "I'd like to have a hat like that," she
said, pointing to a dunce's cap made of the bark of a tree; "I'd
wear that smack on Fifth Avenue," and you knew she could, and
that it would look marvelous on her. She was intrigued by the

costumes of the veiled women who, to her, have such mystery and allure.

We were stopped in the park by an old German actor, who appeared out of nowhere and said he had a wonderful film story for her. It must be really a very peculiar sensation to know that almost everyone one sees knows one by sight.

Now that Greta has come to feel at ease in my company and can rely upon me as a companion, we go shopping around the neighborhood. It comforts her to have someone to stand by and strengthen her moral courage while she looks at a sweater or tries on a pair of shoes. At first I felt extremely self-conscious at being with someone so easily recognized, and it was disconcerting for me to notice the shop assistants winking at one another and whispering her name. I would be more taken aback than she when autograph hunters approached her. But it delights me to see the sweetness with which always she refuses. "No, I never do," she says, with such a melting smile that no umbrage could be taken.

She has perfected the technique of hiding her face, and it is amazing how quickly she sees people who know or recognize her, how adroitly she avoids them. Whenever any stranger advances to talk, even quite affably, Greta moans to herself: "Oh, no!"—as if a child has had its toy suddenly smashed. Her distress is acute; it is like a personal affront, an insult to her privacy. She told of how in a shop today the girls at the counter had yattered: "Is it?" "Of course it is!" "Where?" "Next to you!"—right in her face as if she hadn't existed.

Later, when we were coming into my hotel, two raucous teenage fans chased her up the steps, squawking like parrots. One of them asked me: "Is that Greta Garbo?" I did not reply. The girls were furious and said: "She should be glad we recognize her." I would have liked to have hit them with the Gruyère cheese we had just bought at the delicatessen on our way home. It had enchanted me to go to the market with Greta while she bought her groceries. The list was brought out: "Two celery, two carrots, 'ail.' How do you spell 'ale'?" It is a pleasure always to see how determinedly quiet and private she is in her taste: she does not know what it is to be pretentious. It is rare that someone endowed with riches and success retains such unswerving simplicity of character. Naturally Greta charmed all the store people by her playfulness and high spirits: her laughter breaks my heart.

"Right, then—at three o'clock." "And what will you do if I'm a little late?" I asked. "I'll be lying full length on my sofa making out a grocery list with my hat on." But, although I had to hurry through a photograph sitting for *Vogue* with the Duchess of Windsor, I was not late. We went shopping. The shop assistant asked her: "Excuse me, but isn't your face familiar to me? Have you anything to do with the movies?" "Maybe I have," Greta replied. Later, out on the street, a man nodded curtly. "It's so funny," Greta explained, "they think my face is familiar. They don't know who I am, but they imagine they know me and give a nod of recognition." She always has a realistic approach to everything and can never be flattered.

Greta, wearing a large gray fedora, strides through the park. The afternoon sky is blue and pink with apricot clouds—even the hideous skyscrapers become pink and verdigris. Today we laugh a lot. Greta tells me that she has very seldom laughed in her life before. This great trump card in my hand gives me much confidence and pleasure. When she asks if she might have the sketch of me that Bérard made, I feel I have really won a place in her life.

After each meeting we bid one another good-bye with a tremendous display of waving. Certain well brought up children are taught that it is considered "common" to wave. Greta is generally averse to drawing attention, yet she enjoys this pantomime so much that, as we retreat from one another, we bring out our handkerchiefs and wave our arms until nothing can be seen except a small, white, confetti speck in the crowds.

> One of the aspects of the loving conspiracy which unites two free beings consists in just the material breaking down of conventional repression. Through this return to nature they experience much the same kind of relief as does the Polar navigator when he wins through once again to the open sea.
>
> *René Guyon*

I picked up the telephone and asked for the Ritz Tower, then for her room. She answered. I asked: "Is that my beloved?" She gasped a little, and with rather an embarrassed and happy laugh admitted: "Yes." I took the opportunity of asking her for the first time that very daring question: "Do you love me?" To my astonishment she replied: "Yes." I was so surprised that I felt my ears could not be trusted, for it was so unlike her to respond in this way. I then stretched my luck by repeating the question—and again she said: "Yes." And I went on repeating it until finally she laughed and said: "You shouldn't ask direct questions."

This paragraph is from Benjamin Constant's *Adolphe,* but it seems to be about me:

> Who can describe the charm of love? That conviction that we have found the being who was destined by nature to be ours, that sudden illumination of life, that new value attaching to the slightest circumstances, those swift hours, the details of which elude us in retrospect through their very sweetness, leaving in our mind only a long trail of happiness; that playful gaiety which occasionally mingles for no reason with our general feeling of tenderness; in our love's presence such pleasure, in her absence such hope; such aloofness to all vulgar cares, such feeling of superiority towards all our surroundings and of certainty that, on the plane on which we are living, society can no longer touch us; and that mutual understanding which divines each thought and responds to each emotion—the charm of love! Those who have known the charm of love cannot describe it!

I have discovered that Greta's memory is erratic. Certain events—particularly those connected with California—evaporate from her mind. Earlier ones remain in full detail. She embarks on long anecdotes about her youth. There was a man in Stockholm named Count Cat who was a great fly-by-night, rich and erratic. One night he was giving a rowdy supper party in a restaurant, and some wine was spilled on a sofa. The manager made him pay for the sofa, so when the party was over he and his friends removed the sofa with them. They were carrying it through the streets of Stockholm when they were arrested. "What are you doing with that sofa? Come to the police station for explanations." After some time the revellers were released. Again they started off through the open door with the sofa, and once more they were arrested. Still determined to take the sofa with them they continued on their way. I thought how surprising it would be for Count Cat, if he is alive, to know that his escapade was still remembered. But he had made a stir in Stockholm and such an impression on a young girl that, here in New York twenty years later, we were laughing about it.

Greta also told, with great humor, of how on one of her return visits to Sweden she had gone for a walk with a woman friend on a frozen lake. Greta was wearing a short fur coat and carrying a walking stick. Suddenly they found themselves up to the neck in the lake. Her terrified companion implored her to keep calm while Greta first hoiked out her walking stick, pulled herself, and then her companion, to the icy surface. But now what to do? They were miles from home; would they not catch pneumonia? Should they go to a nearby house and call a doctor? No, there would be press stories: "Garbo Nearly Drowned." "I couldn't face that, so we decided to run. We ran all the way home, and when the woman's husband came back he found me in bed with his wife drinking hot whisky, and he laughed so much!"

She tells stories such as these in somewhat hesitant, halting phrases. At first I felt like prompting her but this, I realized, would be a mistake. It is often touch and go whether she will break off altogether mid-sentence and decide not to impart further information. Sometimes when she describes some event in which she has participated she leaves out all the facts. "I was persuaded by somebody to go in a taxi to a cocktail party." No names given, no indication of the part of the city nor of the world the hosts lived in. But she described how she had chosen to sit at the far end of a room where she ruminated upon the inhumanity of being in the same precincts with other people, yet not greeting them. "It seemed so curious to arrive in a stranger's house and sit on their chairs." I gleaned the fact that, at the cocktail party, Ferenc Molnar, the playwright, had come into the room with a tragic expression on his baby face. Greta described him: "He has charm, is really quite shrewd, sharp, and clever, but he is old. He is not well anymore. He used to be so alive, and he liked smoking and drinking and women. But you lose interest when you do not participate any more, It drives him made not being able to do anything, and he knows it's *finito*."

One of the most engaging aspects of her histrionic gifts is the brilliant way in which she re-enacts some scene which has just struck her as being comic or poignant. She imitates a clown she has seen at the ice show whose sweet smile has particularly delighted her.

Another day she rushes in with stars in her eyes and pure music in her voice to tell me about a huge chimpanzee in the Park Zoo. "It is the sweetest thing I've ever seen in my life! I must take you to see that huge animal. It's so brutal, so colossal! It has two layers of bars to prevent it putting its great monkey arms through and grabbing someone when it gets angry with the crowds. Today it was so sweet and delicate: I watched it untying the shoelace of the keeper" (with furrowed brow and tight-lipped determination Greta does an imitation) "and it concentrated so hard. It was chewing something all the time" (she chews), "and it was bent over this shoe" (Greta likewise), "and with its great big nails tugged very expertly at the laces in the right direction, because it knew if it tugged the wrong way the knot would be made fast. Then, suddenly, in the midst of the undertaking, this giant ape stopped work and cast its eyes to heaven. It looked so desperate, so miserable, all the cares of the world were in its eyes!" (Hilarious imitation.) "Then it shook its head" (Greta shakes her curls) "and went back with frowning concentration to finish the rest of the job."

This evening we dine with a mutual friend, the shy and adorably sympathetic Mona Harrison Williams, who had been so quick to make me feel welcome when I first came to this country. To-night's outing is a great event for me, as it is the first time that Greta and I have been invited anywhere together. Mona makes everything very easy, and her other guests pay no more attention to Greta than to one another. Mona is now living in only a part of her home on Fifth Avenue, most of the vast rooms being under dust sheets. It is in one of these dismantled rooms that—among packing cases and covers, by the light of a street lamp outside the window and to the beat of relayed music from *Carousel*— Greta and I dance for the first time. I am completely ecstatic, like any young man in love who takes his girl out to a night club. "If I Loved You" is the tune that will always remind me of this evening. It became "our song."

When, at early dawn, we left Mona's house, situated so high uptown as to be almost in Harlem, and embarked upon the long walk home, I was in such a state of elation that, in the almost deserted streets, I sang, I improvised ballets and performed all sorts of acrobatic stunts. I leaped in the air and swung on the struts of awnings outside apartment houses and shops. Greta, shocked, surprised, and secretly delighted, would never have guessed that I possessed such prowess—nor would I.

Happily, at this time most of my theatrical work has eased off and I manage to crowd my photography and other business into the mornings in order that by lunch time, or directly afterwards, I can make my way to Greta's hotel. Beaming with anticipation I hurry through the streets, brooking no interruptions from chance acquaintances, until I arrive in the hall at the Ritz Tower, announce my arrival and stand watching the hand of the elevator indicator for the arrival on *terra firma* of the goddess from the skies. The hand of the indicator mounts to Floor Number Seventeen—her floor. Will it stop? Will she get into the carriage? No, it soars up and up. Then on its downward journey it stops at Number Eighteen, then Seventeen. Yes—the hand shows the approach of love. The expected arrival is at hand, close-to, at last face to face. She is undemonstrative, hurries through the hall, and we do not greet one another until, away from the stragglers and out past the revolving doors into the crowded street, we are alone.

Sometimes, instead of a long walk, we go to a gymnasium to do exercises, or we look at a primitive painting by Bombois. (Why she likes this *faux naïf* I can't quite imagine.) Tentatively, I try to persuade her to visit the flamboyant clairvoyant, henna-headed Nella Webb, to hear if the future is as bright as we hope, but Greta cancels the appointment at the last moment. Another day she does materialize—at the dermatologist, Casnati, a raven witch who tends the pores of face and scalp. As we lie back, side by side, in a laboratory while mud packs harden on our faces, we wonder if we will remain encased, unable to talk, like this for life. When the procedure is over Greta remarks: "Well, are we now married?"

_____ *Spring, 1946*

Greta appears and re-appears in a new guise. She does not seem to be a woman wearing a change of clothes, but is rather a different mythological figure every time. Her face is always changing. I am newly amazed at the delicacy of the carving of a nostril; suddenly I am aware of the perpendicular crevice, appearing at the memory of some unhappiness, between her brows.

One brilliantly sunny afternoon we were striding along in

jocular spirits when I noticed a phenomenon of lighting reflected from the pavement on Greta's face. She was laughing broadly, showing dazzling teeth, and she continued to smile while her eyes looked surprised. She was wearing a large gray hat which cast her face in shadow, but which gave her complexion a sort of opalescent incandescence, like porcelain lit from within. The iris of the eyes became a violet-blue, and her expression was of utter happiness—the joyfulness that only children possess. Here was true royalty of form—an alliance of the classical with a dazzling healthy litheness and a perfect honesty.

At last I am beginning to feel no anxiety in our friendship. It is wonderful to hear her making future plans in which I am to join her. We must go and see Molnar together, go to Chinatown to buy pajamas, and this time next year, God willing, we'll go to Switzerland.

Greta likes to make mysteries of quite unimportant ordinary occurrences. Sometimes she brings this to ludicrous lengths.

For example, I happened to know, by chance, that Greta had an appointment this afternoon with Clare Booth Luce, who wished to write a film scenario for her. So it was quite a little comedy when Greta arrived at my rooms and described her afternoon in detail without mentioning any names. She wiped her brow, slumped into an armchair, and exclaimed: "Phew! I've been three hours listening to a story! Why don't people cut it short? They're so lacking in sensibility! I got so tired! It was so hot! I longed for air. When at long, long last the end came, I was asked: 'Did you like that story?' I answered: 'Yes, it's all right, but it isn't written yet. How do you know what it will be like when it's written? I can't say "Yes, I'll do a film of it," and then have you work on it for three or four months only to be told that I don't like it. I don't want any hard feelings or unpleasantness, so it's better if I say now: "I ain't going to do urrtte."'"

Greta then asked me for a drink. She lit a cigarette and we talked about other things. Later, very innocently and casually, she inquired: "Tell me, do you know Clare Booth Luce?" It was difficult not to smile. After a pause I admitted that I did, and that

I had known her since my early days in America. "Why do you want to know?" I asked. "I just thought of her for a moment," replied Greta, inhaling her cigarette, but refusing to tell me that she had spent the afternoon listening to her film synopsis.

One afternoon Greta started once or twice to ask a favor, then decided against it: "Perhaps another day I'll mention it." I was most intrigued. Then she continued hesitantly: "If only you were not such a grand and elegant photographer . . . " I finished the sentence for her: "Then you'd ask me to take your passport photograph?" She looked astounded. "How did you know?" Greta had told me she was planning to leave for a holiday in Sweden, and I realized it would have been impossible for her to go to any ordinary passport photographer without the results being displayed far and wide. Knowing her antipathy to publicity of all forms, resulting in her terror of cameras, I had purposely never suggested that she should pose for me. To take pictures of her has always been my greatest ambition, and this opportunity was unique. However, the sitting must be as simple and private as possible, for to have an assistant with lights would be to over-load the occasion. The following afternoon a screen was placed near a window, while on the outside door of my apartment a notice was pinned: "Passport photographs taken here."

The sitter arrived wearing a biscuit-colored suit and polo-collared sweater, her hair a lion's mane. At first she stood stiffly to attention, facing my Rolleiflex full face as if it were a firing squad. But, by degrees, she started to assume all sorts of poses and many changes of mood. The artist in her suddenly came into flower. She was enjoying the return to an aspect of the métier that had been her life's work. Could I believe my luck? By degrees I was emboldened enough to ask if she would take off her habitual sweater. Then I brought out some "prop" clothes—a pierrot's ruff and white pointed cap—that I had secreted just in case . . . Greta became Debureau. A man's top hat was discarded on sight, though a Holbein tam-o'-shanter was approved once it was bashed into a Chinese mandarin's hat. Every now and again Greta was saying: "That's enough now—got to go." But by the time I took her word as gospel a vast number of pictures had been made.

The results formed a prized collection, though few of them were suitable for passports.

When shown the small contacts, the sitter was pleased. She

pronounced them "strong" and clean-cut and of a good quality. Together we went shopping for a folding leather frame so that I could have my favorites by me wherever I travelled. She put a pencilled cross on the back of those of which she approved and would allow me to publish in *Vogue*. When the selection was sent to my good friend, Alexander Liberman, the art editor, he could hardly believe his eyes. Here was a precious windfall of a dozen different pictures of someone who for ten years had resolutely refused to be photographed. From the rich hoard Alex chose a laughing head to be used across two pages. Surely this did not do justice to the full range of Greta's beauty. I cajoled him into publishing a variety of moods and guises.

Au Revoir to Greta/May, 1946

Greta has dropped the bombshell that she must return to the coast. Could I join her there? No, from California she would sail almost immediately to her native Sweden. "Could I meet you in Stockholm?" "Oh, no!" The idea of her departure saddened me greatly. For the past weeks I had lived only in terms of her. She filled my days, and I dreamt of her at night.

Suddenly New York seemed pointless without her. Frederick Ashton wired me from Covent Garden that he had a ballet for me to design if I could return at once. It was the ballet *Les Sirenes* with music by Gerald Berners. I might as well go home. When I arrived back in England a telegram arrived, unsigned, from Greta bidding me good morning.

Part 4
DESIGNS
for BALLET
1946

On returning home I found myself in a quandary. The ballet Freddie Ashton, a great lover of the works of Ouïda, had asked me to design was to be based on her novel *Moths*. Trouville, at its height as a fashionable watering place, was to be the background, and the extraordinary mixture of personalities on the *plage,* wearing garden party toilettes or period bathing costumes, would give the designer great range. In addition, Margot Fonteyn was to be a Spanish dancer based on the character of *la belle Otero,* Robert Helpmann was to perform as her South American tenor-lover, and Freddie himself, as an Oriental pasha resembling the Aga Khan, would descend from an enormous balloon. Gerald Berners had written an extremely amusing waltz as part of the score. But I had already contracted to be in America to design an earlier ballet by Freddie – *Les Patineurs* – for the New York Ballet Theatre at the time set for the Covent Garden rehearsals. It was not difficult to be persuaded by Freddie to do the Ouida designs for costumes and sets and leave their execution to experts. Therein I made a mistake.

However detailed one's instructions and drawings may be, there are always bound to be major readjustments made once one sees the designs taking shape. What looks well on paper may have to be amplified or minimized in reality; what one dancer can wear, another cannot. And the final effects can be enhanced or diminished by the lighting.

I have, at last, learned that every stage undertaking involves ten times as much work as originally envisaged, and, as usual, on this project the number of designs required increased each week. Perhaps the best theatrical results are always achieved with much pain and anguish but, although my eyes and back ached over the drawing board, and it was sometimes with the numbness of death that I took myself eventually to bed, this was an experience of the utmost pleasure; working conditions can never have been more idyllic. While Gerald Berners worked at his piano in the drawing room of his small eighteenth-century house in Faringdon, near Oxford, I labored, with more detailed love and care than usual, upon the designs in an upstairs bedroom. Lunch was not only a pleasant interlude but a gastronomic treat. At the end of the day I would show Gerald my progress, he would play his score, while Freddie's imagination was fired to further frivolities. After dinner, upstairs again to paint another filigree row of struts in the Trouville pier or more ducks' eggs pearl on Otero's costume.

Feeling confident that I had left behind me a delightful legacy, I returned to the States on the tenth of July. It was with dreadful anguish that I heard, two months later, lukewarm reports of our united effort on Ouïda's *Moths*. Margot, with eyes rolling, tongue in cheek and rose behind the ear, was alluring in her black jet and flounces; some of Freddie's choreography for his Oriental entourage and the bathers was witty; but my designs were considered too fashionable, and Helpmann, bursting into song, embarrassed the Covent Garden audience. Gerald was beginning to suffer from high blood pressure and nervous depression, the illness from which he died, and was no longer at the height of his powers. His perverse and comic music did not carry an evening; it was not in the serious mood of the moment when post-war ballet enthusiasts were looking for something more significant. *Moths* soon faded from memory.

_____ *Patineurs* AND *La Dame Aux Camellias*/*July, 1946: New York*

I am bad at turning down jobs; I know how difficult they are to come by. It has taken me a long while to feel that, as a designer, I have achieved a foothold in the American theatre, but suddenly a deluge of offers had descended on me.

While working to evoke the atmosphere of a Victorian tuppence-colored, Hoxton-toy-theatre snow scene for *Les Patineurs*, a skating ballet set to Chabrier's sugar-sweet music, a more ambitious ballet project presented itself. I was offered the designing of a full-length *La Dame aux Camellias* for Alicia Markova to dance. No sooner had Madame Karinska finished making the fondant-colored tarlatan tutus for the skater ballet than she set her old Russian refugees to work caparisoning *grandes cocottes* of the sixties in the richest silks, velvets, and furs.

I myself could not have chosen a more felicitous subject for my designs than *Camille.* Yet, having accepted the offer, I was bereft of inspiration. My friends in the Public Library produced books of reference by the dozen, and Miss Polaire Weissman, in the Costume Art section of the Metropolitan, even brought out from her fine collection original dresses and undergarments so that our costumes would have the authentic cut. I filled notebooks with details of bonnets, gas brackets, grillwork scrolls, pediments for ornamental vases, pelmets for curtains, fringes for ottomans and trimmings for crinolines, but still no overall conception came to me.

In desperation I took my plight to the Russian painter Pavel Tchelitchew, himself a great scenic designer. Pavlik can be a difficult friend; he is apt to be touchy and fractious. He is terribly jealous—and not only of other painters; public acclaim for almost anyone can generate wrath in him. It was once repeated to him that I said he was even envious of Shirley Temple. One can offend him without realizing it by praising Picasso or Matisse, and for weeks on end one will be in his bad books. (Once, after an estrangement, someone played us a Tchaikowsky record, and Pavlik's Russian heart melted in an emotional reconciliation.)

But Pavlik can also be the most generous friend, showering presents of his fine drawings, giving advice about an artist's work, recommending galleries, and being kind in the most unexpected ways. Without seeming to realize the magnitude of his help, he will knock off from his own work to throw the crumbs of his inspiration to others. Many is the time in the past that he has sent me home with a whole wad of odd scraps of paper, or old envelopes, covered with his spidery little drawings that are the kernel for a whole production. Now once more he came to the rescue.

I showed him my tentative scribbles. "No, it's no use having all that scenery. You must invent a scheme for the dance—a device—that will fill the imagination. This is a ballet, not a stage drama. Build only a light framework: make your changes within that. Be ingenious: forget lifelike proportions: use false perspectives. Recreate a forgotten world, a world you have never seen, so that the audience will gasp with surprise and recognition. Make everything gold and glittering, and rich and dusty. All the whores should be like Victorian jewelry—make one a topaz, another amethyst or sapphire or ruby." Pavlik's fountain pen was skimming over pieces of tissue paper with authority and zest. Each indication was a treasure. "And the country idyll must be full of wheat sheaves and sheaves of corn and cornstalks." Within a few moments the ballet was designed. All I had to do was to go back to my hotel and start to work elaborating carefully in color and detail his marvellous bonework. Pavlik never expects to be thanked, yet how could I ever think of him but with a full heart?

The scenery, involving a ballroom, a countryside, and a bedroom, was made to change to the music in full view of the audience. The ingenuity of the stage carpenters was stretched to its furthest extent in an effort to produce something that had not been tried before. Somehow they achieved a marvel. When the scenes were set and the dancers came on stage in Karinska's ball costumes, enthusiasm turned to euphoria. Pavlik joyously clasped Karinska, his great friend and compatriot, who had made of each costume a work of art. Markova, a thistledown Camille, would surely reach her highest peak. The lights in the auditorium gave way to an impenetrable darkness: the curtain went up on the Victorian jewelry.

The ballet started. As we sat watching, only a few moments passed before we realized that there was no ballet. The choreographer had given the dancers nothing to do. Camille and Armand executed a few cursory steps: the *corps de ballet* performed routines of the utmost banality. It was inevitable that on the following night, in front of a packed house, the evening became a disaster which even Markova could not prevent. Another ballet soon forgotten.

Above, photograph of Anton Dolin and Alicia Markova as lovers in the ballet *La Dame aux Camellias*, given at the Metropolitan Opera House. Below, design for dancers in Frederick Ashton's *Les Patineurs*, presented by the Ballet Theatre in New York.

4 COUPLES

irtuoso Dancers

"Les Patineurs"

Music by Meyerbeer
Choreo-
graphy by
Frederick
Ashton.

Décor by
Cecil
Beaton

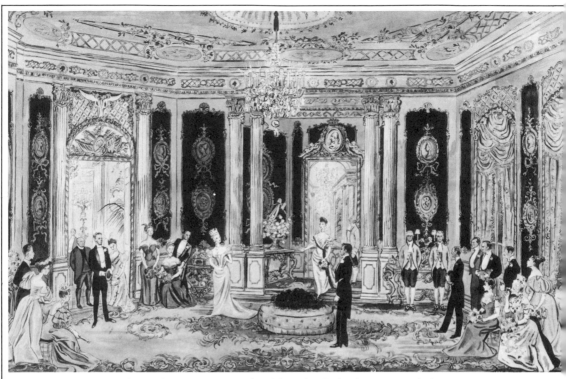

Lady Windermere's Fan, produced by John Gielgud, starring Isabel Jeans as Mrs. Erlynne. Design and photograph for ballroom scene, Act II.

Designs for film *Anna Karenina*, starring Vivien Leigh. Produced by Alexander Korda and directed by Duvivier.

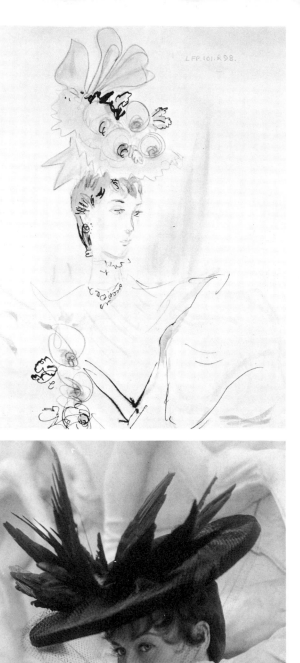

Designs for Alexander Korda's production of *An Ideal Husband*. Right and above, Paulette Goddard, in black-crow-decorated hat and orchid evening dress, playing the wicked Mrs. Cheveley. Diana Wynyard, opposite, cool English beauty, in garden party array and Queen Alexandra brocades as hostess at Lady Chiltern's reception.

Three of Cecil Beaton's backdrop designs for Laurence Olivier's production of *School for Scandal:* above, outside Sir Peter Teazle's house; above, right, Lady Sneerwell's boudoir; below, right, the picture gallery.

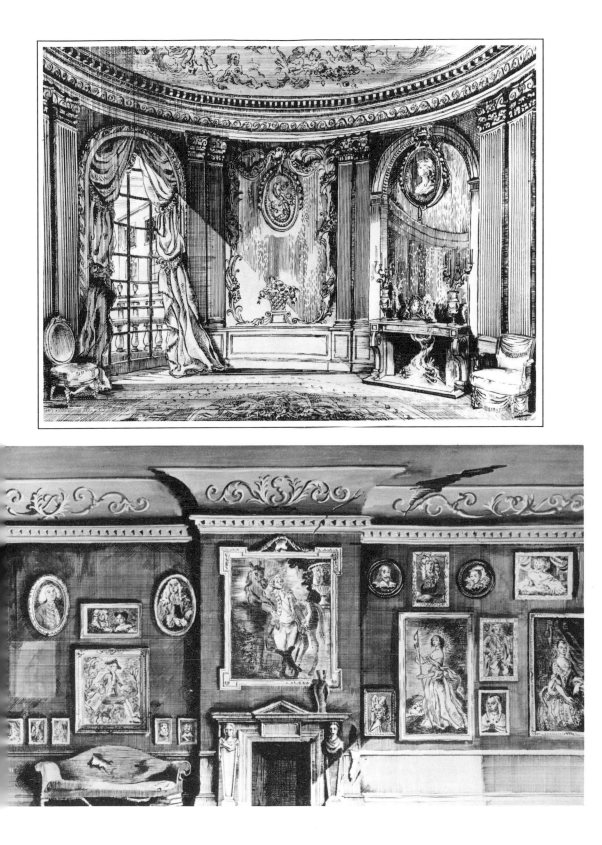

Part 5

CALIFORNIA and NEW YORK

1946

Cruelly enough, while Greta is away in Sweden, other stage work has brought me within a few blocks of her house. Finally it has been arranged that a Los Angeles management, Messrs. Russell and Lewis, is to re-create the London production of *Lady Windermere's Fan* and after a short trial on the coast, it will come to Broadway.

Not only have I been in charge of the building of sets and costumes, but, quite by chance, I have become a member of the cast. There was difficulty in finding a suitable Englishman for the small but effective role of Cecil Graham, the waspish gossip who finds Lady Windermere's fan underneath a cushion in Lord Darlington's rooms. One morning, on the way to the scenic paint shop, I passed the management, Russell & Lewis, in the carpenter's workshop and let drop the idea I had had last night after dinner, sitting out by Cole Porter's pool, that I should play Cecil Graham. "You must have been drunk!" was the director's reply. This gave me the incentive to prove myself. I wired Arnold Weissberger, my New York agent, Maud Nelson, my secretary, and my mother to ask if they advised me to exhibit myself for the first time on the stage. Their replies were all negative, which only increased my determination. After two rehearsals I was given the little plum of a part.

Many times, at intervals between rehearsals, I telephoned to Greta's empty house. There was always the chance that the owner might have returned unexpectedly. In any case it gave me a sort of uncanny fascination to hear the bell ringing unanswered; somehow I felt I was bringing my presence to bear in the owner's absence.

Tonight I carried out my long-conceived plan of visiting the house. Originally I had had the idea of ringing the bell and asking the maid to allow me to plant some bulbs in the garden. I even went so far as to search for lily bulbs, but in vain: the nursery gardens had nothing worthy of representing me in her garden. Tonight I would, at any rate, discover where she lived.

California nights are particularly romantic. I find something exciting in the fragrant atmosphere that is made up of orange blossom, the *dama di notte,* flowering acacia, and so many unnamed, but strongly scented, trees. The small white houses appear at their best lit from within, and the warm glow coming through the windows contrasts with the cold blueness of moonlight.

In my search for 622 Bedford Drive I walked along the palmfringed avenues and pepper-treed drives of Beverly Hills. The numbers changed slowly but, at last, I came to the one to which my countless fervid letters had been addressed. "Six twenty-two" was written in wrought iron in that quavery, witchlike style that is peculiar to Hollywood. This home, squat and low, did not seem a suitable abode for a goddess. It had a whimsical, toylike quality that gave it the appearance of something at a garden exhibition. The rough-stained front door was illuminated by a frosted lantern. Stealthily, I trod across the coarse green lawn. Lights were on in the hall and ground-floor rooms. I peered through the letter box. On the walls were a variety of bad modern pictures; sickening little miniatures were framed in groups by the chimney piece, and everywhere were silver-framed photographs of celebrities: Elsie Mendl, Greer Garson, Ilona Massey, and dozens of blonde starlets. Who could live in such an interior! I left, dejected. There must be some mistake.

I discovered that number six twenty-two, to which I had written all my letters, was not Greta's house but that of Harry Crocker, an agreeable dilettante, friend, and somewhat amateur gossip columnist. This friend of Greta's sends on all correspondence and parcels that arrive at his halfway junction. Here was another astonishing example of Greta's mania for secrecy and her lack of trust in her friends. I was hurt that I had not been favored with her real address, which was then given me by Crocker and to which I made my way two nights later.

Number nine-hundred-and-four (the figures add to the unlucky number) on the same Drive is her real address. This house appeared utterly anonymous with two slit windows, heavily curtained, each side of the front door. I crept along by the garage entrance and found that the garden was hidden behind a high wall. Everything was very severe, clean and white, expensive-looking, and rather agreeable. A wonderful magnolia tree in bloom scented the night.

Later I returned home feeling content that this was a suitable house for so fine a hermit. I could well imagine my friend retreating behind the wall and staying for days on end hiding even from her servant. The picture brought her closer to me.

The more I see of the suburban intrigue and invidious standards of Hollywood's film colony, the more remarkable it is that Greta exists, after fifteen years, completely unsullied or untouched by the influence of this ingrown community.

It was to be expected: before my photographs of Greta were to appear in *Vogue,* word got around in journalistic circles of the imminent scoop. I imagine Greta's "little man" had asked why she had allowed me to publicize her. A week before the magazine was to be on all the newsstands, Greta sent me a cable from Sweden saying that if more than one of the photographs were to appear I would never be forgiven. I had not understood that although she had put a tick to OK many of these pictures, she had intended that only one was to appear. Frantic calls to my friends at *Vogue:* "Stop everything!" It was too late: the copies were already bound and on their way throughout the country. Greta's telegram was later followed by a letter saying she was deeply distressed at the idea of having any costume pictures of herself published unless they had to do with her work. She was after all a serious person.

It was impossible to prevent her from feeling completely betrayed. My abject cables and letters, telephone calls, and flowers sent to her in Sweden went unanswered.

I felt as if I had committed a murder.

At this juncture it was fortunate that I was able to derive much satisfaction from my career in many of its various aspects: to realize that life can be satisfying even without all that one wants. After a sluggish start my creative efforts seemed to have built up a force that was pulling me forward with excitement. It gave me the realization that it was not just a question of work for work's sake, or money, or even fulfilling some of the ambitions I had formed at Cambridge. It was more a feeling of achieving substance.

The success of *Lady Windermere*, and the leap forward that my photographic activities now took, led to many promises of jobs from the States and France. I had much to please me.

_____ *In the* Lady Windermere *Cast*/*New York*

When *Lady Windermere's Fan* opened in Santa Barbara I was almost numb with stage fright. By the time we had moved to San Francisco, however, I had acquired some confidence. Los Angeles audiences are notoriously unreceptive and I learned what it was to play against impossible odds—as on the night when the city's electricity supply gave out and our brilliant ballroom scene was played in semidarkness with only the theatre's portable generator to come to our rescue. But once the production had been acclaimed in New York the routine of appearing at the theatre for each evening and matinee completely delighted me. Novice that I was, I soon discovered that one must be always on the alert to what is coming from the audience; that each performance differed because at any moment some surprise element would promote an alteration of tone, voice pitch, or pace. It was exhilarating to find oneself making discoveries in the craft of acting. I wondered how on earth I had spent my evenings before this opportunity arose for enjoying myself in the most exciting, and exhibitionistic, way before going out to relish that well-earned drink and supper after the performance.

_____ *Silence from Greta*

We had not been ensconced in the Court Theatre on Broadway for more than a few days when Greta landed from her Scandinavian holiday. I telephoned her at the Ritz Tower. I was kept waiting a considerable time by the operator: doubtless Greta was talking to someone else. At last the operator said: "She don't answer," and I suspected that Greta was hiding from me.

My feelings were a combination of such misery, loss, hurt, and despair that my stomach asserted itself. I could neither eat, drink, nor sleep. All day and every night I found myself being haunted by memories of our happy times together. I remembered so many unaccustomed aspects of her face: the pouts of compassion, the feckless gaiety, the frankness of her laugh, the allure of the smile with lowered eyelids. In my room I kept imagining that she would suddenly appear round a corner, looking startled, defiant, or aggressive, in all sorts of strange garments. In the streets my mania did not leave me: every woman coming along the avenue would have something of Greta in her, but as the stranger approached I would see that in every way she was the antithesis of my idol. Yet I would be reminded of aspects of Greta's simplicity or some human quality even when watching a conventionally smart woman, with choker pearls and a ridiculous flowered hat, tottering along on high heels. Perhaps Greta had changed her style and decided to wear a different sort of hat? Now surely that *profile perdu* belongs to her? But the chin under the hat turned. It belonged to some quite coarse, ugly woman.

The search continues. Time and again the same mistake is made: nowhere am I immune from the fateful possibility that Greta may be nearby—hidden in the crowd in the theatre or in any surroundings, however unsuitable. Everything I see, every place I go to, brings back to me the times we spent together. Central Park has become an absolute nightmare of memories: each tree has its specific associations, and each mountain and hillock reminds me of that advent of spring when we welcomed the first rays of sun and celebrated the coming warmth by lying full length on the grass.

Now there is only silence. I fill the void by working excessively hard and making for myself as many distractions as possible. But every book I try to read manages to conjure up her image. Lady Murasaki describes Yūgao, a mysterious lady called after the white flowers known as evening faces, with petals half unfolded like the lips of people smiling at their own thoughts: "about her too there was something fugitive, insubstantial. Genji was obsessed by the idea that, just as she had hidden herself in this place, so one day she would once more vanish and hide, and he would never be able to find her again. There was every sign that her residence here was quite temporary. He was sure that when the time came to move she would not tell him where she was going."

I am certain there will be no response to my notes but, nevertheless, I write. I refrain from telephoning too many times in order to avoid the inevitable agony of being told by the impervious operator that there is no reply. I know the situation is hopeless. Will time make it more bearable?

Descartes wrote: "I love—therefore I am. When I no longer love I am no longer anything."

Greta by Telephone

It was almost a relief when I heard indirectly that Greta had returned to Hollywood. Now I could walk down the New York streets without being haunted by her ghost. But I was still miserable. Six weeks passed before I summoned up the courage to telephone her in Hollywood: "She don't answer." Still no replies to my repeated telegrams or letters. I arranged for a friend to put a note under her Beverly Hills front door at six o'clock one morning. No reply. I began to realize that this beautiful bird had alighted on a branch in my garden, been frightened, and flown away for ever.

I was lying on my bed. This was October 7th (one of my lucky numbers, perhaps my stars were good). On the spur of the moment I lifted the telephone receiver and put another call through to California—and the miracle happened! The operator had informed her that "New York" was calling, not that it was a personal call from me. Perhaps she thought it was to be "the little man" at the end of the wire. Before she realized it we were talking. "Why, Mr. Beaton? Why, why, why? How very surprising!" "What are you wearing?" I asked. "Nothing." A good deal of "Mr. Beaton-ing" and "I don't know nothink," followed. Then I asked: "Did you enjoy your holiday in Sweden?" "I won't tell you." But, by degrees, the thaw took place. We laughed. Soon it seemed as if there had never been a breach. In her rather cruel, playful way, knowing that two thousand miles separated us, she said: "Come on over now." "Not now, but can I come later?" "Now, only now." She said she had received a letter from me but that she couldn't decipher my handwriting; there was cruelty in that, so I said it appeared that she enjoyed making me suffer. She said: "I wouldn't do anything to any human being to make him suffer." Eventually we seemed to arrive sufficiently near a reconciliation for me to ask if I was forgiven. By the end of the call I imagined that all was as well as before, and that our relationship remained as strange and violent and intuitive as only happens when two people meet who are magnetically drawn to one another.

_____ *October 26th, 1946*

After many further vain attempts to speak to Greta on the telephone (I would call at all times of the day, and I could hear the operator being told by Greta's sad-voiced servant that Miss Brown was not at home and she did not know when she was expected back) this morning I was again fortunate enough to gain my quarry. At first she was exasperated and treated me as a tiresome burden that might as well be disposed of once and for all. "This is no good," she said. "We are too different. By your action you have deprived me of a friend." "Who is the friend?" "You were!" She did not wish me to telephone, she had nothing to tell me. Desperately I adlibbed: "But I don't want you to tell me anything—I just want to talk to you." "Well, we never talk on the telephone here in California—only in New York we talk on the telephone. I'm not being cruel or vindictive, but things have changed." "I haven't changed, have you?" I asked. "No. I'm a very strange person," she replied, "and I can't change, and I don't think I want to very much either, so you had better not call any more." I was fighting for my life. "Then may I write?" "What's the point?" This was pretty near to disaster for me, but by banter and repartee we eventually returned to better terms. Greta suddenly showed that she was curious, if not jealous, that someone had sent me tuberoses to the theatre when I had my first night on Broadway. "Are you shocked with me for exhibiting myself on the stage?" "No, not interested," she replied, but a little later she said: "You'd better get off that stage." When I said that unfortunately I had to leave the cast, I was to be under contract to work in films for Alexander Korda in England, and I'd soon be sailing home for nearly a year, she said: "When are you going? And have you got a cow?" "No, I haven't even a house in the country any more." "Well, I don't know how you'll make out." I said I wished she would fly to New York but that it was too cold for her to come just now. She said she liked cold weather. The more I elaborated on the reasons why she should not come, the more anxious she seemed to be to do so. It was a long and sad conversation in some ways, but I prayed that if I could overcome her mood, and make her forget her present attitude towards me, all would be as before.

I didn't telephone her again for over a month. I knew that if I did she would feel I was chasing her, and that if I remained quiet she might possibly be more interested. Although I longed many times to talk to her I did not do so until about a week after Christmas. She was surprised to hear that I had not already returned to England. She was frankly delighted to hear me and accepted my advances without reservations. "Of course I wouldn't go home without telephoning to you," I said. I described how it was snowing as I looked out of my hotel bedroom. Oh, she longed to come to New York; she had hoped to come "over the holidays," but "too late now," she said, with what sounded like a pang of regret.

From now on I telephoned to California very often. Sometimes I would hear the bell ringing unheard in her pantry. On the Thursday, when the sad-voiced maidservant was out, Greta became quite abandoned in her invitation for me to "come right over, to come—come—come!" It was a typical taunt, yet a sign of forgiveness on her part. She knew she was safe herself, but was putting me in a difficult predicament. I laughed at her invitation which was like the ticking of a clock. "How do you sleep?" I asked. "I sleep well if I go to bed early enough: I retire with the chickens." "What have you been doing?" "Just pottering—I haven't had time to stop." She laughed, she talked nonsense. "Ah, we're all bound to our duty, we're soldiers fighting for 'les beaux arts.'" "Well, keep your pecker up. I'll call tomorrow to find out how you are." "No, you mayn't telephone. No, no! That ain't cricket. Just send me a wire if you're in a stew."

_____ *My Mother in New York*/*November 20th, 1946*

Returning to my grand and elegant hotel suite late tonight I am very touched by a pencilled note I find on the table in the small hall. It is from my mother to say how much she had enjoyed the evening, seeing me play in *Lady Windermere.*

My first impression of the States had come to me in childhood from my parents. Soon after their marriage they had made journeys across the Atlantic and the accounts of their visits to New York, to Florida, and the deep South had filled me with such a strange romantic excitement that I yearned for "the promised land." The sort of America that they had seen—staying with the Barrs, some wealthy friends who were possibly, like my father, in the timber or lumber business, and other well-to-do hospitable friends, living on plantations in carefree happiness—was the one that first occupied my mind. It is very different from the one I now enjoy. Since I have come to spend so large a part of my life in the States I wanted my mother to see how I lived and carried on in an atmosphere so far removed from that at home in England. After the austere war years, and after being incarcerated for so long in the depths of the wintry countryside, I thought it would be a treat for her to have a glimpse of the luxury of modern Manhattan. It would be the last opportunity for her to see me on the boards, too, for, much as I was enjoying myself, I had to return to England. While in New York I had negotiated with Alexander Korda to design film productions for him, to advise him behind the camera, and be of directorial assistance, the contract to run for seven years.

But the contrast between my mother's life and mine has become too great. I realized this at once when I caught my first sight of her on the New York docks. Her boat had landed earlier than had been expected, and already she had seen her belongings (packed in my discarded suitcases) through the Customs and, looking quite bewildered, was trying to follow an impatient porter through a seething, jostling, shouting crowd. With her pale-blue puzzled eyes, her gentleness and trust, and still wearing the orchid—now completely dead—that someone had given her in London for a bon voyage present, she was as unlike the people around her as if she had come from another planet.

After the initial shock of seeing me—the first familiar face since she had boarded the liner one week ago—she became less anguished. But she has been unable to cope with the noise and the pace of the New York of today. She wonders why I am always in such a hurry, why I talk so fast and become impatient. I have tried to make things agreeable for her, and friends have rallied round, but I have failed in not devoting myself to her with more understanding and patience. The sad fact remains that she has become too old for the New Yorkers' way of life. It has been a baffling visit for her.

Perhaps when, in a few days' time, we sail back to England she will forget the flaws and will enjoy telling her family of the fuss that was made of her, of the presents and the flowers she was given, and I can comfort myself with tonight's little note which is something that I shall always keep.

January, 1947: London

A few days after I had returned home I telephoned Greta from London. She heard my voice with incredulity.

"You're not to do it—I told you not to telephone!"

"Why?" I asked.

"It's too far."

"The ends of the world are not too far."

"Well, I won't give you my address in Norfolk, Virginia, unless you promise not to telephone. . . . Well, good-bye, and thank you for your call. Do you miss me?" she asked, like a child speaking its piece.

"Yes. Why are you going to Norfolk?"

"I haven't an idea in the world."

"What have you been doing?"

"Nothing much. Just walking."

"Who with?"

"The alley cats—and the alley dogs. You'd better have stayed at Plaza!"

Part 6

FRESH FIELDS in ENGLAND

1947

When I had first gone to see Alexander Korda in his rooms at the St. Regis, New York, it was with a certain amount of misgiving. I did not want to work in films. "I want to buy you," he had said. "But I don't want to be bought—and I'm terribly expensive." I told him of my past film experiences in London studios. I had enjoyed designing *Mr. Kipps* and *Pitt the Younger* since I had the delightful Carol Reed as my director, but Gabriel Pascal had created many complications for me with an attempt to design for *Major Barbara*. In other cases not only was the director without an eye to the visual aspect of film making but also the technicians were disinterested in making anything appear authentic and had no wish to listen to my attempts to help. He looked piqued; he is not accustomed to people refusing his advances. "Well, I think I'm the only person who can utilize all your talents and give you the opportunity to fulfill your ambitions as designer, director, photographer, writer, or what you will." Naturally I was flattered. The more I thought about the idea, the more it seemed feasible. I went to my lawyer and a whopping great contract was signed.

Korda and I sailed to England together on the *Queen Elizabeth*. At every meeting I found him more charming, and I was surprised that anyone with a motion-picture background could be so well read and generally intelligent. He did not seem to wish to talk about films and their making. In fact, whenever I broached the subject of my working for him he was vague and abstracted. He shrugged: "You just do your work where you want, but when the film starts I want you on the floor with me." At first he intended to do a film of Oscar Wilde's *Salomé* and to direct it himself, and in the preliminary discussions with his talented brother Vincent I saw that we were heading for trouble. The two brothers were afraid that I would follow in the steps of Allah Nazimova, whose Beardsley setting for *Salomé* had been panned. It seems to me impossible to do this period "purple patch" in a straightforward, serious vein. "Why not put it into an *art nouveau* frame? By making it even more curious the effect would be less ridiculous." I had dropped such a spanner that the whole project was slowly abandoned.

Sir Alexander Korda on the telephone.

"How are you, Saisille, old boy? When shall I see you?" drawled the Hungarian voice.

"Whenever you want."

"What about this afternoon?"

"Anytime you like."

"What about this morning?"

"Whenever you say."

"Twelve-thirty? . . . . Twelve o'clock, old boy, would be even better."

When, after battling through the snow, I arrived at his office in his landering, great Piccadilly house Sir Alex was pacing up and down the large room trying to keep warm. He was wearing his overcoat; there were no lights on. We were enjoying a peak of the Shinwell winter season, and the gas and coal supply had given out. Emmanuel Shinwell, then the Minister of Fuel and Power, had not been prepared for one of the coldest winters England had known for many years, and the suffering endured, especially by the elderly and the sick, was tragic.

"Hullo, old boy!" He peered at me through the gloom. "Well, I've got two pieces of news for you. One good—one bad."

"Tell me the bad first." I braced myself for the shock.

"No, I'll tell the good first. You've always tried to bully me into making *Ideal Husband* as a film. Well, we're going to do it. That's the good news. Now for the bad: we start shooting in three weeks' time."

"But that's also good news," I said with genuine enthusiasm.

"I want you behind the camera with me—and of course to do the costumes and all sorts of odd jobs. Start right away. We'll do it entirely in the period of when the play was written—1895."

Out in the snow again I took up my position at the end of a long bus queue. The nineties seemed to me so much longer ago than a mere fifty years: in comparison with today's life in England under a Labour government it could have been as remote as ancient Rome. What a self-indulgent era it had been! The blessings of equality were unknown, neither had the virtues of austerity been recognized. With altogether too much pleasure and leisure, most people overate and drank too much, and wasted the hours in conversation.

One bus after another, filled to the ceiling with steaming wet humanity, went by without stopping. The queue remained static. What a worthwhile job lay ahead—to show, by innuendo, how unenlightened in comparison to ours those old days of horse-drawn carriages had been. Snow and mud from roaring cars and motorbike traffic spattered the still motionless queue.

At last a bus hove in sight in which I was able to find an inch of space on the running board. Holding tight to the rail I thought about Victoria as Queen of England and Empress of India, and how an empire had ruthlessly dominated the world. The bus skidded but I was thrown clear. I put up my umbrella and staggered on into the semidarkness towards South Kensington.

Home at last, I discovered that I had run short of drawing paper. At the nearest art-store their quota of paper had given out, neither had they India ink in black, only orange. I did my first designs on the insides of cardboard boxes in orange ink. Two days later Sir Alexander looked at the results.

"Did the women really look like that then? How horrible!"

His brother Vincent, always depressed and always depressing, puckered his forehead at the sight of the furnishings of the period. "Look at all those fussy dust-catching knicknacks! Where can we get candles today? Hothouse flowers! Who's got hothouses? No wonder, with those sideboards groaning with ortolans and quails, so many of the Victorians had to go to Homburg or Baden to have their livers cleaned out."

Working on preparations for the film also brought further proof of the fact that we are living in the modern world. The slips of young girls who came to portray the privileged guests in the ball-room scene in no way resembled those enormous Boadiceas, full-bosomed and well-cushioned, who could scarcely bend, so encumbered were they by their boned corsets, barbaric jewelry and dozens of yards of heavy silk. It was not easy to find among our utility materials, docketed cretonnes, or nylon household goods, anything to simulate those thick brocades, cumbrous satins, and quilted damasks; because of the war and the need to expend all our energies and resources on the production of absolute essentials, nothing that was in any way considered a luxury had been manufactured. Asking the wig master if he could emulate the Victorian coiffures by adding false hair to modern pates, he shrugged: "Hair? We've had none for years!" We fought on manfully.

Korda did not start work in three weeks' time and there were the usual delays. But much of the work of research, design, fittings, of conferences, was a revelation to me, and my enthusiasm was sustained. Then, suddenly, Korda gave me the added responsibility of designing all the costumes for *Anna Karenina*. Although I considered the Garbo films of *Anna* among her best performances, the costumes for both the silent and "talkie" versions seemed to be lacking in Russian and period flavor. This would put me on my mettle and be an opportunity to design something more authentically "solid" and heavy in atmosphere. When it became impossible to find costumiers in London who could undertake the work at such short notice, Korda suggested that the leading actress's dresses and hats should be made in Paris. Here I found that the great Madame Karinska had handed on her dressmaking genius to her daughter. The confections that she created for Vivien Leigh as Anna were masterpieces. Likewise, Madame Paulette made free adaptations of my sketches for hats that transcended anything that I could have desired.

_____ *February 1st, 1947*

It is the greatest possible treat to be working in such an agreeable manner while staying again with Duff and Diana. Laurence Olivier had come over to join Vivien to see Jean-Louis Barrault in *Hamlet*, a production in which he was interested since he was preparing his own film version of the play.

Returning late from fittings one night, I realized I was starting a bad cold. My throat tingled, my eyes burned, and I had nothing to take for it. I asked Laurence Olivier and Vivien Leigh, who had just come in from a rout given by some French theatre people, if they had any cure. Alas, they had nothing, not even an aspirin. Next day I was stricken. However, it was a relief to give in — to be able to call a halt.

The Oliviers/*Friday*

Still stricken, and with a temperature, I was disappointed that there would be no *Hamlet* for me this evening. (The Oliviers had got me a ticket and I was looking forward to seeing Jean-Louis Barrault.) However, Larry Olivier gave me a lot to think about as I lay in my dreary state. He trusted it wouldn't offend me to be offered second choice, but if Roger Furse, to whom he was obligated to give preference, were too busy with the film of *Hamlet*, would I care to take on the stage production of Sheridan's *School for Scandal*, which he was to take to Australia and New Zealand and later bring to the New Theatre in London. This is one of my favorite of all plays, so full of charm, wit, and kindliness. I would certainly jump at any such opportunity. Larry would be an interesting Sir Peter and Vivien would look adorable as Lady Teazle. My brain started working overtime with ideas for sets and costumes. I became impatient with my illness for not allowing me to get straight to work.

Saturday

Still in bed, but with throat less painful. I was able to read a lot. Larry came in and chuckled about our behavior here in this grand house. He said: "For the first few days I was so bloody serious because I was shy. It would be so awful to make a joke in the British Embassy and find you'd gone too far." And "I find it difficult when Duff comes into the room not to straighten up to attention too much or, alternatively, to be so casual as to ignore him almost entirely and finally greet him in an offhand way." The burlesque he did of himself was quite a cameo.

I became somewhat restless in bed and felt I was missing so much amusement downstairs. I telephoned to ask Diana, "Can you talk to me now?" "No, twenty people in the room." However, I was not lonely for long. Fellow house guests dropped in: Juliet

Duff to pick up a magazine she had lent me, Louise de Vilmorin to give me a book on Ledoux. (She, too, has been *alitée*. Her *"bronchoscopie,"* in which tubes, lights, and scissors are put down her throat to the bottom of the lung to investigate some inexplicable inflammation, had taken place on Friday.) After dinner the Oliviers brought up with them the two chaps who are here to work on the filming of *Hamlet:* Roger Furse *(décor)* and Tony Bushell (manager). They had spent the afternoon discussing plans and designs and had thrown out two weeks of Furse's work. But they had made a valuable discovery: instead of building whole sets they would decide what would be the most suitable and pictorial background for each shot and reverse shot, then they would only build the necessary. This seems to be logical, yet is a complete reversal of the normal procedure of building an entire room, then wondering where on earth are the right angles to shoot.

"Abstract," Larry answered when I asked how the production would look. He then proceeded to describe the film in hearty schoolboy phrases. With arms flailing he emulated with a big "whoosh" a great curtain falling down here—a pillar "pffutting" down there—"a hell of a lot of smoke and emptiness all over the place." Instead of using words that could be found in a dictionary, he would illustrate his intentions by making prep-school sounds— of pops, bangs, and corks being drawn, of internal combustion explosions, farts, and all sorts of other coarse noises. The camera would "raspberry" down onto the castle at the beginning of the film ("an old-fashioned idea, but then I'm old-fashioned"), and then "raspberry" away at the end—and the castle that was shown wouldn't necessarily tally with the sets but the atmosphere would be the same. Larry is, heaven knows, serious about his career, but the project on hand is referred to only in ribald terms. No question of "Would it be beautiful to have . . . . ?" "Mightn't it be extraordinary to . . . .?"—just: "A great blob here (bang! bang-ho!)"—"A great cowpat there (bungho!)"

It was a most gymnastic performance that we were treated to. Larry's imitations have about them something of the original clown or, at least, the essential entertainer, who can be found in some remote music hall or performing in the street outside a pub. This was the real Larry—the mummer, the ale-drinking Thespian

—not the rather overwhelmed and shy cipher with wrinkled forehead that goes out into society.

_____ *Sunday*

Disappointed in myself. My throat again agonizingly sore and my condition weak, no question of getting up. Vivien spent the afternoon sitting on my bed and regaling me with stories about her stage experiences. Larry was meanwhile working with the *Hamlet* chaps in his sitting room. Later they all came in to show me the tentative designs. They are less abstract than Larry had described, and I thought Ophelia was too positively Holbeinesque. But Furse can be relied upon always to do a thoroughly professional job, and his drawings are always sensitive and in fine taste.

While the others were out at a dinner at the Louise de Vilmorin house at Verrières, I enjoyed looking through illustrated eighteenth-century books with Sheridan at the back of my mind. But I could wait no longer for the others to return, so went to sleep.

It was not long afterwards that Larry, rather muzzy, came into the room and regaled me, in the darkness, with stories of the evening. It had not been entirely successful. Diana, furious that the men had not mixed with the women after dinner, said: "The English have corrupted French manners!" "The Game"[1] was played, and the amateurs and professionals were at war. Juliet had previously confided to me how badly the actors perform in "the game," and tonight the professionals complained of the slowness of Juliet's reactions. "You silly old goose, do something! Act, Juliet! Go on—oh, go *on*, Juliet!" Vivien came into the dark room, surprised at our chortles, and joined in the tirade against Juliet. "Oh, she was so slow! She wouldn't give an indication of what she was!" When, later, Vivien and Larry were fumbling their way out of the still black room, Larry, behind the bedscreen, stumbled across the bolster which I always throw out of my bed before going to sleep. "What on earth is this here?" he demanded, and I amused him by replying: "Lady Juliet Duff, by all that's wonderful!"

_____

[1] An elaborate form of charades.

Diana said: "Should I play the Queen in *Hamlet?*" (Larry had invited her to do so in his forthcoming production).

"No," said Louise de Vilmorin, "it would ruin a lovely film for me. I'd be too nervous to see it."

Sunday

I have the days mixed, but no matter. Still in bed but decided to get up for lunch. Duff in his nicest mood. He has perhaps the most civilized mind of anyone I know: his intelligence, erudition and general knowledge make me feel inadequate. There is no subject — even photography or design — about which he does not know more than I; even after all these years I am shy with him. He can be alarming, for he does not suffer fools gladly and at any moment his temper may get the better of him, and then the result is stupendous. But generally he is the most docile of people. He is never hurried and has the born writer's gift of leisure. He manages to get through an enormous amount of work, yet always seems to have time for reading. I broke into the library the other morning to find him sitting peacefully at his desk reading Horace. Diana, on the other hand, must be "doing" something.

After lunch today, unable to relax and do nothing, she arranged for Duff to read aloud. Diana sewing a piece of black and white watered taffeta; Vivien and I listening to Duff, in dry, slow and rather sad voice, read three stories of Elizabeth Bowen. Outside a forlorn, melting snowscape.

On the Korda Set/ Spring 1947

At long last we assembled on a certain cold Monday morning at the Shepperton studios outside London for the initial day of shooting of *An Ideal Husband.*

For me it was like going to public school for the first time. Korda's brother gave me word pictures of some of the people we would be working with. "Perinal, the camera man, is the Nadar[1] of cinema photography. He can always get the rich tones of the

---

[1] The Victorian portrait photographer and balloonist.

master, but he has no enthusiasm, for he is always a pessimist. Madame Natalie Kalmus is the abandoned wife of the man who invented Technicolor. She is a great bore because, having money and nothing to do with her time, she wants power. She enjoys motoring all the way down from her flat in Park Lane with an eye filter to put a few useless spokes in wheels about color separations, vibrations, etc. Don't pay too much attention to her idiotic talk. Her assistant Miss Bridge, a color expert, runs about with odd microscopic pieces of material and a lot of shop talk." Vincent himself, sad, weak, and disillusioned, gives the impression of having sold his soul to the devil. He has been in the film world for twenty years and shakes his head from side to side and says: "It's a terrible pissiness, this." I discover that he has a heart of gold and a great deal of tact. He expounds the disadvantages of fighting with the people with whom one is working.

Miss Bridge is soon confiding to Korda that Madame Kalmus does not approve of Paulette Goddard's ball dress. "Why?" asks Korda. "It doesn't give her enough lift." Korda smiles. "Why, I'm even proud of having myself suggested that Mister Beaton should drop those shoulders." Defeat of Madame Kalmus. Two days later Madame Kalmus and Miss Bridge gang up on me again. "We want a little talk. In your pink boudoir set you are having a yellow evening dress. Is that not so? Well, will the colors harmonize? . . ." Korda interjects: "Mister Beaton on his own has now decided against the yellow dress." "Oh!" Complete bafflement of Technicolor experts, and a lie.

Clarissa Churchill,[1] who during the past two years now has been a close friend, has recently been given a nebulous job by Korda ("You will find your own niche," was all he explained to her), and together we went through the "breaking in" process. Together we started off for the motorcar journey in fog or early morning mist to Shepperton Studios on the distant outskirts of London.

Soon we became exhilarated and interested in watching Korda's direction. We were full of admiration for his quickness, perception, subtlety, and flair. But by his choice of cast he gave himself insuperable difficulties, and when the hard job of acting had to be faced, he discovered that two of his leading actors were com-

---

[1] Niece of Winston Churchill later to marry Anthony Eden, now the Earl of Avon.

pletely inadequate. He soon realized that Paulette Goddard, who
was to be the wicked Mrs. Cheveley, could not possibly play the
part as an Englishwoman (her attempt to be a mixture of Lady
Diana Cooper and Sylvia Ashley Fairbanks—a blend suggested
to her by Noël Coward on the boat that brought her across the
Atlantic—was really rather painful) so I was told to look through
other Wilde plays for reference to Americans. We interpolated a
few lines from *The Woman of No Importance* to make a joke
about, and justify, Paulette's accent. Martita Hunt was called
in to coach Michael Wilding in the refinements of elocution, but
she professed no confidence in the success of her results. "He's
too common for the part," she said. "All the people who see the
film will be common," said Korda, glib in reply. But an easy
comeback is a mistake. By degrees I began to realize how readily
Korda excuses himself when he is in the wrong. His intention was
to make the highest quality film. When I complained about a
library set being particularly phoney and vulgar he shrugged:
"Well, the Chilterns are *nouveaux riches.*" That is not what
Wilde intended them to be. That is not why we went to Paris for
the hats and to Wildenstein to hire Louis XIV tapestries.

One evening after the shooting, Korda was shown rushes of the
previous week's work on a faulty projector. Perinal had been
told to produce some particularly striking lighting effects in order
to submerge the gaudy bookcases in the library set. Now Korda
thought the effects too dark: the actors' faces were out of focus.
Korda has been working until three o'clock each morning on
projects for three other pictures that are about to be simultaneously put into production. No wonder he is exhausted. He raised
hell: a week's work was wasted. Everything was blamed: everyone was summoned to give advice. Then, of course, chaos broke
loose. "Paulette's head looks too small." "The cape's too 'musical
comedy,'" said Paulette. "It's because of the orange velvet Mister
Beaton has designed," said Madame Kalmus. "Why not make it
blue?" suggested Miss Bridge. Madame Kalmus and Miss
Bridge had a field day. The discussions were disastrous. Perinal
was told to lighten the background. From then on his work on this
hideous set was entirely ruined.

When Korda saw the offending rushes on a proper projector

a few days later, the results were as richly "Nadaresque" as only Perinal could make them. But it was too late now to alter his instructions, and all the scenes in the library were shot with its vulgarity carefully highlighted.

My admiration for Korda was soon mingled with astonishment. At the time that he was most engrossed directing and producing *An Ideal Husband* (by no means a small production) his company directors were getting desperate to call a meeting, but Korda was busy negotiating a lawsuit in Hollywood. Suddenly, just as the *Anna Karenina* production was about to go before the cameras, Korda at last got around to reading the script that had been written by Jean Anouilh and Julien Duvivier (the film's director). He at once realized their efforts required work.

Hell let loose. Korda again sleepless. Constance Collier, with magnificent ram's profile, important nostrils, and prognathous jaw, has come from her house in Hollywood where for many years now she has abandoned her illustrious career on the stage for the screen, to play the part of Lady Markby on the *Ideal Husband* set. Today she bared her salted-almond teeth and chuckled: "Look at the lamb: he's not with us at all. He's not directing this film, he's directing Tolstoy. Look at him reading *Anna Karenina* between shots." Sure enough, there he was, with Tolstoy pressed close to his myopic eyes, oblivious of the electricians and grips moving dangerous equipment within inches of his head. Occasionally he would make a mark in the margin. Constance bared her salted almonds again. "Look! He's making a few notes so he can impress them at the conference and let them know he's read the book." After one *Ideal Husband* scene had been taken, he called for a stenographer and sat on the stage under an arc light dictating.

When the result of this dictation appeared a few hours later it was a revelation. In spite of the conditions in which he had been working, he had written an absolutely brilliant analysis of Tolstoy's book. He pointed out where the Anouilh-Duvivier script had gone wrong, and why and where it must be rewritten. These notes showed him to be endowed with acute sensitivity and an appreciation of fine literary nuances. It was also a passionate appeal to respect the true Tolstoy.

I felt that from now on, however much I might differ from Korda in certain aspects of taste, it was up to me to concentrate on his best points and to realize how remarkable a man he is.

A few days later I discovered that Korda had given his notes on the rewriting of the script to a writer generally regarded as a hack who had just completed a bad picture. When challenged by Vivien Leigh on the wisdom of this Alex said: "If I give the job to Rodney Ackland, or a good writer, he'd produce *his* version of *Anna*. I want my outline to be copied faithfully." The result, which appeared ten days later, was certainly better than the former, but naturally, since it was a rush job, was not really up to the mark.

—————————————————————————— May 7th, 1947

Korda in a bad mood: all sorts of irritants make him like a bear with a sore head. Our set is teeming: over two hundred guests are assembled on stage in their expensive finery. Lord and Lady Chiltern are receiving at the head of an imposing staircase. For the fiftieth time the ghostly-looking butler rings out: "The Earl of Caversham." The beautiful Diana Wynyard does her extraordinarily ugly, but charming, grin: C. Aubrey Smith bows with as much spontaneity as if he were running through the performance for the first take. Suddenly Glynis Johns, who plays the part of the ingenue Mabel Chiltern, cannot be found. "Who allowed her to go for breakfast?" screams Korda, and the two men responsible for giving her leave to go to the cafeteria are given a fine display of temperament. "Now where's Miss Goddard?" "In the Medical Aid." The technicians around the camera are on their guard against more disasters. One of the electricians calls sotto voce to an unseen figure among the lights aloft: "Save the scoops and trim your arcs when I tell you to, for God's sake, or there'll be bloody murder."

Volte-face of Miss Bridge: "Mister Beaton, I must tell you I like your costumes—even if others don't."

"Don't others like them?"

"Well—Madame Kalmus doesn't."

"Why?"

"Oh, well—she never likes anything she doesn't do herself. You know, a leopard can't change its spots. Now, if you like a thing you stick to it. There's no mystery about Technicolor, it's just the same as color in life except that it intensifies or glorifies color."

Rushes: The projection room is empty except for the hairdressers and others of the make-up department. As they watch the rushes they interrupt the on-screen performances by the stars whom all the world adores.

"That wig join's better." "What about that mount in front?" "The dye's come off his tam-o'-shanter." "That shot was taken late in the evening: he doesn't look shaved: he'd been hanging about all day and was just leaving when they called him onto the set, and there wasn't time to touch him." "Oh, I'm sick of her by now! She has such huge jowls, and the neck goes into three great creases every time she turns her head. What's more, she's got a moustache, and her skin is just a bed of acne." "There's too much rouge on the poor bugger's lower lip." "The poor bugger can't keep his eyes open, he's got such a hangover."

Without a word of warning I arrive, in full battle cry, on the *Ideal Husband* set—to find the place deserted. Korda has called a halt while he flies to America to fight that lawsuit. A postponement of two weeks, complete dispersal of crew, high tension slackened.

The elusive English sun now does its summer's work. For two weeks we are bathed in a heat wave. On the *Anna Karenina* set they are wearing furs and laying snow on the ground to be seen through windows on which the prop men are nailing icicles.

Vivien Leigh, so companionable and perky in private life, becomes sadly changed as soon as the strain of picture-making begins to tell. There is no fun anymore. The difficulties are overwhelming and absorbing. I go into her dressing-room one morning, confident of finding her in a great state of elation, for the newspapers have just announced that her husband has been knighted.

I open the door. "Oh, I'm so happy for you about the great news!" A face of fury is reflected in the mirror. "Really, it's too stupid! Would you believe it—the dressmaker from Paris was

waiting at her hotel the entire day yesterday and the studio forgot
to order a car for her. Really—I've never worked on such a film
as this!"

Later, Vivien instructs me: "Please tell Clarissa how to behave
when she brings journalists on the set. I don't want them turned
off, but I want to have them announced first and presented."
When the message is relayed to Clarissa, she has already received
it from half a dozen other sources.

It is difficult for me, working concurrently on two large productions. There is no camaraderie between the two companies. If I
excuse myself: "I have to go to the *Ideal Husband* set," I am told:
"Oh, leave them to it!" It is particularly foolish to plan to shoot
two of the most elaborate scenes on the same day. For the *Ideal
Husband* hundreds of elegant extras representing the world of
fashion in Hyde Park are strolling up Rotten Row while phaetons,
broughams, every sort of curricle, bicycles, and horseback riders
are also on tap. There are guards parading in full dress, Salvation
Army bands, horses, dogs, etc. The studio is not geared to this
pitch of work. Yet on the *Anna Karenina* set fifty ballroom guests
have been lined up complete with hairdo, jewels, etc.; director
Julien Duvivier snarls: "They all look like English girls that
haven't had enough to eat. (Rationing is still in force.) Get some
full-bosomed girls that look like Russian aristocrats." This criticism,
coming at this time from a Frenchman, is not considered tactful
by the wardrobe department who, having worked all weekend,
now have the impossible task of re-fitting all these costumes.

In fact, Duvivier does not get the best out of his helpers: he is
said to be unkind to the underdog. He snaps off heads when his
minions speak up and make criticisms or interruptions that are
part of their job.

Eventually the unit revolts. Union meeting. An uproar is abated
by Duvivier's offer to give a dinner and film showing of one of his
earlier productions to the entire unit. Another union meeting to
decide if the invitation should be accepted: grudgingly, it is. The
company decides it will get as much out of the unpopular director
as possible. There is no love lost anywhere. A double horseshoe

table is set up, and a good dinner provided with a great supply of wines and spirits, but the drink only increases the ill humors. Speeches are made with very unfortunate references to the troubles that have existed earlier in the week. Cheers for other members of the unit, half-hearted for the director. Duvivier wise-cracks bitterly. An impasse of drunken embarrassment.

An earlier film directed by Duvivier—a French one—is shown after dinner. Many refrain from seeing it: others are too drunk. The evening is interrupted by the noise of men falling from their seats.

Work next day is worse. Half the wardrobe staff are away with hangovers. The director's temper is fierier than ever.

Later: The wardrobe master is in hospital. His condition is serious. He is on the danger list. He is dead.

Saturday afternoon: "The boss is arriving! Any minute now!" "He's at the gate! He's here!" Korda has been met at the airport and driven forthwith to the studio. About a dozen different units try to get his attention.

Momentous decisions must be made immediately. In the face of the *I.H.* and *A.K.* representatives, the *Bonnie Prince Charlie* set have nabbed him. It seems as if they have received a shock. The rumor has it that, after weeks spent on location in Scotland, the film will not be made.[1]

The publicity men now have hold of Korda. The war leader is with his chiefs of staff. When the leader turns to one of his entou-rage the rest fall back. As the honor is conferred for a brief moment only, it is up to the lesser light to make the most of the occasion—also to prolong it as long as possible. The leader is taken to inspect a new set. "No—it has no atmosphere and it's too big. It must be rebuilt by Monday morning."

On the *Ideal Husband* exterior set: we are waiting for a big cloud to pass: for days now we have been watching the gray skies. Each hour costs Korda an astronomical figure for the time of so many people, animals, and period carriages. The women's clothes are crushed and dirty, and their trains have trailed in the mud and the horse dung. By now, everything that was once sparkling and

---

[1] Rumor proved false. The film was made, with David Niven in the lead role.

elegant looks sordid and drab. The spirit seems to be knocked out of all but the principal actors; they have enjoyed a rest and have only some comparatively easy scenes to do.

Everyone—society-pedestrians, coachmen, bicyclists, brass bands, platoon of guards, etc.—is ready at last, except Paulette Goddard. Her make-up girl explains the delay: "I've been cutting an eyelash for her."

At last the sun! A frenzied rush for the golden seconds to be used to their best advantage. Suddenly the scenes are "in the can." The ghost of Korda smiles. Only one more day's work inside the studio and shooting will be finished on *Ideal Husband.* Then Korda can give his attention to the troubles of *Anna Karenina* and *Bonnie Prince Charlie.*

——————————————*Weekend with Laurence Olivier/Spring, 1947: Notley Priory*

Vivien is away visiting her former husband: Larry was busy all Saturday with business plans for his Australian tour, but intended to devote Sunday to going over the details of my *School for Scandal* designs. Larry would have preferred my production to be rich and realistic with mahogany doors and built fireplaces, but, since the scenery will have to travel throughout Australia and New Zealand before coming to London, it is more expedient to use *trompe l'oeil.* This gives me much more scope for invention, and I am delighted at the prospect of doing all the sets as if they were eighteenth-century engravings, even introducing the hatching strokes into the costumes.

Meanwhile, I listen to Larry and his accountant. "We're banking on every performance playing to capacity. Now, how many are we?"

"Forty-one—that's one too many."

"Can't we take one extra?"

"That extra fare will cost £1,000 by the end of the tour."

"Then suppose Vivien and I don't go?"

But in general, L. is very businesslike, with a minimum of jokes and interruptions.

Later he talked to me about acting. "In my opinion acting is a question of range and taste. Let me give you an example of what I mean. Margaret Leighton is a most brilliant actress. She can do anything. She does everything quite naturally. It took me two years to walk round a chair with ease; it took me another two years to laugh on the stage. I had to learn everything: what to do with my hands, how to cry. Leighton can do all those things automatically. When I was playing Hotspur in Shakespeare's *Henry IV,* I had a very short time for study. I gave a sketchy performance, and one place in particular, where I knew I was horribly banal, became quite obnoxious to me. I had to say: 'Well done—give us another song,' or something like that, and I had thought of nothing better to do than applaud. One evening I thought 'I won't do this again,' and I suddenly had the idea of seeing Margaret Leighton weeping and being jovial to hide her sadness, and saying: 'Come, let's have another song,' to cover up her misery. So as we sat listening to the first song I whispered: 'Weep—weep as much as you can!' and after a few moments great big tears were coursing down her cheeks. She couldn't have done that unless her range was enormous, and I consider the question of taste made all the difference to that scene."

Larry also told me of his early struggles on the stage. Wearing a discarded suit of his uncle's cut down to fit him, with one pair of shoes and an old hat, he would go the rounds of the managers' offices. For years it was a question of getting an extra ten shillings a week and an extra line. Then he got married and the situation was more acute, and he had to accept all sorts of parts that he knew were not suitable. Noël Coward told him to play in *Private Lives,* saying, "It'll run for years and you need the money." Now it amused him so much to be lionized by "Society." Last week Sibyl Colefax[1] had taken Vivien and him on to a supper party after a Rubinstein concert. Olga Lynn, a diminutive singer who had sacrificed music for society, had come up to him and said: "Do you know Maggie Teyte?"[2] "No." "Then stay right here and I'll bring her up and present her to you." "And an old girl, 'Lady Abercrombie,' [Lady Aberconway,[3] in fact] cornered me and was

---

[1] The energetic wife of Sir Arthur Colefax, who brought together a variety of famous people from all worlds of creative activity.

[2] Said to be the most accomplished *lieder* singer whose technique, taught to her by the famous Jean de Reszke, has served her throughout the years.

[3] Wife of Lord Aberconway, a London personality, a hostess, and a lover of the arts.

being very sympathetic, and at one moment lowered her eyelids and said: 'Oh, Sir Laurence! — Sir Laurence!'"

Larry finds now that he can assume the responsibilities of a country squire and talk as man to man with the farmer next door about the water system, the costs of supplying neighboring farms with drainage, etc. It is rare that one comes across an actor whose self-assurance doesn't border on crass bumptiousness. Perhaps more by strength of character than natural ability, Olivier has succeeded. Now his problems are ones of how to sustain his success and how to save money for his old age. But the architecture of his professional life seems pretty solid.

Dégringolade of Gerald Berners

Gerald Berners is fading fast. Once so full of fun and wit, given to all forms of unexpected eccentricity, even to practical jokes, he is now sad and morose. He has such talent in so many fields — music, painting — and recently he has proved that he is a writer of exquisite stylishness. His amusing short stories and novels have not been estimated at their real worth, but he should continue. Yet he does not seem to have the will to live. He leaves his house at Faringdon with its statues decked with artificial fernery, the cases of stuffed birds, and the pigeons dyed all colors of the rainbow, and he goes to his London doctor. "I don't want you to return to the country tomorrow," the doctor tells him. "I want you to agree to stay under my supervision at the clinic for the next month. You've got to look after yourself. We received the cardiogram and it shows us quite distinctly that you've had a clot — a thrombosis — which has pressed near your heart. It's dispersed now, but we must watch you very carefully as this is the thing that people die of, so it's worth your while to give up the next four weeks to being quite quiet. Now you'll come along tomorrow afternoon, won't you? You'll get into a taxi, and you've got someone to lift your bag down, haven't you? You'll please me a lot by saying you'll do this. Good. I'm very relieved to hear you've made the right decision."

Gerald comes blinking into my room in his London house where I am staying. "It's really quite serious. It's the sort of thing that people die of. Oh well, it's not worth getting upset about, but I might as well take a month off for, after all, health is everything, isn't it? And it's never quiet at Faringdon with Robert[1] about. I've been very worried there lately. I've had to bring a law case about two people who wouldn't move out of one of the cottages on the estate, and it's been difficult to keep calm. There's always such a lot to do. The bore is I'm missing the spring there. Now, let me see—when I come out of the nursing home it will be June first. The syringa will be coming out and the greenhouse peaches will be ripe."

Pathetic Gerald! When he returned to Faringdon, life was no easier for him and it was not long before, in desperation, he turned his face to the wall.[2]

_____ *Looking for a New House*/October, 1947

Since I was thrown out of Ashcombe I have been somewhat forlornly looking for a small house in the country to take its place. But where on the entire earth could I find such another remote and beautiful a treasure as Ashcombe? Particulars came from estate agents by every post: "Imposing Georgian style mansion only thirty-seven minutes from Piccadilly Circus . . . ." "Tudor gem — oak porch—all mod. cons.—billiard room and solarium . . . ." "Converted Gothic lodge with indoor fives court . . . ."

I went, by expensive hire-car service, to Sussex to see deserted, pebble-dash haciendas decorated indoors with wrought-iron work, and to Surrey to admire slate-turreted maisonettes with cinder paths curving among the sparse beds of pampas grass and mombretia. I determined to remain faithful to Wiltshire. "No, Messrs. Rawlence and Squarey, I did not fall in love yesterday afternoon with that mustard-and-pepper brick house at Quidhampton. Why? Because, well, to begin with—it's too near the railway, and those pylons make a beeline for the garden." Eventually I became embarrassed at having to refuse so many of these "unique offers."

But even more embarrassing were the visits, recommended by my relations and closest friends, to the houses of people they knew, who were either feeling the pinch, wishing to make a

_____

[1] Robert Heber-Percy, a vivacious young friend who lived with Lord Berners and eventually inherited all his property, much to the dismay and surprise of the Berners family.

[2] Lord Berners died in 1950.

change, or settling into something more "in keeping with the times." In spite of its much vaunted monkey puzzle tree I loathed "Redlands" and wished desperately that its occupants, still in residence, were not so obviously avid to sell to me. I felt trapped. It was incumbent upon me to admire the gnarled beams, the granite chimney piece and the stained-glass lattices, the rockery and ponticums beyond, yet the praise must not be laid on too thick — for then my eventual escape would be made all the harder. No matter what I said, there was nothing to be done: when I tried to leave "Redlands" without a promise of "something down on account" the owner's son-in-law tried to set the dogs on me.

After a while, in a recurrent nightmare, I dreamt I was being blackmailed into buying some such overwhelming monstrosity as Royal Holloway College or a sinister Victorian workhouse.

However, Edith Olivier, who eighteen years ago had found Ashcombe for me, now wrote to me of a small Wren house not far from her in Wilton which belonged to the National Trust, and which she had heard was available for rental. Perhaps Edith could mark up a double . . . . Edith Olivier was a Wiltshire clergyman's daughter and a remarkable character, who late in life became a literary figure, publishing many books on local life and entertaining men of letters at her house in the park at Wilton.

The aftermath of the war has brought with it our relief and gratitude, yet few joys. We in England have all endured what must be one of the most uncomfortable phases in recent history. People are undernourished, yet the food prospect is dark. The financial crisis is appalling and our debt to America increasing, yet under the Labour Government money is racketed away. According to Churchill, the Socialist policy, apart from abandoning well-tried traditions, is to spread class warfare and to reduce us all to the dull uniformity of a prison. We are in trouble in Palestine and Greece, and already the Germans are cutting up rough so that our troops must remain in vast quantities and at crippling expense. Continual crises hit hard our export trade. Each month brings further humiliations: these are our last days in Burma, we have left Cairo and lost India. Mr. Attlee's gang has brought disaster in practically all forms upon us, and a White Paper, just issued, prescribes no remedy from present ills. The excuses advanced for the Government's chronic mistakes are blamed on years of Tory misrule, and the only consolation offered is that we must all work harder.

To add to our winter of discontent the whole land has been suffering from a plague of cold, another ice age. Under the auspices of Mr. Emmanuel Shinwell, Minister of Fuel and Power, the coal supply has almost completely given out: gas flickers weakly—even hospitals are without hot water. Edith Olivier and other elderly ladies have not been permitted to switch on their electric blankets, and the death rate from pneumonia has rocketed.

Not surprisingly the train from Waterloo to Salisbury on the Saturday morning was unheated. Edith had to knock the icicles off me when I arrived—and found, most thankfully, that she had still a supply of logs for her small but hospitable hearth. Fortunately Edith's cheerful spirits and courage were in contrast to my mood, and her rabbit pie warmed me and gave me enough strength to set off with her on a polar expedition through the iced snow before dark enveloped us.

At first Edith's small motorcar would not start; our breath made clouds of steam as, in turn, we cranked the ineffectual handle. By degrees the frozen tubes thawed; eventually we jerked and skidded over the ice towards the village of Dinton. A noble edifice, somewhat Palladian, with a magnolia pinioned to its yellow stone walls, presented itself. On closer inspection the property was altogether too grand for my taste or my pocket.

The light weakened and the thermometer dropped. On the somewhat dejected return to Wilton we passed through the village of Broadchalke. Here had lived John Aubrey, the seventeenth-century antiquarian and historian. Aubrey wrote that the village possesses "one of the tunablest ring of bells in Wiltshire which hang advantageously, the river running near the churchyard, which meliorates the sound." Edith's car ground to an abrupt halt in front of a miniature palace which I had often admired when living ten miles away. In fact, each time I came upon this Charles II rose-brick frontage I stopped, with screeching brakes, to admire the design of what must have been originally built for a king's *nid d'amour* or hunting lodge. Apart from its quite exceptional façade, with its elegant stone pilasters and the bust of an unknown poet in the broken pediment over the door, the house had always had added interest because of Mrs. Wood, its owner, and the mother of the remarkable painter Christopher Wood. Although Mrs. Wood was wary of snoopers, and had an unwelcoming manner with visitors, she retained in the attic a huge collection of her late son's canvases.

Mrs. Wood had recently died, and it was rumored that the house was about to be sold. It was, therefore, with a feeling of adventure that this cold late afternoon Edith boldly rang the front door bell and, after a moment of *pourparler* with an unfriendly servant, was bidden to enter.

At first, in the last light of day, the interior of the house disappointed us. The hall was cut up into several partitions comprising a gun room, corridor, and a minute enclosure with a gate-legged dining table. Oak beams warred with the classic lines of the exterior, and a clumsy mock Elizabethan chimney piece of modern red brick protruded out of all proportion. We could not understand why, in such a rambling way, rooms were placed on different levels. We shivered as we went from one disused parlor to another, then up to the dark and sinister attic where cockfighting used to take place in the eighteenth century. We peered in the gloom at the pens where the prize birds were kept before being let out into the blinding light of candles to fight for their survival.

Then again we braced ourselves for the Alaskan elements in order to view the garden and terrace. The dark sky made everything appear bleak and cheerless: a dirty snow-covered hill seemed to avalanche precariously close to the house. Edith, purple-nosed, did not wax enthusiastic; neither was I, as I had been at Ashcombe, a victim of love at first sight. Nevertheless, when we had returned to Edith's hearth and were huddling over hot drinks, enough enthusiasm was kindled to suggest summoning my mother to give her opinion on the place.

On the Monday morning, for the first time in many months, the sun shone on England. Everyone's spirits soared, even one's hatred for Mr. Shinwell turned to mere contempt. On the second visit to Reddish House I was elated—and my mother too. Her heart went out to the house of warm lilac-colored brick and she loved the way it lay with the garden rising to a paddock, the long vistas of lawn sheltered by a double row of limes and elms and the kitchen garden enclosed with a typical Wiltshire wall of chalk topped with thatch roof. From across the village street the property con-

tinued across a meadow to a stretch of poplars and willows border-
ing the river Ebble, once stocked with crayfish by Aubrey, and
where the trout, two feet long, were considered by Charles II
to be the best flavored in England. My mother also enthused over
the vast yews cut to look like plum puddings, the topiary trees
shaped like chessmen, the well established nut walk, and the
clumps of beeches. Two adjoining thatched cottages, surprisingly
like Ann Hathaway's, with their own gardens, were also part of
the property. My mother saw the possibilities of making the terrace, with its southern aspect and old-fashioned roses growing
over a balustrade, into a sheltered spot for outdoor lunch or tea.
In fact, we both considered that the loss of Ashcombe from which
we were both so acutely suffering might be partially compensated
for by this new acquisition.

Of course Reddish House did not possess the wayward romantic
remoteness of Ashcombe. Instead of hiding in folds of wooded
downland it presented its extremely formal exterior onto a village
street. But just as I was looking out of its old glass windowpanes
a dogcart trotted by, and children were returning from school;
the village life seemed to have a delightful Miss Mitford quality.
Moreover, the house was a real house—not a fantasy, makeshift,
pretense like Ashcombe. This was the abode of an adult person:
perhaps it would be a good thing if I started living up to my swiftly
advancing age. But could I afford to buy a real house? And particularly one like this which must surely be so much in demand—
small, compact, but of a fine quality? The fact that it was included
in eighteenth-century books of engravings as a gem of domestic
architecture gave it an extra cachet and value.

Although I had never made his acquaintance, I sent a telegram
to Dr. Wood commiserating upon the recent death of his wife,
then boldly asked him for the first offer of refusal of his house.
I discovered that the property had been left by Mrs. Wood to her
daughter, who did not wish to occupy the house herself, yet was
unable to keep her father there in solitary misery. She wished to
sell her legacy as quickly and as painlessly as possible. No doubt
if she had advertised in *Country Life* the house would have
fetched more than the ten thousand pounds she asked me and
for which, with alacrity, I bought it—only later wondering how I
would find the money to foot the bill.

Soon my enthusiasm to convert the house to my own taste had fired me to the extent that a dozen times each night I would switch on the bedside light to record a note or an idea about the way the hall could be enlarged, rustic oak beams covered, and extra windows inserted.

When my Ashcombe furniture appeared from storage out of the vans, most of it had immediately to be sent for sale in the Caledonian Market, whence much of it originally came: what had been suitable for weekends of charades and folly was not suitable for Reddish. Besides, the made-over junk had not worn well. Reddish House dictated a more sober style of decoration, and its contents must be more respectful to all my predecessors whose histories I was busy piecing together from the voluminous deeds—dating from 1599 and beautifully inscribed and decorated with calligraphy and waxen seals—which came to me with the house.

Restrictions on travel allowances are now lifted. Being able to fly to Paris gives me the feeling of independence that has been denied, and here I have found on the Left Bank chairs and tables that delight in form, color, and price, and in the Flea Market there are all sorts of old curtains and materials of a quality not to be found in England, even with coupons to spare.

Broadchalke promises another great new interest: I am in love and life seems good.

Noël Coward

Picasso

Christian Bérard

Anita Loos

Frank Fay, star of *Harvey*

Princess Bera

Lady Diana Cooper

Gertrude Stein

André Gide

Part 7

NEW YORK IDYLL

1947–48

Sanatorium atmosphere of Atlantic boat trip: fellow passengers nonexistent, long sleep, meals (potatoes in their jackets), no mental taxation, nerves gradually padded. Return to health and strength somewhat retarded on arrival by cruel Customs chaos on the dock. At last freedom.

The New York light is so harsh it makes your eyes feel old. The colors are the primary ones: butcher blues and vermillion on hoardings, in shop windows, or on the children roller skating. They do not fade impressionistically into the distance. All is sharp, crisp, hard, without subtleties of gradation. The taxi stops at a crimson light by a newsstand. Typical of the brash, relentless, conscious anti-art use of color is the border of scarlet on the cover of *Time* magazine. This frame would destroy the pictorial effect of whatever it contained, but it strikes exactly that discordant note of commercialism which even the more enlightened people understand, and even respect.

After the really terrible squalor of the back streets, the immaculate sidewalks of Park and Fifth come as a shock. Everything seems so prosperous: the shops highly polished, the merchandise gleaming; the men in sharply pressed suits, the women with freshly set hair and new fur coats. But the eggshell smoothness has no real character.

From my hotel room I telephone immediately to the Ritz Tower—to the person who has occupied my mind for the last two years. "Miss Brown don't answer." Why is she hiding from me again? I am in despair. How to get through the day? Are my hopes dashed? Will I never see her again? Next day I telephone a hotel. My heart is pounding while I wait to be put through to her room. An unfamiliar voice replies, very gay and laughing and high-pitched: "No, I am not well. I have got sinus trouble. You can hear it in my voice."

"It is a year and a half since I have seen you."

"Is it really? How terrible—how sad."

"Did you enjoy Europe?"

"Ain't going to tell you."

"I rang you up yesterday but they said . . ." She interrupted me: "'Miss Brown don't live here anymore.' Well, she answered today. I'd love to come and see you. Are you in the same rooms?"

"Yes."

"Well, it can't be today and then tomorrow is Saturday."

"You're still busy at weekends?" I asked rather bitterly, knowing that she has to be at liberty when "the little man" is free.

"It may not be before Monday."

"Well, I have something for you—a lot of things." (Meaning all the letters I had written and not posted since her silence.)

"Are they matches?"

"Matches?"

"Don't you remember, when matches were difficult to come by, you gave me a big box and they have lasted all this time."

"And my red pajamas I gave you—do you ever wear them?" I asked.

"No, but I look at them sometimes."

"I'm so glad, honey."

"Honey?"

"Yes, honey."

"Hohney-chile."

It is all so easy and I am relieved; it might have been the terror, the silence, the return to emptiness. I am now at the beginning of a new offensive; if I am clever enough not to force the issues I may win through.

"Perhaps I can come to see you between three and three-thirty?"

"Fine," I answered.

"Will anyone be there?"

"No one. It will be a morgue of silence, solitude and secrecy."

"Now don't overdo it."

October 3rd

One of my happy days. Luckily I was busy with the morning's chores so other things took my mind off my obsession with the coming encounter. Then I made preparations as for a marriage. Flowers in the room, Old Golds placed around in profusion. I wore my second-best suit, my favorite being kept for another time — for now I would rely on the impact of the shock of reunion. I came back early from lunch and waited. What would the next hour bring? I had remained in an uncertainty for so long; I had had to reassure myself with great difficulty at times that only circumstances were against me, and that all was really well. But the uncertainty that things might have changed has recently grown. Lately quite a few friends have met Greta on her holidays abroad and my news of her has consisted only of second-hand reports from them. (All I had to reassure myself was the memory of a very welcome, gargantuan box of chocolates sent to Pelham Place from Beverly Hills. When Greta had arrived in London there had been photographs of her trying to duck in and out of Claridge's wearing a vast, conspicuous white hat. This hat was subsequently seen in many parts of the city — but not by me. Each day I had telephoned. Sometimes no reply, sometimes a hurried talk and she would call me when she could see me. Meanwhile Bobbie Andrews, the actor, told me he had taken Greta for a long walk in the park; she had been wearing the huge, white hat. I was extremely jealous. One morning, when I had been out, Greta had left word with my secretary that she would visit me that afternoon. I had at once become almost frantic with nervous apprehension. The film studios had telephoned summoning me immediately to see Korda. The command was rejected. Another call came from Claridge's to announce a delay. I lay flat on my back trying to calm my nerves, then another brief message to my secretary: "Unable to come around today." The following morning the huge, white hat had left England.)

Perhaps the same sad game would be played this afternoon. Prostrate on the sofa with my eyes closed I visualized the arrival, the wandering around, the sitting in this chair. My heart started to thump so violently that it was almost alarming. I looked at my watch: ten minutes had passed, the longest ten minutes I had ever experienced. The watch again — five more minutes had passed. A bowl of fruit was moved from a side table into the center of the room, some books were rearranged. Pages were turned of *La Divina Proportion,* but how to concentrate? Perhaps she would not be coming after all, and my punishment must be taken

sweetly. Nothing to do but to await with fortitude the next opportunity. I began to feel quite sick. Was there time to go to the loo?
From the bathroom I wandered into the bedroom and looked
through a mound of carefully assorted photographs. Then, at last,
the bell. I must put down the photographs one batch neatly on top
of another. Again the bell. She was impatient! Only a thin slice
of wooden door now separated us.

> What fortitude the soul contains
> That it can so endure
> The accent of a coming foot
> The opening of a door.

Now I would open and know my fate. Now the certainty of
reality gave me the incentive to act with decision and even a
certain coolness. I had rehearsed all sorts of welcome: "My, my,
my!" or "Well, well, well!" (in her idiom), or "At last, after all
this time—what a long time it has been!" or "What a charming
surprise!" Then would we fall into one another's arms, or would
we remain formally distant and circumspect?

I teetered towards the door; with a sweep I opened it. I was
not disappointed, but my heart withstood the impact: I still survived. She was wearing a black peaked hat and a falling dark
coat, her mouth was very red, her face peakier than I had remembered, the nose more pointed. Her body had become a shred—
there was hardly any flesh on it. Bowing formally, my reflexes
caused me to exclaim: "What a charming surprise!"

"Surprise?" She was surprised.

I stood my distance: she was again surprised. But I could not
allow her to remain long in this state and soon she said: "So you're
massaging my back again, are you?" All the while she was taking
in various aspects of the room with an extraordinary intensity.

"You remember this old sweater? I haven't worn it since—
this is the first time I have put it on. It is very warm today and
I have been hunting."

"Hunting?"

"On Third Avenue and Fourth Avenue. You get so many smuts
in your eyes, and it's so noisy and dirty."

"What are you looking for? Your lighter? Holder?" The Old
Gold is lit.

"I expect you think I'm so busy?" she remarked apologetically
about the preparations for smoking.

"Well, have you had any great emotional or spiritual experiences since I have seen you?"

"*La vie.*"

"And what do you want most out of it?"

"Generally or specifically?"

"Specifically."

"It would be foolish to tell you and I am not as foolish as all that."

"A Frenchwoman would tell me."

"Oh, let's stop all this *badinage!* What is that word in English?"

"Tomfoolery."

"Tomfoolery—oh!"

We continue to yatter about nothing. It is pleasant enough, and I must play this coolly and not force the issue, not ask for explanations of the long past silence.

"And so you met my friends David[1] and Michael[2] in the South of France, and you laughed at Michael's impersonation of Queen Mary?"

"Fantastic—it's so true—so funny!"

"Did you like them?"

"Very much, and I love the British—the way they speak and their manners."

"Then what a pity you allowed so little time for your English stay."

"Don't let's discuss it. But a terrible thing happened at Claridge's. I let the bath overflow, and I was so afraid the ceiling below would come down, and it took forever to swab the floor with towels and my poor little sponge."

Even taking into account her love of secrecy, it was a bit baffling that nothing important was discussed. It was as if she were living on a different planet. But her practical side came out when, touring the apartment, she put things to rights and, as darkness fell, drew the mustard velvet curtains.

Our meeting had changed to a calmer atmosphere when anecdotes and questions were exchanged. She even asked: "You enjoyed working with Korda?"

---

[1] David Herbert

[2] Michael Duff

"Up to a point. He's a man of charm, but a cynic — and it's difficult to work for someone who changes his mind to suit the situation; eventually the personal temperaments on the set made things difficult." I related how, only recently, hearing Korda's voice on the telephone had made me quake in my innards. The idea of being at his beck, however polite his call, was anathema. After this interval I felt more qualms than ever at the prospect of getting into the trap again, yet my finances are such that, if some fairly substantial sum of money doesn't come in soon, I shall have to sell the new house in the country. Greta said: "If you feel like this after a three months' interval, imagine how I feel after eight years!" We both aired our anxieties and dread at the prospect of her working for films.

"Yes, film studios are obnoxious places." The information that Korda had re-made the film of *Anna,* with Vivien Leigh in Greta's part, in no way interested her. "You see what it was for me to be in such a jail all those years."

"And how was your visit to Sweden?"

"I felt uprooted, knowing no one except a certain friend on whom I daren't call under the present circumstances."

"Why?" I asked, my curiosity getting the better of my tact.

"It's a tricky subject. But the U.S. uproots one: I have been here so long. Oh, well — what's it matter? In any country there are only one or two people one likes. One has one's work or, if not, then life is made up of unimportant details. There's no difference."

I was then bold enough to confess: "The Swedish newspapers rang me to know if we were engaged to be married. Did they worry you about me?"

"No, they never asked me anything." (Such a relief!)

"Then why didn't you answer my telephone calls?"

"I don't approve of the telephone."

"But we can't just rely only on the spiritual bond. Life is passing by quickly," I stressed. "Look how moth-eaten and haggard I've become! You don't want to wait until I'm a total wreck."

"Don't you know that Shaw said that old age must never be mentioned?"

Changing the subject, I asked, "And did you find the delights of Paris unalloyed?"

She gave the impression of having been lonely. Lunch and

dinner, two dress shows, a horrible waste of time. "I can't travel. I don't know how to do it. I never see the bill. The little man gets all the tickets, makes the arrangements. I just go along and pay my share at the end."

In her hotel room she had tried to study French, but she told amusingly of how she went into a shop for a cardigan sweater and asked: *"En quelles couleurs?"* The assistant said abruptly: "Oh, we have them in all colors."

Before having left for Europe Greta had been exhausted — painting the windows of her California house. Her hands had become chapped with deep lines. She had scraped the window ledges with sandpaper and then a knife, gouging big flakes off until they looked like fringes. Then: "Oh, so tiring to do the painting! To go on smoothly, and not to let it drip!"

In Europe she had become painfully thin, having caught a bug. Now at dinner in New York she looked almost simian with untidy hair and large, smudged, red mouth.

Greta's due at four o'clock: I wait in my room expectantly. The bell rings: a messenger with an envelope. The bell rings again. She is looking very white but poignant. She describes having come from three male interior decorators. They are old acquaintances but their language offends her: "They say things *stink,* and they call people *bitches.* And I don't like that, but don't want to offend them by remarking upon it. Now I can't stay long. I've got a lady calling for me here. We're going on somewhere three blocks down Fifth Avenue." The woman arrives. She is a Mrs. Sanson from Santa Barbara, in a fur coat and a smart back-tilted hat — the last sort of woman one would expect to be a friend of Greta's. Florid-complexioned and reddish-haired, with a large diamond brooch, she proves to be a rollicking good sort, but without any imagination or claims to understanding of the "artistic temperament." Mrs. Sanson takes in the situation in a flash. Greta refers to me as her fiancé. In the ensuing conversation Greta lets drop the information that she had seen *Lady Windermere's Fan* on Broadway, but after I had left the cast. "Oh, you go flitting about too much." Mrs. Sanson, however, had seen me on the first night in Santa Barbara. The atmosphere has changed completely, the tension has disappeared and there are no more complications—instead jokes and pleasantries, cushions thrown across the room, and roses and kisses.

"I am so busy!" she says on the telephone.

"Doing what?"

"Hunting. All I need is a horn and some dogs."

"Then you are too busy to see me today?"

" 'Fraid so. You take me by surprise and get me too muddled. But I haven't had any air. Suppose we go in the park again? I haven't been there this winter. Where shall we meet? How about the Zoo? How about that archway? I'll be there at four punctually —I might lose you under that archway if I'm not on the tick."

I am having my hair cut. I look at my watch. How favored, how blessed I am, that in half an hour I shall be keeping a tryst with that most rare and elusive creature! I go to buy socks and a pair of gloves. I look at the clock again. In fifteen minutes I shall be waiting under that archway. I rush back to my rooms at the hotel. Miss Cleghorn, surprised at my hurry, hands me a sheaf of telephone messages, but I do not look at them. "I'm going out for a walk in the park." She appears even more surprised at this information.

The winter sun has faded. It is now past the best of the day and the air is very cold. I mistake a number of women for the person I have in mind. She has not yet arrived. I stand about. My nose becomes mauve and icicled: there is no more drafty place than under that archway. I wander towards the Zoo and go into the Lion House; it is warm in there, but smelly. I must not remain more than a second in case she has arrived and is already waiting. No sign. I sit on a park seat and watch an old woman in a fur coat feeding the pigeons and squirrels. I go into the even smellier warmth of the Monkey House, but not for long. When I come out and walk by the cages where a few scruffy animals are being watched by the nursemaids and their charges, I see that divinely proportioned figure coming towards me. It is, unlike the rest of humanity, so utterly romantic. It is wearing a dark blue coat and Pilgrim Fathers' hat, a large black bag slung from a shoulder, gloves, and sandals. The passers-by spot her so we cannot draw attention to ourselves. As we approach we give discreet signals with our hands. Then suddenly we are together. I about-turn and arm in arm we are rushing through the gritty parkland. We chatter like six-year-olds. When some pigeons get into her path she becomes very English and refers to them as "these bloody doves." We march in double-quick time as far as the Museum, then stand panting.

"Shall we go in and look at the tapestries?" I ask.

"How smart you are! How did you know they are on view? Well, we won't go in—we'll go back."

A woman with a pram shouts at Greta in Swedish—she receives no reply. A man who dogs us for some distance, and then asks to take a photograph, gets a very sweet and gracious refusal. As we near my hotel she remarks: "By the law of gravity this should be Sixty-Fifth Street."

We part, but only for a short duration, she to go to Sixty-Third Street to buy some plain biscuits for our tea before joining me in my rooms. She does not wish to be seen coming into the hotel with me. I order tea from Eugene, the floor waiter, and light the candles, and dismiss Miss Cleghorn. Then the bell rings frantically—she is out of breath, her hair all awry, the package under her arm. She has been discovered coming up the back stairs by Serge Obolensky. He seems very surprised and engaged her in conversation. I am amused at her panic. Her face is still cold from the park. The tea arrives from Eugene.

"Don't ask questions," she says. "Don't scrutinize." She keeps looking at her watch.

"Isn't it awful to be with someone who is always following the clock, and is so strict, and won't let you ask questions or scrutinize!"

November 4th, 1947

"Miss Brown don't answer." It is as if I were falling through space. She cannot have left the hotel so early. I try again throughout the day. No—surely we are not back to where we were?

When, eventually, Greta does answer my call, she will give no explanation for her evasiveness during the past week. She merely asks me: "You know Alan Porter at the Museum of Modern Art?

I haven't seen him for ages, and this morning he rang me up. Well, we are meeting at the Museum at four o'clock; would you like to come?"

Tea and cookies were being served to a lot of old Helen Hokinson women with floral hats and hearing aids in the penthouse lounge. Greta and Alan were sitting deep in gossip behind a large ficus plant. Greta wore layer upon layer of woollen garments—an assortment in, roughly, mushroom colors. She was exerting herself a great deal and making most of the conversational headway while Alan kept saying: "Wouldn't you know it!" But eventually Alan started asking blatant questions that I have long since learned to avoid. For example: "Who was that crazy man I read about in the papers who has died leaving you his farm and fortune?" It seems Greta had never seen the nut, and he had merely ended by giving her a lot of bother, for the residue of his will may amount to about half a goat; her lawyer is dealing with it. "But who is going to look after the lawyer?" asked Alan. Then he brazenly talked about her film work—a subject that all her friends quickly learn is taboo. "Your early pictures—*Joyless Street* and *Gosta Björling*,—how old were you then?" Surprisingly enough Greta supplied the information: "Not yet eighteen—and I had such a lot of puppy fat! My arms were so well covered, and my bosoms were full and round and were supported very high up like a pigeon." Alan: "You wore a black wig." G.: "Oh no, I never wore a black wig! I've always had my own natural hair, except once for *The Torrent* when it was dyed—oh, it was horrible! But, imagine this—we are talking about myself—that's bad!"

I walk Greta home, but she makes no definite date for another meeting. Has she been forbidden by "the little man" to see me alone? Has she decided that I must be dropped? Yet she is not the sort who quickly grows tired of a friend. I am baffled and worried.

Mona's Advice

Mona Williams is one of my oldest New York friends; there is nothing I do not confide in her. One evening I confessed that I was as deeply in love with Greta as if I had been a man half my age smitten for the first time. I explained that for so many years now, my relationships of an amorous nature have not seriously involved my deepest emotions. Suddenly I have realized how inexperienced I am at coping with a situation that others of my age would have conducted with considerable maturity. So naïf and gauche am I that I am incapable of utilizing unexpected situations to my best advantage. Only very rarely in any former romantic relationship have I felt that my physical presence has played a dominant part in the situation. For generally it was the other person who was the magnet; I was regarded primarily for my attributes of companionship, affection, or love on a more platonic plane. Suddenly I realized that I was emitting some sort of electric power. Now that I knew that I possessed this extra strength, I recoiled from it. I was embarrassed and felt that it gave me an unfair advantage which I did not enjoy and did not wish to use. No doubt this was foolish. In a fight for survival in love perhaps one should avail oneself of all odds. But, having acquired this mysterious gift, I tried to minimize its magic.

I told Mona that I felt Greta was more than intrigued by me, but the agony of never knowing quite where one was with her was almost beyond endurance. Suddenly one day Greta could not be found. Without any valid reason she had disappeared. . . .

Mona gave me the kind of advice I could only find in New York. "You're being a dope," she said. "Stop it—it's not getting you anywhere. Surely you know what a bore it is to have someone waiting for you—always at your beck and call, never cutting up rough or keeping you guessing. You just play her game—behave with her in the same way that she behaves with you. Don't call her up, and when she calls you say you've been busy. Be nice to her, of course, but be rather casual. If it doesn't work you've lost nothing, because as it is you haven't got anything. But you'll find it will succeed, believe me. I don't wish to be a traitor to my sex, but women are so much less nice than men, and you're my friend and I see her game so clearly. She knows you are just hanging about waiting on her, and if she feels in the mood she will come around, just for an hour. But you've got to get her worried. You've got to get her mind, and her mind's got to worry about what's going on in your mind. When first you see the results working, don't have any mercy. It's crucial; you can't afford to be dopey about anything that is important in your life. Why do you think I've been able to keep Harrison interested all these years? He is the arch-teaser and I knew where he was trying to get me. But I played my cards better than he did. He's guessing all the time, and that's why he is so intrigued and happy."

_____ *Monday*

I didn't telephone — my usual sentimental call of habit. I didn't telephone for four days. I was flat on my bed when the telephone rang. "Can I come around now?" she asked. It was pouring with rain outside, the traffic disorganized. I didn't sound welcoming. "It's too rainy for you to sally forth, and I've got to go out." This refusal worked like a trick. "I'll be right over." The pep talk from Mona had given me assurance: it was as if I'd employed a magic potion. The doorbell rang and, instead of hurrying to open it, I walked very arrogantly and slowly around the room in a stiff manner, amused as I watched my progress in the looking glass over the drawing room chimney.

"So you've been busy, have you? Well, what have you been doing?" Smiles, uncertainties, embarrassments on her part. If only temporarily, the tables were suddenly turned. G. said: "I knew instinctively that I ought not to have waited so long." Her fears about my being faithless had been corroborated, according to her. I sat back and smiled.

For a year and a half I had felt unsure of myself, but now I was enjoying my pathetic little victory. I mentioned that I had been out until three o'clock in the morning with somebody. *That* made an impression. I told her I was dining tonight with Mona. *That* went well too. Questions were asked about other friends, and after certain admissions she said: "You're stepping out in all directions."

We talked more like two old friends for, suddenly, we were exchanging information instead of mere childish gibberish. All at once she said: "Damn that party! Why do you have to go? I want you to stay here." Yet I felt sorry for Greta: she looked somewhat impoverished, like a stray kitten, very wet with a fur-lined mackintosh and hood that had shrunk. She wore a lot of woollen scarves and waistcoats over her dark blue jumper. Greta is too frightened to go into Saks alone but the other day, accompanied by her friend Mrs. Sanson, she had mustered sufficient courage to buy a new skirt. The skirt had the "new look," long and flowing, but in the rain it had become longer, the waistband was too loose and it kept falling, and it appeared almost like a peasant's skirt with her rubber high boots below. She said everything was the wrong length, her new expensive coat was now too short and couldn't be let down. "It's very sad to be a woman."

Suddenly she asked many questions about my mother and about my life and my house in the country, and what would happen if she lived there. There was no note of confidence in her voice. I had to steel myself not to show my sympathy and to decide that I must leave forthwith for this cocktail party which I knew would be hell. We walked out together into the rain. Greta's gloves were made of gray cotton and looked poor, with pointed finger tips that were wet. She made a picture of misery and courage as she went back to her ivory Ritz Tower, alone and baffled.

Later: I must be firm and not allow myself to telephone for several days while my new position is being consolidated. The novice continues the horrible campaign.

I am dozing at six o'clock one evening when the unforgettable voice is heard again on the telephone. I perk up. "Are you still as busy as ever?" I answer: "Oh yes, very busy." "Well, I'm laid up—I'm in poor spirits." Commiserations. More questions asked about whom I'd seen. I described Mona's beauty—her skin so blooming and in the pitch of perfection, and her hands so smooth and beautiful. G. gasped: "*My* hands are so rough and wrinkled and lined. Ask Mona what she puts on her hands, will you?" Vague plans are made for the future. She can't get seats for *The Winslow Boy,* which has been brought over from London and is an enormous success on Broadway. Have I any pull? "Of course I have." "Then we'll go on Monday. And what about seeing the Royal Wedding on the screen?" We talked on the telephone for an hour. At one moment I said: "So put that in your pipe and smoke it." Greta said: "You're not to use such rough expressions to me. I'm feeling downtrodden enough as it is. I'm not a bit chipper" ("chippurre").

An angry voice on the telephone: "Are you trying to mesmerize me?" "What nonsense—what are you talking about?" "*Were* you trying to mesmerize me?" "No." "I suppose you were quite busy—never thinking about me at all." She continued: "Well, why should I telephone you? I can't see you today." Nevertheless, we made vague plans about meeting, or rather not meeting, at a party tonight. My evening was as free as air but I had suddenly decided not to go to this party, not because it would be dull, but mainly because if she went, as I expected she would, she would wonder why I wasn't there.

I do not telephone her but rather wait for her call. It makes life much happier not having to hear that death knell: "She don't answer." Sometimes the bell rings and I pick up the receiver: there are strange intakes of breath, muffled giggles, and small squeaks, and I know whom to expect on the line. My name is reiterated in a bird chirp: I no longer retort with her name. Today she would come along at five o'clock; she arrived a little before.

I accepted her compliments in silence, and whenever she asked me some point-blank questions I avoided a straight reply. She laughed: "You're so afraid of committing yourself!" It is still somewhat of an effort to assume consciously a different role from that which one has played for the last two years. How different the state in Denmark since I arrived here, when everything had been so frustrating! Now, in fun, she said: "I think I shall have to make an honest man of you!" "No, it's too late—you're not the marrying type," I rejoindered, almost gritting my teeth and clenching my fists in a farcical effort to follow Mona's tuition.

Although perhaps even to confide such thoughts to paper may be unwise, there are times when I feel that the possibility is within sight, that one day I might get her worked up sufficiently to rush off to a Registrar. For myself I am not only willing, but desperate, and confident that we could have the infinite joy of making a new and successful life together.

I dare not feel pity for the battle is still too desperate: on so many points I'm likely to give way. But isn't it rather abominable what a difference a change of tactics has made? Greta used never to ask me to call her, and if I asked if I might, she would say: "No, I'll call you." Now she asks me to telephone her tomorrow to tell her about the opening of *Antony and Cleopatra*. "Tomorrow ring me anytime—ten-thirty, eleven, whenever you want."

I telephoned as late as possible. At the end of our talk she said: "Thank you for calling me." The following morning she telephoned me: "I must go out for a bit so that they can do the rooms—they are getting dusty after four days. I looked out of the window yesterday and it appeared so crisp outside; but I can't come and see you today—I look too pale."

—————————————————————————————*December 1st, 1947*

I went to Boston for two or three days to photograph a gentleman cook on Beacon Hill for *Vogue,* but I did not call Greta before leaving and gave no hint that I would be away. I liked to think the telephone would be ringing in my absence. On Thanksgiving Day I had delivered a vase of white orchids with one of the long letters that I had written to her while I was in London when I had no knowledge of where to send it. She would certainly acknowledge the flowers but, as her hotel operator had said to me so many times, mine would give the same: "No answer." Sure enough, when I returned from Boston there were many messages to say "Miss Brown" had telephoned. Soon after I had finished my breakfast on Monday morning the telephone again rang and, while I was talking on one line, Miss Cleghorn came in from the sitting room to say that Miss Garbo was on the other. "Is it all right for the theatre tonight?" Greta asked. "Would you like me to come around early? Very early—five o'clock?" "Five o'clock."

The day was a particularly pleasant one: it was the first of December. I had said "Rabbits" before any other word and I felt that augured a lucky spell. (When one is in love one becomes not only more fatuous, but more superstitious.) In fact, the day was spent in the most agreeable way of all—dictating, writing and reading until the last possible moment; it contained no traffic problems or anxiety at arriving late for appointments. Just time enough to bathe, hurry downstairs to have my hair cut, and return to open my door to the most fascinating and intriguing creature in the whole city. Instead of my making all the over-tures, and perhaps receiving only monosyllabic or elusive replies, it was now her turn to take the initiative. She asked jealous ques-tions that were always hidden beneath a veil of jocularity but, nevertheless, evinced real interest. If my replies were distasteful to her she did not fail to show they were so by the play on her face.

Outside it was dark and cold, but a few rays of street light came in through the mustard velvet curtains. They cast an extra-ordinary glow as they fell onto the head as it lay resting like a particularly fine ship's figure-head, as though made of incan-descent alabaster, with hair flowing back and long neck curved against the waves. I became almost dizzy and mesmerized by the huge eyes, eyes that stared long and continuously with barely a flicker of the lids.

Of course there was the usual last minute rush to a restaurant —an Austrian place that was empty except for ourselves.

Greta wanted our theatre seats to be near the stage; I managed to get them—front row center. She was so pleased that she said: "I think I'll have to take you to see the minister." Throughout the play she stared at me, and I remembered how I used to stare at people with whom I have been in love and how annoyed they became. *The Winslow Boy* was a good choice, for the play is so essentially English, and I explained that its atmosphere was similar to that in which I had been brought up. "Did you have that sort of furniture?" she asked. I nodded. She was impressed by the English teamwork acting.

On the way home, at Doubleday's bookshop, I pointed out a picture of herself in an album of cinema stars of the last decade. "I don't give a damn," she laughed. Then, putting her arm through mine, she chirped: "I like you, I like you—it's not a big word, but I like you, and whenever I say good-bye I want to see you again."

_____ *December 2nd, 1947*

Now that I am ostensibly so busy, Greta is no longer as busy as she was while I was not busy. At 3:30 P.M. she would meet me at Sixty-Third Street and Fifth Avenue. She was wearing a mink coat. "Isn't it obnoxious?" she said; "it's so *frauen.*" I must admit it wasn't suitable: it made her appear thick on the bosom with square shoulders. We strode into the park. Soon the lights started to fade and the landscape had no reality. It was like time out of time: a leaden gray sky with scurrying apricot clouds grew dark and tempestuous: it was as if mankind were going to be exterminated in violence for its wickedness.

It was a strange walk and we seemed to have a relaxed feeling that we hadn't enjoyed before. Occasionally we would stop dead in this cold winter landscape to kiss one another, but Greta was worried in case we were being watched, and when it became quite dark she was scared lest we should be· "stood-up" and robbed. At one interval for embraces she said: "Are you eaten up with passion?" and then laughed and explained: "Nobody but myself would say that, and yet it's quite feasible and natural." We walked back to the Plaza and had a chaser, but she could not stay, she had a date that I believe she was not looking forward to.

_____ _December 3rd, 1947_

Telephone: "If you've got anything better to do today, I'm in rather poor shape so please make other plans." "No, I've already put off Mrs. Kahn, and I hated lying in my teeth pretending I had a cold because she's such a great old woman. No, I've nothing better to do, and please remember we've asked the Turkish lady to come and see us at six."

We met at a gallery to see the strange picture I had bought by that Englishwoman, Eleanor Carrington, who lives and paints in Mexico. G. liked the paintings very much. "What an extraordinary 'funtussie' she possesses!" said Greta who, without claiming to be a connoisseur, readily describes the excellencies or defects in any canvas. Although not particularly initiated in modern art she is surprised and shocked by nothing—but rather is in full admiration of the latest demonstrations of force and vigor. G. told me of some of the paintings she has accumulated: a Rouault, very skillfully painted—"a packed canvas"; a Renoir; a blue-period Picasso "of a horrible looking woman"; and she likes abstract subjects. "Where have you hung them? In your bedroom?" "No, in a room that I seldom go into: I never look at them."

We then returned to the hotel to await the Turkish Princess.[1] Suddenly Greta had the usual qualms: "Why did we ask her? It was a mistake." But the visit of the immensely tall and handsome Princess with the important nose of her ancestor, Suleiman the Magnificent, was a success. It brought G. out into the open and made her talk freely of when she was young and about to make her first picture in Turkey, but instead went to Hollywood. G. longed to return to the East for she felt that "those people" were so much wiser than we, who became sidetracked hunting the dollar and leading such superficial lives. G. had sent a locket of her hair to two young men in Benares so that she might one day go there; she felt that there she would find most sympathy and respect.

The Princess, extremely shy by nature, sat with the nape of her neck very straight and her blue eyes staring with surprise as Greta fired a barrage of questions at her. "Are you very religious?" "Are you Hindu or Mohammedan?" "Does it give you great peace?" "I expect you eat healthy meals. How clean your food is! So appetizingly served on palm leaves!" The Princess threw back her head in a great girlish laugh. "Your entire way of life is so immaculate. It is typical that at the end of each meal the remnants are burnt." Again the Princess roared. "I'd like to end in India studying with a *swami*. It's not too late either. I knew a middle-aged woman who returned to Hollywood a completely transformed person, at peace with the world; she exuded serenity."

As G. later remarked, the Princess, although not a garrulous talker, had proved to be a person whom you knew had warmth and understanding.

As usual G. was in a hurry not to be late. We went to dine at the *bourgeois* hour of 6:30 P.M. "If we are later there will be no table," said Greta. We dined at the Golden Horn, a Turkish restaurant, where a lush appeared and embarrassed us in the extreme. G. remembered an occasion when a drunk came up to her companion to know if she was with Greta Garbo: the drunk

---

[1] The Princess of Berar, with whom I had become friends in Hyderabad during the war.

remained shaking hands and left, perfectly contented, without his answer.

We went to the movies, out of curiosity, to see a Cecil B. de Mille opus. First some trailers of forthcoming movies were shown: Tyrone Power in "the sensational all-record-breaking, etc. etc.," and a shot was shown of a group of palpably phony historical characters. Greta said: "Oh no, I can't go back and get mixed up in all this sort of thing again!" The big film incredibly boring, but the evening was made momentous for me by the fact that I was sitting next to her, holding hands and behaving like any small-town teenager.

We soon left and wandered up Broadway, lost in anonymity. We stood outside a music shop listening to the records being relayed; we bought pears at a delicatessen and disliked the Christmas displays in all the windows. We walked home to her Tower. Then, when we said good night and I left her, I was amazed to hear some laughing woman follow me. I thought it was a prostitute and did not bother to turn around. It was Greta. She had decided against going into her hotel: "The night is still young."

_____ ___ *December 8th, 1947*

We were going to a theatre and were late, but luckily Eugene hurried a room service meal through in record time. Eugene is a nice, ugly little man with sad eyes and a nose like a toucan. Perhaps he is sad because he intended to be an electrical engineer, but after eleven years he gave it up for "waitering." He could not resist six dollars a day plus tips. "It's not much of a life," he says, "and I haven't got far, but my son is nine years old and will do better." Eugene is helpful and treats me as a favorite, but even he cannot improve the hotel food. We ate lamb that was rather like discarded chewing gum as we talked about ourselves in slightly veiled terms. I was enjoying turning the tables on her. "You are so unreliable," I said, "I couldn't ever marry you. You are not serious about me."

"What a rebuff! And I adore you, Cecil—I love you—I am in love with you!"

We both laughed.

The play was one that was contrary to everything that either of us enjoy—a raucous comedy about Mary loving John, with irate senators and their outraged wives, and the young getting into amorous scrapes and going against the Army system. The audience squealed like pigs, but we laughed only occasionally, and then with weak hysteria, at some piece of ludicrous stage business. The play has been running a long time, and the actors and actresses have become so stylized in their performances that they were almost inhuman automata.

G. generally runs home early and is resentful of being kept up beyond her usual bedtime, but tonight it did not take much persuasion to inveigle her to a night club. Of all the hundreds in New York we could think of none that was suitable, so we precipitated ourselves into the hubbub of an overcrowded Blue Angel. A cabaret performance was in progress and we were shown to seats so close to the performers that we were within range of their breath and spittle. By degrees we became accustomed to the close quarters and enjoyed each other's reactions to the performance: I, out of the corner of my eye, admiring the flowing rhythm of the profile that watched the proceedings with such compassion or unquestioning happiness. Only when the night club was empty did we walk out into the crisp, refreshing night to visit Hamburger Heaven. Here we remained only for a short while, and ate only a crumb for Greta found the lights glaringly harsh, and a drunk came up and asked for her autograph. "No, I never do—so sorry!" The drunk bowed. "That's quite all right." G. turned with a blank, amazed expression. "You see the unfairness of life. I have to apologize to him for coming up to bother me when I'm having my private supper."

On our way back Greta suggested: "Would you like an apple? I'll give you a couple of apples," she said. Before I knew it, I was for the first time in the sacred precincts of the rooms in her hotel. They were pretty, light-colored rooms with large windows on most sides displaying a panorama of New York. Everything was better than she had described. It was fascinating to discover what books she was reading, what appurtenances of life there were about the room. She would not allow the lights to be switched on so I peered into the gloaming: there were some of her hats lying around, a few bills and package slips, and copies of *Life* magazine and *The New Yorker.* All the mail was addressed to "Harriet Brown." "I live like a monk with one toothbrush, one cake of soap and a pot of cream." Greta went to her kitchenette and, in secret, prepared a meal. Everything was very immaculate and healthy: sweet butter unsalted, Swedish bread, ham and cheese. We drank beer and talked without restraint or inhibition. She discussed the passage of the years. "Something has happened to time; suddenly it goes so fast, so quickly."

I walked almost in a trance: for the past ten hours I have been in the highest realms of happiness. Now I wondered how the present situation could be consolidated into something definite and binding. Thus it is that we always try to pin down something exquisite and ethereal. No matter what happens there will always be the memory of big eyes gazing, and the broad big smile.

Miss Cleghorn, wonderfully tactful, calls me at the studio, in the middle of a frantic fashion sitting, from my hotel room. "I thought you would like to know 'Miss Brown' called you." I hurried through the rest of the sitting, the models suddenly appearing so colorless and banal. When I returned to my rooms she said: "Miss Garbo called you again." I telephoned the Tower. "Would you like to come for a walk?" she asked. I dashed out. The lights were up on Third Avenue while the sky was yellow on the horizon and periwinkle blue above. The El rushed along at alarming speed, making a ghastly noise. "This is hell," Greta admitted, yet it is where she chooses to spend most of her time. To me it is inexplicable that someone who loves the country-side, with the feel of grass beneath her feet, must trudge along these squalid pavements. We peered into the windows of really awful so-called antique shops where nothing was what it pur-ported to be; everything was *nachgemacht,* to use her word. She went into one such shop to see about a lamp she had bought, a pink Victorian vulgarity for which a shade must be made. I longed to tell her to stop wasting her time among this junk, but it seems to absorb her, so I must look on with benign countenance.

At last in one shop, owned by a rather pathetic young English-man, I noticed a pink and red tea cup and saucer which, since these were her favorite colors, I wanted to buy for her. But she tried to convey that she didn't want me to buy them: she kept winking and saying: "There's too much white in it." "But they're your colors," I persisted. "Don't you like it?" Outside I again asked: "Don't you really like it?" and she said: "I told you I thought there was too much white in it. And I meant it. It's a very simple fact ("fucktte"). I wasn't trying to explain an Eastern theory. I just meant what I said: 'There's too much white in it.'"

The night descended. It was too late to go into the park: she was scared—quite rightly—of unseen things. So we walked along looking into more windows, although we did once enter a shop to buy some Swedish bread and cakes. Here Greta was served by a young Swedish blonde and, for the first time, I heard her talking her native tongue. It was both delightful and comic to my ears—like birds spitting. The whole atmosphere of the shop was very charming, simple and pure, and gave the impression of being far from New York.

In side streets we suddenly stopped still and embraced, then we would walk on with a businesslike tread, and my ears would tingle with the sound of my name whispered against my ear.

———————————————————————— *Wednesday, December 10th, 1947*

Seats for the theatre are a good way of binding her down to a certain date; otherwise promises are apt to be vague. Tonight *Antony and Cleopatra* tickets—a five o'clock rendezvous. I had become absorbed doing some sketches of my room and, only when I stopped, realized I had become chilled to the bone. In order to thaw myself out, I started to drink a cup of tea. I opened the door with a cup in my hand. Her face was cold from the rawness outside. She had bought some face powder, or some unguent, that smelled of gardenias—very foreign to her.

We found ourselves once more battling with the clock. No time to go to that nice little cellar off Third Avenue. We descended into the bowels of my hotel and had an elegant dinner in the red and orange glow of the night club. The place, as well as being convenient; was sympathetic.

Our talk suddenly became intent. What was there to stop our living the rest of our lives together? It was so easy. "No, it's not easy," said Greta. We almost found ourselves arguing with each other. "You have not had a difficult life as I have. Everything has been smooth for you. It's easy for you to be gay and happy. Occasionally you may have been sad, when someone has not loved you as much as you loved them. But life has been difficult for me." Greta explained: "You must realize I am a sad person: I am a misfit in life."

"But if you were to come to Europe, and live among creative people and congenial souls, you wouldn't be like that. You are so out of your element here with the pavements under your feet and smuts in your eyes."

"Perhaps it was all that could happen."

"Maybe if you had made films in Germany or France, things would have been easier. You have succeeded in spite of Hollywood taste, but it's only natural you hate everything about it."

"I don't hate Hollywood—any more than I hate Louis B. Mayer. I don't hate anyone, of course, but I don't like Mr. Mayer— although I see his point and I don't blame him for doing to me what he did."

"What did he do?" I knew that to ask such a point-blank question was extremely risky, and I waited anxiously the interval before she replied slowly:

"Well, he made me sign a long contract—five years—and I was terrified and very unhappy, for it seemed like a life term. When I had finished the contract I said to him: 'This is the end. I don't want to continue. I want to get out of pictures.' He and his minions were all so worried! They had these long discussions with me, and we walked up and down outside the sound stage, and they said: 'You can't quit now; we won't let you. You're at the very peak of your career.' But I was all set. I was so unhappy. And then, in 1928, the bank where I had all my money failed. That was the time of the Wall Street crash. Somebody joked that Mr. Mayer made my bank fail so that he could get me back. I had to sign another contract with Mr. Mayer, but I told him to do pictures that I'd like, and he agreed to pay me for half my next picture in advance. He wrote out the highest check I have ever seen. But I had nowhere to put it—no pocket, no bag, so I tucked it into my open shirt and went home to Sweden while they prepared my next film, and that was *Christina*."

Twice in her career Greta had come to the crossroads: once

when she had wanted to leave, and again when the war cut off the European market and her last film, *The Two-faced Woman,* through no fault of hers, was a complete and deserved failure.

The fact that she is, I suppose, financially independent, is an incentive for her to turn down every script that is now offered. "It's so much harder for me now. I had it all my way and did it in my own fashion. I never rehearsed with the director. I used to see him going through the script with other actors, but I couldn't do it if I had to rehearse—it frightens me. I could only do something when it was strange to me: I didn't even know what it was all about; I didn't like to know what the lines meant. Sometimes I would cross them out. Whenever the script read 'Listen,' 'Listen to me,' or 'So then,' I would shuffle over to the next thing. I did anything that came into my head and made a kind of fantasy of it, but I never knew what I was doing, and I didn't want to know the people I was acting with. I couldn't go out to dinner with my leading man and hear about his wife and family. I just wanted to meet the others as strangers on the set. Now, perhaps, it would all have to be different."

She then talked of the inadequacy of her achievement compared with the high hopes she had had as a girl when first under the spell of Maurice Stiller (only, of course, she did not mention him by name). She would never recover from his death, for he had had such a great influence. In her family life there had never been any interest in the things that she liked; it had been a revelation to know him. Then when she had arrived in Hollywood she was abysmally disappointed. The light was reflected off the pavements, off the walls, on all sides. It was so hard—so different from one's fantasy! "I spent my first night in the Hotel Biltmore, looking out of the window, frightened and alone. Then I went to Santa Barbara and I became friendly with a nice person who asked me to marry him, but thank heavens I didn't—we would have been miserable!"

She went on: "I used to quake at the knees when the studio called me up, and once inside those gates I was so sad. I would be called for a conference and they'd sit around the table, cigars in their mouths, and they'd growl and bark: 'Now, Garbo, we've got the script and we think you'd do it well. Now read it, but, first of all, imagine how different it will be.' Then they talked by the hour, and we wouldn't get anywhere. Well, if I disliked it all then, what would I feel about it now? In those days I didn't have to bother about camera angles or anything. Now I'd feel so forlorn with everyone staring at me; I'd be conscious of all the things in my face that weren't there before."

"With a good cameraman you'd be far more beautiful than ever."

"That's not the point—I'd know the way I look. I'm a perfectionist; it would make me uncomfortable if things weren't as they should be. I'd be humiliated. I remember the first time I made a film in Sweden. I was with older actors, and they were horribly frank about the things that happened to their faces in front of the camera. They described how their chins would go out this way if their heads went that way, so they asked that I should walk round the other side of a table in order that they could show their best profile. It was horribly tedious! But what would happen to me? Even if the public didn't notice these things, I would! And that would be obnoxious! No—in certain ways I miss the life, but I'm not an actor who must go on in any circumstances. I'm quite modest in my demands, and I don't have to do it, so what's the point?"

She admitted she was still discussing the possibility of playing George Sand, but the script is not ready. I could see Greta wearing velvet trousers and smoking a cigar. From Joan of Arc to Christina of Sweden, the idea of women in cavalier clothes has a visual aspect that is appealing to her. She would have liked to play St. Francis of Assisi, also Lorenzaccio and Dorian Gray. Disguise has obviously titillated her and, since early days, she has enjoyed wearing the more romantic of men's apparel in her films. Ventriloquists' dolls and pierrots possess an ambiguity that delight her sense of the perverse. This is, no doubt, the reason why stories have been circulated about her having odd tendencies. Any individual in the public eye is likely to be gossiped about by those who enjoy muddying the waters, and nowhere is rumor and scandal more vicious than in the home of moving pictures. It is not to be wondered that Greta should be accused of "everything in the book." She certainly enjoys adulation, and is flirtatious by nature. Her appeal is not restricted to the opposite sex. Her studio considered that the greatest part of her box office draw was to women.

"George Sand could make a wonderful story, but it's eight years since my last film; the war came in the meantime, and there are such difficulties in the world today. My mother country is in such a poor state—everyone's money frozen there—and in France and England there's so much unrest and lack of responsibility—perhaps the same here. . . . There is nothing to go to California for—just an unfurnished house with dreary rayon curtains that are too short and the ugly, ready-made sofas."

Yet, although she has long been away from work, she is still most coveted by the film world. Her name is a symbol, a standard of comparison; of this she seems utterly unaware. The greatest impresarios throughout the world would give her anything to work for them but, she says, she has grown old, wrinkled, and haggard. The impresarios protest: "You are the *Divina.*" Oblivious of this fact, alone she strides along Third Avenue, a lonely figure, on her humble errands while a whole world waits for her to carry the torch to brighter vistas.

Later that evening, at the theatre, she said: "Isn't it strange that these actors enjoy getting up and performing in this way night after night, shouting, ranting, and working themselves so hard."

I had previously heard her admit that she dislikes actors for talking only about themselves, and I had been surprised when once, on Fifth Avenue, one of her former leading men had walked towards us. I murmured the name, "Robert Montgomery," and Greta immediately ducked. I must admit that Montgomery also looked steadfastly across the street.

Tonight I realized how utterly foreign she is to the actors' code of life. We sat in the crowded, overheated theatre in seats that were too far back to make it anything but an effort to listen to Shakespeare. The actors, untrained in classical verse and with little knowledge of voice production, did not help to clarify the meaning. G. could not bear the mumbled butchering of the lines by the minor actors and became exasperated at the amount the central characters talked. "Why doesn't Katherine Cornell just ask the messenger his news instead of talking to him by the hour? And they're so busy! Why do they keep running in and out?" Greta could see only an abstract design of movements. Her attitude throughout was down-to-earth, and even as the tragedy moved to a crescendo, she was not moved. In fact, while Cleopatra was being hoisted high into the monument to take the dying Antony into her arms, a man behind us suddenly had a noisy attack of indigestion, and we were shocked into gales of forbidden laughter. His belchings and rumblings and explosions were so appalling that tears poured down our cheeks and our shoulders shook like jelly, while the man, at the back of our necks, continued to make these awful stomach noises.

When, at last, we left the gloom of Egypt it was to go to the Ritz Tower and drink beer while squatting in semidarkness. Greta said: "How sweet that, for me, you sat through that play for a second time! Now, you wouldn't do that if we had been married five years." Greta elaborated on life after marriage. "You would say: 'Run and get the spray, will you, dear; I see these roses are beginning to get the blight!' Eventually, I'd get so tired of fagging after you that I'd say: 'Jehovah, come here!' and there would be standing by a little Negro boy who would do all the running about."

Suddenly G. said, "Isn't it strange to come back to these rooms tonight and find they have hung up entirely new curtains, and now I cannot for the life of me remember what they were before —and I've been living here for two months."

Six o'clock nonarrival (generally so punctual). At last a moonstruck clown presents itself with wild eyes and hair parted in the middle in haylike wisps. "Mister Tennessee Williams came to call on me, and we talked about nothing—the weather— and after a bit I said: 'Well, I've got an appointment,' and he said: 'Isn't there a bar anywhere around here?' And I said: 'Would you like some vodka?' so we both drank vodka. But that didn't loosen him up—we hadn't got anything to say. He's not interesting as a person: he is just a little man with a moustache. The Heavenly Father didn't make him in the round. He is just not an enlightened person."

Williams is anxious that Greta should play Blanche du Bois in his *Streetcar* film. But she finds the character—a liar—a difficult and unsympathetic one. She went on to explain. "In a way I've always been a dreamer. In my childhood I came across brutality and the result lasted with me all my life, but I'm an honest, clear-cut person and see things very lucidly. I could never be an involved and complicated person: I'm too direct and too masculine. I couldn't bear to tell lies, and see things round corners, like that girl in the play."

Williams, obviously dejected, suggested that perhaps Greta pays too much attention to plots. She told him that since she left the screen, there had never been anything that she could possibly play—all parts are too unlike her conception of life. "The only thing I would ever like to do is *The Eagle with Two Heads.* That has an atmosphere that appeals to me and I've always wanted to play Elizabeth of Austria."

I kept looking at my watch. Two o'clock. Two ten. I left the restaurant and at the corner of the street the lights went red. Nothing to do but wait. Suddenly, at the same moment that she saw me, I saw Greta on the other side of the street. She looked at me with utter amazement, eyes absolutely wild and mouth wide open. This is the first time we have ever met accidentally on the streets. New York is so rambling, and its inhabitants so fast moving and quickly snapped up in its canyons, that one seldom sees friends or acquaintances by chance. We greeted one another while, simultaneously, an *opéra-bouffe*-looking Italian gentleman with a pointed moustache came up with an autograph request which was refused. We started our walk, veering towards the west side from which one sees unexpectedly pretty aspects of the park. Greta told me that she had just been into a drug store and had said to the assistant: "I have a very peculiar request to make to you. Could you let me have a piece of string?" She now proceeded to put the string around the waist of her mink coat in order to keep it from flying open. What other woman would be so direct and unaffected as to think of tying up her mink coat with string?

We passed the animals in the Zoo. Greta said that one of them looked like me. It did. Again, at the Natural History Museum, she saw an animal—stuffed this time—that also looked like me.

I still cannot take in my great good fortune of having won her affection. However, the first electric excitement of our meetings has given way to a more natural and cozy feeling of friendship. Today in the cold we stopped at isolated places to embrace one another with tenderness rather than fervor. When we had to part company we did so with reluctance and a grand display of waving. The people on Sixty-Ninth Street thought us demented —and we were. But it was fun to wave at Greta's diminishing figure. A fluttering glove became a smaller and smaller speck until she was finally hidden in the traffic morass of the city.

Later that evening, I was hurrying on foot towards my dinner rendezvous, somewhat entertained by my thoughts, when in the dark I saw Greta and her friend flashing towards me. They were black shadows against the half-light, and they strode like mountaineers. "The little man" was wrapped up as if in the Arctic, but Greta was like a great goddess striding along. They must have seen me in the distance and were both staring and amused. But Greta flashed me such a wonderfully broad and generous smile it was like a gay handshake, so full of friendship and friendliness. It was a moment of exhilaration for me, and I was delighted to see how these two were walking along with a large space between them, whereas when we walk we are hand-in-hand with our elbows brushing.

_____ _____ *Saturday evening, December 13th, 1947*

I got back from the *Volpone* movie to find that "Miss Brown" had called. I rang back, in fear lest I should wake Greta who has been ill with a bronchial cold. But no—she had put out the light hours ago, had not been able to sleep, had turned on the light and read a little, then later had still not slept. She said that a great gust of sorrow for herself had overtaken her. She felt wretched. I had given her Pavlik's[1] recipe of camphor, iodine, and alcohol to *faire Écossais* on her chest. She had done this, and she said she was painted like a savage. I then advised her to put a sock or something around her throat. She suggested: "A rope?" She couldn't think why she couldn't sleep, except that she had known I was at a movie and therefore wasn't thinking about her. However, now that we had talked she would,

_____
[1] Pavel Tchelitchew, Russian painter.

like a child, put her mind to it and use her will power to lose consciousness.

"Will you pray that I'm better in the morning?"

"I certainly will. Do you pray?"

"Every night."

"Who do you pray to?" I asked.

"Jesus, but I don't hang onto the end of the bed."

"Don't you pray to the Almighty Father and the Holy Ghost?"

"No, I skip the Ghost."

"Goodnight, my archangel."

I was at a loss to know what do do with myself, for Greta was unable to see me today. The poor thing is really ill and must rest and take things calmly. However, if by afternoon she felt better, we might perhaps go out to breathe fresh air together. I waited most of the afternoon for her call, then, having idled time away, I decided to go out for a haircut. Of course that caused the telephone to ring. "Cecil, are you busy? Are you doing anything?" It was such a strange voice speaking in pathetic, plaintive tones that I was worried. She had seldom before started a conversation by using my name, and this resembled a wail. She sounded utterly dejected. "I'll meet you on Fifty-Eighth Street by the cinema," she said, slurring her words. "How are you feeling?" "Oh, wretched—very bad," and there was a catch in her voice. I ran out of the hotel to meet her, anxious about the condition I might find her in. After a minute out of doors one's features were frozen. It was far too cold for her to be out; the doctor had told her to stay in until she could take a trip to Florida. I ran along the street and in the distance saw a very forlorn figure dragging towards me. As she approached her face was turned somewhat sideways with an expression of great sadness. Weeping, with large tears coursing down her cheeks, she was *in extremis*, unmindful of passers-by. I did my best to comfort her there and then, and with my arm around her brought her back to my room. She appeared to be in a strange state. Later I discovered what had happened. She had been out to breathe in some fresh air but soon, finding herself frozen, had returned to her room. To overcome her numbness she had taken a swig of vodka which, because of low resistance, had gone straight to her head. She became dizzy, then lachrymose. Even now she made little sense and kept throwing her head back and flicking her hair. Her eyes were dazed. I wanted to give her hot milk and cover her with a rug, but she said "no" to every suggestion. She was sweet, childish, and pathetic and, after a time, calmed down. Later she lay on the sofa while I read letters from home to her. I had this morning received a batch of press clippings from London unfavorably comparing Vivien Leigh's *Anna Karenina* with hers. I thought, misguidedly, that Greta might be interested, but she was only sorry that, having worked so hard on a job, the new film was not a success for me.

When, later, I took her back to the Tower she had recovered, though she was still alarmingly weak and tired.

_____ *Monday, December 15th, 1947*

Another empty day was filled when, suddenly, Greta called to say she was well again. In the morning sunlight we set off in high spirits to walk in the snowy park. It was cold and our noses were red, but she said: "I don't know why it is that I love snow so much. Perhaps because, as a child, I lived in a country where, for months on end, there is snow." We walked for several hours. We talked about deportment, and her having taken lessons on the Butler method of straightening the back, and the correct and healthy way of walking. She had once seen the actress, Ina Claire, another Butler pupil, walking in a peculiar way. "What are you doing?" Greta had asked. Ina had replied: "I'm re-hanging my body."

Greta talked of *The Paradine Case* movie about which she had been to see Selznick in his office with a view to playing the leading role. On being told the story she had said: "I don't like people who commit murders. It is not interesting if someone puts poison in a glass by the blind man's bedside. I don't want to destroy—I want to be of help to people. I want to be of help to you, Mister Selznick." "Are you kidding?" he had asked. "No, I'm quite serious." So she had left his office without the part —or any regrets.

On our way home she was worried when I conducted her across

Park Avenue with the traffic light in our favor so that the onrush of cars had to stop. She asked: "How do I know they've got any brakes?" We wended our way to Second Avenue to see a carved angel that she had ordered for a Christmas present. On several occasions now we have visited this antique shop to make inquiries about the angel which was being stripped of some of its dirty gold paint. Each visit had been in vain. Then she was told: "The angel is not here; the man who is stripping it wants more money if he is to do any further work on it, but he wishes you to see it." So today we went to see the angel by appointment. We mounted some rickety stairs to a downtrodden attic, opened a door, and there, on the floor, the angel confronted us. Greta gave a moan of great pain. She was in the most extreme state of misery: it was as if she had witnessed the death of a friend. "Oh no! They've ruined it! It's horrible what they've done! Oh no! How awful! No—we can't stay here now." And before the villain appeared, Greta had gone down the stairs again. She turned to me as I followed and looked up with eyes larger and more tragic than ever. "It was a beautiful angel, and they've ruined it. Oh, that's a crime!" Although she asked: "Do I have to pay for it?" it was the wreckage of a work of art that upset her so much, and she added: "I couldn't give that to anyone now."

Later I asked her if she had rung up the antique shop about the condition of the angel. "Oh no, I avoid unpleasant subjects. I adopt the ostrich policy: I turn away from anything I don't want to face. But that doesn't solve anything."

_____ *Christmas, 1947*

As Christmastime approached we ventured on shopping expeditions as far downtown as Macy's. Here Greta tried to buy bargains, but anything cheap struck me as being hideous. I couldn't pretend to be sympathetic to much of the junk put out as bait to desperate shoppers, and the heat and jostling humanity were somewhat overwhelming. It all seemed rather futile, but Greta enjoyed the challenge for she takes her Christmas seriously. In Sweden, she said, it had been lovely: dark by three o'clock in the afternoon, and all the rooms lit up, and fires and presents. This was the first year she had not had a Christmas tree. "Are you religious?" I asked. "In my own way. We each have our own ideas. I don't go to church and I don't know how the Heavenly Father works, but I have my own instincts about what is right or wrong." She asked herself, without reply: "Can there be any afterlife? Do we continue after this? Is there any resurrection?"

Coming away from the hectic crowds, we were distraught at the sight of an old woman who had fallen flat on her face in the street. She had misjudged the depth of the curb and fell on her nose, and her teeth and lips were covered with blood. As we helped her to her feet Garbo said, "Oh, how sad life is!"

Although Greta had trudged along all day, she was still game to walk in the park. I dumped all our parcels at my hotel and joined her for a twilight stroll. As the day faded from the sky, the lights in the surrounding buildings appeared like diamonds in the icy fresh air; underfoot were the crisp, crackly noises of frost. Except for ourselves the park was deserted. Greta remarked upon the paradox of the nearby mass of humanity, the noise and airlessness, while just around us was isolation and peace.

We came back to my rooms to drink vodka and laugh and play-fully taunt one another. When it was time for her to leave she delayed, gossiping nonchalantly in the doorway, and our mutual friend, Serge Obolensky, passed by. At first he looked a little surprised, but he greeted us charmingly and then walked on down the long corridor. "Well, I do have the rottenest luck!" she said. "I bet 'the little man' will see me next time, then my goose will be cooked." Greta returned to my room and telephoned "the little man." Later she explained: "He isn't feeling at all well. He is sick of having to look after all the difficult people in his business, and I guess he's tired by the end of the day." This was the first time that she had talked to me about "the little man," and I wondered hopefully if perhaps her friendship with him had not become something in the nature of an obligation. I asked: "Does it make it easier for you if I try to be friends with him? Shall I ask him in for a drink?" "Better try to be friends," said Greta sadly.

I was waiting inside her hotel, having missed her at the door. She returned, rather panicky, and at once saw me sitting on the hall sofa and spotted that I did not look well. I had been fighting a cold for two days and had taken a lot of aspirin and now felt exhausted. "Where are we going?" I asked. "I won't tell you." In fact, her intention had been to take me to see an Odilon Redon which perhaps she might buy, but its owner had gone away. Instead she directed me to a bookshop with a special Swedish gift department upstairs. We looked at the most hideous Swedish toys, painted glass, "artsy-craftsy" decorations on aprons, and paper tablecloths. Only the little bundles of sticks for whip-ping sauces and cleaning pots delighted me. Although critical of the taste of almost everything here, I was appreciative of the senti-ment that was at the back of our visit. It touched me quite a lot to have her want me to share her enthusiasm for an old-fashioned Swedish Christmas.

She was utterly charming and natural with all her fellow-countrymen serving in the shop and seemed to feel quite at home and unharrassed by them. When she speaks in her native language she becomes very smiling and relaxed, and her face brightens. She bought some Swedish magazines and then we went on to the Swedish cake shop that smelled of cinnamon and sweet spices and was festive with busy activity. "How sad it is to see these things transplanted from their native hearth," Greta regretted. "It is so different from one's childhood; all the colors are wrong: those cartons used to be dark red—now they are too pale and yellow. Everything has deteriorated." But the cakes look delicious, and we bought ginger biscuits, and each gave the other a huge lucky heart.

We returned, parcel-laden, to her rooms in the Ritz Tower. After a moment her doorbell rang, and the porter brought in a lot of packages for "Miss Brown." "Would you mind if I opened that one now?" she asked, holding a large box. "There may be flowers in it, and they oughtn't to die all cased up." She opened the box and a look of displeasure came over her face as she read a card, then glanced at the flowers as though she hated the sight of them. "Don't you like them?" I asked. "Oh no, they're Holly-wood ones," and she produced four huge mauve orchids. I have sufficient vulgarity and inherent bad taste in me to feel these most expensive of hothouse flowers have a certain Boldini-1914-*grande-cocotte* glamour about them. But, for her, they are everything that is artificial and unsuitable.

I asked why she went to such lengths as having her parcels addressed to a pseudonym? She did not reply. And why did she not allow even her friends to allude to her as Greta? Personally, I found their talk about "Miss Gee" very self-conscious. Greta remarked that she intensely disliked her first name. "Then," I asked, "what shall I call you in future?" "Wife," she said, as she went to fill a vase in the bathroom. I raised my voice above the running tap and, as if calling her in the garden, shouted: "Wife! Wife!" But she remonstrated: "No, no—you must be very quiet; there is never any sound in this apartment. It's as if no one ever lived here: never any noises at all." I could well believe it.

_____ _Christmas Eve_

In bed all day with my wretched cold never improving, I felt sluggish and lifeless. Greta said she would come in sometime during the afternoon. She appeared, her face like velour and her eyes rather lined. She had not fallen asleep until four o'clock in the morning. At two-thirty she had got up and smoked half a cigarette, then had a drink. Today she had been out early, battling for presents in the crowds. She had even been down to Macy's where, she said, the poor shop assistants were now in a coma.

"They are?"

"Why sure, the poor things have been on their feet all this time, and they just look at you in a daze and they don't know what they're doing. And I saw two men—they were so drunk! I have never seen men so drunk, and one was trying to hold the other, but they couldn't keep up, and they were already wet when, suddenly, they fell right in front of a car, and they just scraped the snow off the mudguards. Oh, it was terrible to see them so drunk."

Greta took off her coat and folded herself at the foot of the bed. She hid her face in a mop of hair, like Susy, my mother's dog at home. She became coy and stammered: "You must be quiet and not get yourself worked up; it's not good for your cold." But I said that I was only preserving myself for her: then, peeping out through her hair, she replied that she had no answer to that one. She did not wish to come near me and catch my germs, nor for me to see the spot she had on her nose. "I'm so conscious of it," she said, "that when people on the street said 'Happy Christmas,' I squinted and couldn't see beyond my nose."

For Christmas breakfast tomorrow she has arranged with "the little black and white friend"[1] (Mercedes de Acosta) that I should join her. "Mercedes must have been rather intrigued when she heard you were bringing me?" I said. "Oh, I didn't tell her who I'd be bringing. I merely asked: 'Have you room for an extra lost soul?' and Mercedes said 'yes.' 'Are you sure you have a plate?' I asked her. 'Yes, but who is it you are bringing?' 'It doesn't matter who it is—you'll know soon enough so long as you've got the extra plate.'" I was amused, yet appalled that Mercedes always plays the wrong cards.

_____ *Christmas Day*

My cold almost recovered, but the habit of staying in bed takes a hold, and I found it was an upheaval to get to Greta's by midday. G. had again slept badly, and her face was so white that it made her hair, which fell in a mass of curls, appear darker. Greta's room was filled with packages and a lot of slowly dying flowers; some sweetheart roses were jammed into a coffee pot. Greta had been up since seven o'clock tying and sorting packages and now had a vast cardboard box filled for Mercedes. While waiting for her I opened the kitchenette door, partly out of idle curiosity, but this gesture brought from her a violent admonition. "I hate curiosity. I dislike it intensely if people don't mind their own business." I felt utterly crushed, and it took a long time for me to recover.

The arrival at Mercedes's went off at half cock. Mercedes did not appear surprised or particularly delighted to see me, and her apartment seemed small and crowded and the atmosphere rather unpleasant and strange. Mercedes, unable to hide her anxiety, was extremely preoccupied with the thought of having to prepare a meal. Greta, sensing the climate, at once took control and entertained us all with a most amusing and adroit performance. She sang snatches of songs: the lugubrious Swedish Salvation Army hymn, and "Nobody Knows the Troubles I've

_____
[1] So named because her face is always powdered white and she wears only black clothes.

Seen But Jesus." She recited, sprawling with legs high on the sofa, short poems by unknown writers and bits of hymns. In contrast to all her random, higgledy-piggledy outpourings, she was also very executive and when Mr. Everley, the fourth guest, arrived, she went off to the kitchen and, with a towel around her hips, cooked ham and eggs. When she returned she was still in an authoritative mood and forbade Mercedes to distribute the presents. "No, we do that later, and we don't make a mess of the room."

Later, when the meal was over, and everyone had given his gifts, Greta produced her large box of prizes. Then with adroit but apparently casual introductions, she offered to each the presents she had chosen with such care. "This is ten cents store"— "This is wholesale"—"This hasn't got the price on, has it?" When Mr. Everley gave Greta his present she read the card and said: "Oh, Mr. Everley, haven't you been rather lavish? Your phrasing is over-extravagant." Greta, even now, was careful not to give anyone the impression that she could be on intimate terms with them. Mercedes, poor dear, always at her worst in Greta's presence, in a rather too canny way, overtly bragged of their friendship: ". . . that time when you wouldn't let me buy that coffee pot . . ." and ". . . that pink vase you liked so much . . ." or ". . . that holiday we spent together in the desert. . . ." This was not lost on Greta who rather abruptly put her down. Mercedes, however, did not seem to resent any rebuff. Greta alluded to me as "Mister Beaton," and Everley as "Everley"; but under her breath she said to me: "Don't you dare ever call anyone 'darling' but myself!"

With wonderful timing, and in a very casual way so that no one would suspect ("sussect," as she says) that there was any method in her madness, Greta started to leave the party punctually at three o'clock for, it turned out, she had an appointment. We walked home arm-in-arm; but when we neared the 'danger zone' I had to wait while she walked on ahead lest "the little man" should see us together.

At first Greta did not wish to go out to meet friends of mine; but neither did I like the idea of my friends gossiping among themselves about my "secret" life. By degrees, the burden became almost too heavy and I wanted to lighten it by proving that it was real. It would be a relief to decant some of my bottled-up emotions. As usual, Greta proves unaccountable. After she has refused to meet my Russian friends, Pavlik and Natascha,[1] whom I know she will find understanding and sympathetic, she decides to change her mind. Once having decided she would like to go out to dinner, or to drinks, she prepares for the occasion with great excitement. Always a great to-do about what she shall wear from her "poor little trunk." Once we arrive at a friend's home she comports herself with the greatest ease and seems to take complete charge of the situation, treating everyone to a virtuoso performance of charm and magnetism.

Greta needed little coaxing to go and see Nicky Gunzberg's Balzacesque apartment. She liked it not only for having a highly civilized style and patina that is rare in New York, but also for being somber and cozy. She seemed to be relaxed and enjoying herself. Then Natascha started to retell the latest New York scandal of the little grass widow from Paris who, in the absence of her hostess, a woman of violent temperament, went to bed with her host. The wife's discovery of the two caught *in flagrante* is a classic farce situation, but made melodramatic in this instance by the wife's bringing out a whip. We all had our contribution to add to the saga which had been on many lips, especially since it had been alluded to in the columns. I noticed that Greta had become silent, and when we left the apartment she said: "Oh, Mister Beaton, I've still got to teach you so much! How can you degrade yourself to the level of telling such ordinary, boring details of gossip? Why did it interest you? What's so funny?" Greta considered it unworthy to take cognizance of the fact that two people, a man and a woman, were found in bed together. "It's not important! It's a natural thing ("naahr-turrel thingge") to do—it's the law of nature! The poor little man suddenly feels in need of a woman and so he goes to bed with one. The fact that it gets into the papers is the reason why you're so interested, but it's not interesting really. It's a biological fact

---

[1] Princess Paley, married to J. C. Wilson

("fucktte"), and it happens all the time; behind all these windows it's going on now," and she waved her arm at the surrounding skyscrapers. "It's nothing—of no importance; it's just a biological fact."

We went to an exhibition of Pavel Tchelitchew's early pictures, mostly zouaves, clowns, acrobats and other circus figures. She admired Pavlik's technique, but refused to be entirely impressed and considered his color too morbid. She liked the portrait of Natascha Paley. "It gives her a wonderful, mysterious, and spiritual quality that she does not possess, and the veiled eyes produce a strange look. It is like a stepping stone to death."

_____   _____ **Visit to Erich Remarque**

If one pokes into odd corners of this city one can find posses of Italians, Germans, Moors, Greeks, and Finns living, in spite of their present situation, much as they might be in their native haunts. Tonight, in Erich Remarque's suite in the Ambassador Hotel, a group of Germans sat drinking—not the usual whisky —but delicious Moselle. Surrounded by Remarque's collection of Oriental pictures, *objets d'art,* Persian carpets and Chinese pottery, which gave such character to this otherwise anonymous apartment, they conversed about politics, the theatre and wine as only the most civilized of Germans could.

Greta is permanently endowed with what is known as star quality and this works for her whenever she enters a room. By the time she had placed herself on a sofa, with Old Gold held aloft, and imparted the information: "I never call anybody by their first names, but when I discovered that Maria was Remarque's second name I never miss an opportunity to use it," she had the half dozen men present completely "Garbonized."

The talk in German and English (Greta speaks German fluently and makes the language sound melodious) was mostly of foreign interests and personalities, and the theatre and the movies in Berlin and Vienna in particular. It showed me that although Greta has lived—twenty years, is it?—in this country, her instincts and real tastes are middle European. When Oscar Homolka, the actor, confided to her that he would like to live in England, where people were "real," Greta seemed impressed and sympathetic. The drinking continued, and the empty, elegant, tall-necked bottles were put in a row on the floor: soon a regiment had assembled. Four hours passed. The talk was splendid, continental and witty. Each time Greta suggested maybe we should leave, another bottle of Moselle was brought out. The room was filled with smoke: ash trays became piled with cigars and cigarette stubs. I was bemused, but with the uncorking of the tenth bottle of Moselle, I began to balk and became tired without being drunk. Four o'clock struck. At last the others were becoming slightly tipsy. I knew that Greta would remain till dawn if I didn't make the move.

When we left Erich's re-creation of Berlin we were surprised to find ourselves on an almost totally deserted Park Avenue. On our way home there were only one or two people to be seen, so we had plenty of opportunity to embrace, on doorsteps and at street corners. Whenever anyone did happen to heave into sight, we argued in simulated Brooklyn accents, and in loud voices, as we stood gesticulating violently. "Now listen, buddy, you can't tell me nothin' about stocks." "Well, I'll tell you what— put your money where your mouth is. All the action is in footwear and ready-mades." "Now listen, twenty bucks will bring you a hundred before you can say 'Parcheesi.'" "And then what?" "Now listen to me. You put ten thousand in the rack, and you can tell any buddy where the hell to get off. . . ." Then we laughed and clung to one another like limpets: it was almost impossible to drag ourselves apart. The walk home in the surprising cold was delightful. Greta waited on her doorstep to wave until I was out of sight. Back at my hotel I at once telephoned. We laughed with surprise as we recapitulated the events during our twelve hours together. Tomorrow we are to spend even more time together.

She was sporting her "new look" skirt, by now much too long and baggy. With this she wore three sweaters, and stuck between her brows was a frown plaster.

In spite of everything, Greta, in her unself-conscious way,

proved the most alluring, fascinating creature. She aroused in me feelings of protectiveness, amusement, and desire.

Out into the ice-cold night for dinner at a Brazilian restaurant called Semon. The atmosphere was convivial, the food savory, and we were both hungry. Greta's mood was joyful and I was in good spirits. She told comic stories—she has a fount of them—the sort that no matter how many times I hear I can never remember later. If I try to tell a comic story in return, she stops me if the premise is not probable. "Nothing is funny to me that isn't a possibility."

I entertained her by telling her how effeminate I had been as a small boy, and of how distressing it must have been to my father to discover that I showed no inclination to follow in his footsteps and become a great cricketer. Rather, I acquired an abnormal interest in women's fashions. Somehow I even managed to wear the regulation preparatory school caps and felt hats so that they resembled those of the ladies appearing in the *Sketch* and *Play Pictorial.* Also, being stage-struck, I developed an intense interest in actresses' make-up. Whenever, on family birthdays or at Christmas, we went to musical comedies or pantomimes, I would peer through the opera glasses to marvel at the eyelids painted turquoise blue and the little dots of scarlet at the inner corners of the eyes.

My mother's dressing-table drawer of powder, rouge, mascara, and false kiss-curls held an uncanny fascination for me. Once, on the annual summer holiday in Norfolk, on my way down late to breakfast in the furnished house which we rented for a six weeks' duration, I stole into my mother's bedroom, opened the imitation-old-oak drawer, and painted my face like one of the pierrettes in the troupe we had been taken to see the night before. This was not an attempt at a joke, and somehow I imagined that the transformation my face had so hurriedly undergone would not be noticed by my parents, busy with their eggs, bacon, and fried bread. But my father, on leaving the dining room, caught sight of this cosmetic mask coming down the stairs. He became so enraged that I was locked for the day in my bedroom. The punishment did not unduly upset me. I resented such unfair treatment—nobody understood me—and I would just as soon miss the usual outing spent on that miserable, gray Sheringham beach, sitting in an east wind on uncomfortable pebbles, or dashing into the icy North Sea. When eventually released from my imprisonment, I casually threw to one side a watercolor portrait I had painted during the day. It was of my theatrical love, Lily Elsie. It was the best portrait I had done to date, with my heroine looking over a shoulder in a Vermeerlike pose, wearing a huge Greek chignon, and with red dots in the corners of her blue dusted eyelids. My mother nodded to my father as if indeed she had given birth to a young Vermeer. My father, too, was impressed with the likeness and the azure background.

Greta sympathized more with my father than with me. "Are you very affectionately demonstrative to your mother?" she asked. "No, we love one another but can't show it. I'm very self-conscious with her." Greta conceded: "Parents make it so difficult for us."

I also talked about the first indefinable, mysterious stirrings of love at Harrow, and the lack of sex at Cambridge University in those days. Greta asked if my mother was worried about me, for, she said, it must be terrible for parents, who only wish for their offspring to lead sheltered, conventional lives, to find them being so strange.

Instead of becoming morbid about the subject, we started to laugh at the idea of my having been such a sissy while, at the same time, always being so wiry, energetic and, if put to any challenge, extremely headstrong. This had led to my involvement in complicated situations with all sorts of unsuitable women— when, for instance, some gesture made in a mood of bravura was interpreted more seriously than was intended. "You're so violent! Sometimes during the day your fingers around me are like steel, and they almost break into my back. It's a wonder you're safe. Your mother must worry when you rush ahead quite madly. So far you've got along all right, but I don't know what keeps you preserved."

All barriers of reserve seemed to be down, so I ventured to steer the conversation to expound my views about why we were good for one another. I started off: "I'm poor in worldly terms, and have nothing to offer you—nothing, absolutely nothing but salvation: in fact," I said, "I am the Salvation Army." I didn't get any further for she laughed so much there was no possibility of being serious. We left the restaurant, lingering en route to the Tower. "Call me when you get back home," she said. When her hotel operator asked me: "Who's calling Miss Brown?" I replied: "The Salvation Army." When Greta picked up the receiver she was still laughing.

We met outside my hotel. Greta had given Miss Cleghorn a message that she wished to show me a certain painting in a gallery nearby, but she had changed the plan, and now wanted to explore the freshly snow-covered park. But I was wearing thin shoes with no galoshes. I telephoned from the downstairs hall for Miss Cleghorn to throw the galoshes out of my window into Fifty-Eighth Street. It was not at all a typical New York scene that was watched by a gang of road cleaners and passers-by, for I believe one can be heavily fined for throwing anything out of a window. But the incident was made unforgettable for me by the changing expressions of surprise, alarm and childish glee on Greta's face as, surreptitiously, she was witness to the proceedings. Terrified of being noticed in the center of the hubbub, she could not yet altogether extricate herself from the excitement. Miss Cleghorn's spectacled white face appeared above. One black object hove nearer and nearer. A tremendous thud! Then another! The galoshes had arrived without accident. "That's one way of getting a pair of overshoes," said a truckman.

We trudged through the high snowdrifts and enjoyed watching the kids on toboggans, skis, and sledges. They had transposed the whole park into an endless playground and the scene was like Breughel pictures of winter with small black figures moving in every direction. Greta's mood became so euphoric that she even made jokes to passers-by. Once she followed a mother pulling a child on a dogcart and cooed: "Look at its boots! Those feet are to me all of childhood." Then she went up to one baby and looked in its face and did the most enchanting imitation of its surprise and wonder at seeing her face in such close proximity. We were fascinated by the skaters and the youngsters sliding down icy slopes on their backsides. "I used to do that as a child and ruined my coats, and my little mother used to be so upset."

As we were walking home some young hooligans shouted her

name and ran after us, their cries of "Greta Garbo" ringing through the park. I wanted to chuck snowballs at them, but Greta said no, we must just do nothing but "suffer." "If we show we're angry they'll be after us. They'll have fiendish sport, but if we do nothing they'll have no fun—and I know: I was awful as a child! We used to do all the tricks of ringing door bells and running away, and next door to us was an embittered old spinster and she made the mistake of going for us. Then we let her have it! We were a gang, and we threw water at her windows, and sand, and I was the ringleader. I wasn't at all like a girl. I used to play leapfrog, and have a bag of marbles of my own—a tomboy."

By now the sky was dark and the lamps came on, looking, as Greta remarked, like a Valentine with the falling snowflakes dotted around. Walking through the snowstorm was strangely peaceful and calm. We came back to my room with cold faces and glowing health before going on to the little Brazilian restaurant for dinner. Here we shared a bottle of Chilean wine which made Greta very communicative. Our first meeting—in Hollywood—she confessed had left little impression on her, except that she remembered my soft white leather jacket. This, under the strange circumstances, was quite surprising, and not at all flattering. I said it was better, perhaps, that we had preserved our real relationship for later on in life when I was more experienced. But she disagreed. "No, I think it would have been very nice if I had let you come and eat spinach with me, as you suggested, the following day. I should have been intrigued lest you fall into bad habits, and you might have been so surprised at having this relationship that you would have been unlike anyone else." She said she had left it till late if she was to be married, though a Frenchman had said he liked his women "like a salad, *un peu fatiguées*." Women getting on in years were so grateful for a lover! We talked about a mutual friend's recent marriage. Suddenly something happened to the man, and he was able to give that woman something no ordinary man would have been able to—complete and utterly pristine love, and oh, she was grateful!

_____ *December 26th, 1947*

"*Il neige*," she said on the telephone. That was a euphemism. New York was buried under snow. Friends called up to discuss the sensational storm outside. No buses or taxis running, the life of the city at a standstill except for men scraping a passageway through the streets and a few enthusiasts skiing down Park Avenue.

I had invited a dozen friends in for drinks. The reason for the party: to dissipate the bogey of "the little man" by inviting him to bring Greta to my rooms. All day the snow continued to fall from a soup-brown sky; a strange silence pervaded the town and nothing moved. I wondered if Greta herself could come. Yet I knew in my heart she would arrive, for she enjoys violence in the elements: storms and blizzards excite her. ("One never knows if the roof will be blown off.") She appeared, covered with brilliance and sparkle, with "the little man" accoutered like a mountaineer. Her cheeks were pink, her eyes bright, her skin flaked with snow drops, her clothes all gray and shiny black. She wore gum boots, a nun's coif around her face, and on top of that a black seafarer's hat like the old-fashioned advertisement for Elliman's Embrocation.

Apart from Pavel Tchelitchew, who reported, at various times of the day, that the snow was mounting higher and higher, and that it was "disaster," and Mona, who telephoned during the festivities to say she was marooned, everyone whom I had invited materialized. The fact that they were incarcerated here gave the gathering a curious atmosphere. When the writer George Davis, who has eulogized Garbo for years, arrived, having been in a subway that wouldn't function, he found that the experience of meeting his goddess for the first time was even more dreamlike than he had visualized it. George said: "She's the only one who has this dream quality of unreality, and it's fitting that I should have had such difficulty in getting here today—that I should meet her in these Scandinavian conditions." George later remarked that Greta still possesses a unique quality, that she would always evolve, that it is nonsense to say she belongs to one epoch . . . like all great artists she can change to become part of the next phase of artistic activity.

The room was filled. Vodka and slivovitz were the most popular drinks; soon everyone was warm to the cockles and enthusiastically applauding the late arrivals. Greta's honesty is often mistaken for wit. She answered in good faith Dali's inquiry: "You-h, Garbo-h, skee-ee?" "Yes, but only on level ground,"—at which everyone went into roars of laughter. I paid little obvious attention to Greta, but when I did sit next to her she turned and, like a woodpecker, repeated an affectionate phrase in whispers.

"The little man" seemed ill at ease, and his eyes never met mine with any confidence or honesty. On his arrival he said: "You must have asked an enormous number of people to get this crowd here." Throughout he emanated a troubled, electric aura. Even the drinks did not give him any false faith in me, and he was quite correct in his surmise. When, accepting another drink, he said: "I'll just have a sip to show there is no ill feeling," I whispered to Greta: "Is it going all right with him?" and she said with infinite conviction: "Oh, yaaish—yaaish."

Long past their dinner time, the party guests, wrapped up in their coverings of wool and mackintosh, started the trek home. I was able to have a quick encounter with Greta while others were fitting on their snow boots. When I tried to kiss her she said: "Oh, don't be so foolish!" and a look of terror came over her face. "When do you telephone?" "Tomorrow."

_____ *Monday, December 29th, 1947*

We walked to the Twenty-One restaurant and were thrown into a rowdy *melée* of people. Greta was very gay and taking everything in her stride. The great tall impresario of the place said: "I'll give you a nice quiet corner in the shade." To which G. replied: "No, we've come here to be in the lights and in the center of everything!" I was quite as amazed as the tall impresario. Some sawdrill-voiced woman came up to Greta and rasped: "You've given me so much pleasure, what is it your name is?" Greta did not help her out and considered she was being classed with Bob Hope and Betty Grable. A beat-up, gin-sodden wreck, at least twenty years older than Greta, teetered up and, without wishing to be wounding, confessed: "Oh, Miss Garbo—I used to worship you when I was a teensy, weensy, bitsy 'lil girl!"

I couldn't help being irritated by the busy young man opposite who, with his girlfriend beside him, spent the evening telephoning from their table. "Perhaps he wants to show her how important he is; maybe he doesn't feel secure, or maybe his mother is very ill. You don't know, you just jump to conclusions, you may be wrong." Her advice to be calmer, more generous, was friendly and well meant. "You are apt to be critical and outspoken. Others encour-

age you to show off and be audacious. But who are you to judge
people who may be doing their best? It isn't very intelligent of you
to behave like that: to put it on its most superficial plane, it doesn't
pay off. You see, I had a very troublesome, difficult time in my
youth, and I learned a lot of these things then. It doesn't do to ask
for an eye for an eye—not that I've read the Bible since I was a
child—and then I was so shocked by Abraham and all that incest."
I marveled at Greta's strength of character and at how she is
impervious to anyone's behaving badly to her. She will never meet
wrong with wrong.

This all sounds as if we had a heavy and quarrelsome dinner
but, in fact, I felt we had achieved an added sympathy for each
other. She has taught me much, and I encourage her to continue
the course of lessons. One of my luxuries is that I quite enjoy airing
my shortcomings; I sometimes boast of my ignorance, my weak-
nesses, and faults of character. I admit that I rely too much on my
instinct, that I am incapable of analysis, and am not the deepest
of wells. I am grateful to Greta that, with her guidance, I am able
to scratch a little beneath the surface to look for the meaning of
things.

We walked home through the streets of ice. An Alaskan gale
was blowing: a full, brilliant moon shone into G.'s room. We drank
the nice cold beer, and I remained dawdling only a little time as
I felt weak from the effects of my cold. I whispered in her ears in
the dark, and in a cloud of tenderness dragged myself away.

_____ *New Year's Eve/December 31st, 1947*

It being New Year's Eve today we felt the longing to celebrate
together. But Greta had promised to dine with "the little man"
and I had arranged to go to Mona's grand party; perhaps if Greta
were free she would telephone me at Mona's. During the grand
formal dinner the butler came up to me and bowed. "It's Mister
Thompson on the line." This is just one more of the names Greta
uses as a disguise. "Mr. Thompson" was already by ten-thirty back
at his hotel: "he" had been weeping and had shed so many tears!
Would I join "him"? Mona was large-hearted and understanding as
ever, and I soon disappeared without bidding the others good
night. In the taxi on the way down Park Avenue, with its long
centipedes of brilliant Christmas trees, I watched the merrymak-

ers hurrying to their midnight revels. I felt that I was the luckiest person alive to be keeping this tryst with the one person in the world I wanted. Greta did not appear as if she had been weeping, although she looked serious. She said that she had been very cruel to "the little man." He had become devoted to her and was the best friend she'd ever had, but she couldn't be tied down like this. "Oh, I've said such wounding things to him, but I couldn't help it. I became quite hysterical, and I laughed and I cried, and all my mascara ran and I looked such a sight." Enough of this.

We hurried out through the merrymakers and came back to my room to celebrate the arrival of the New Year by drinking some 1840 whisky that Margaret Case had given me. I gave a toast to our marriage and our life together, but Greta did not take up this theme and smiled a little diffidently. Our embrace was tender, but we did not have enough arms to entwine round each other's shoulders and waists.

All the sirens sounded and hooters hooted, and even the ships in the port made their bellowing noises. We stood at the window and watched the colored sky, and wished and 'skolled' and drank, and by degrees I became quite drunk. I'd had champagne and brandy at Mona's and was now digging into the old whisky, and I became very full of life without any inhibitions, using rough language and rather rowdily galumphing about the place. At moments we stared at one another as if in a trance and felt taken possession of by some devil. Greta was gay, liking my attempts at jokes; sometimes we sniggered close together like children forbidden to laugh in church or in class, and laughing so much more because of the hopelessness of the situation. Then we stood stiffly facing one another, she with her feet wide apart and her hair hanging partly over her face. Then she looked at me with lowered lids and one eyebrow raised—a typical and alluring regard of hers which has been copied by half the women of the world. When I caught sight of myself in the mirror I was appalled by the swollen, bloated face that confronted me, lips all smudged with rouge and eyes bunged up. I said: "How is it possible for you to like anyone who looks as awful as I do?" She made a kind reply, and I clasped her again. "Don't ever leave me again—don't make me unhappy again, I beg of you!"

We walked back to the Tower and the town was filled with drunkards; we laughed at some of the people wearing comic hats above sad, ordinary faces, and one elderly man with a long feather on his head was the most ridiculous sight in the whole city. The intense cold reminded me of Russia. Even our heaviest clothing seemed suddenly flimsy. Soon my ears were hurting with frostbite and Greta could hardly get her breath. She pretended that she was quite tipsy, but she had had only a few sips of the ancient whisky. Suddenly she went up to a large and hideous old dog wearing a heavy coat. Greta screwed up her face and said: "Oh, the lovely little doggy!" and shook her head at it. The dog's master, an aged confirmed bachelor, was so surprised, but delighted, to have his dog admired that he shot a row of false teeth at us in a terrible semblance of a smile. We both doubled up with laughter. Outside the Ritz Tower we dawdled, and then I went up with her in the elevator. In her rooms she stripped to become a Madison Square athlete with white socks, small red slippers and tight underpants. She put on my hat and gallivanted about in the extreme of circus clowning.

When I returned to my rooms "Mr. Thompson" telephoned to say that he had just read in the papers that New York marriages were undermined by drink.

Next morning "Mr. Thompson" telephoned me again. "I'm not up yet—haven't got on my mascara; you've never seen me without it and I look naked. My lashes are pale like an albino, and I look so surprised and open. I'm never going to let you see me without buckets of mascara on; I'm going out now to buy tons of it." ("toorns uf utte").

I related to Greta how I had been awakened from my first sleep by a woman in the next room giving vent to the most agonizing sounds. I realized the woman was in the throes of love-making and that the cries, so heartbreaking to hear, were part of her enjoyment. Ecstasy is revolting if it comes to this. Greta said the man must be a brute, then added: "And I know how strange the noises of the night can be: the laughter, people fighting in the street below. I sometimes lie with my heart beating like mad—it's so awful, I feel life can't go on."

Greta came in at a little after six o'clock; Michael Duff was here sitting bolt upright awaiting her arrival. Greta enjoys the "British Empire" aspect of Michael. "The British have such reserve; they don't say all they mean, they're nice. I get that feeling, and I know I'm right." Michael inadvertently gave a delightful picture of my home life in England, of my mother and my "divine" Aunt Jessie; Greta seemed pleased. Together they made a comic team, and it was interesting to watch each individual's considerable charm working upon the other. With every discovery about one another these two characters came into closer harmony. I have seldom seen Greta as demonstrative; she told entertaining anecdotes, laughed at him, and kissed him on both cheeks. Naturally Michael was quite bewitched and, when leaving, tried to nail her down for future occasions—but, of course, she was as mercurial as ever.

When I answered her ring at my door, she was not there but hiding around a corner. This is typical of her. When I leave a restaurant a minute after her she is nowhere to be seen, but a few seconds later emerges from her hiding place. Today, on her way through the snow, a young man had come up to her and said: "Did you see such-and-such a film? Because, if so, don't you think I overacted in it?" Greta had looked astounded and said: "I'm so cold, I can't talk to you now." She laughed about the incident. On account of the snow and dearth of taxicabs I suggested I hire a car to take us to the theatre tonight, but she was horrified. "No, we must go on foot: we are students." That is how she likes to see herself. She hates getting into a taxi and seldom does so. "They are full of germs and are obnoxious."

On the way Greta recounted how once she went to the opera with Mrs. Sanson. Mrs. S. generally appeared at the opera in a chinchilla coat with tiara and orchids. "But not this time!" Greta laughed. "What we looked like! It was raining, pouring in torrents. I was wearing a salmon-pink mackintosh and a mackintosh hat and snow boots, and we unpeeled ourselves by layers." She told me of other incidents when she went out with Mrs. Sanson to various unsuitable places, and that Mrs. Sanson had little sense of humor about appearing at a disadvantage.

It was too cold to talk much during our park walk today but, at one point, I raised my hat and said, as is customary when I am about to touch her cheek with a kiss: "Am I permitted to draw attention?" and she said: "I was just about to do the same thing." With lips pressed down in a child's moue, her eyes darting in all directions to spy any strangers who might be approaching, she gave me a loving peck. Suddenly she said: "Got to go now. I have to see somebody or something." Instinctively I guessed that the something was the re-showing of her film *Ninotchka*, now playing at the little Carnegie Cinema.

I went alone to see *Ninotchka* and was very self-conscious for fear that, by chance, she and "the little man" should be there too. After ten years *Ninotchka* is still a funny film, and the range and variety of Greta's performance is masterly. Now that I know her well, I can see what a lot of herself she gives to the part. The tragic, touching, honey-sympathy quality of her voice comes across the microphone in an amazingly lifelike way. Lubitsch is the first director to show that Greta has a sense of humor. It is doubtful, however, if future historians will be able to tell from this picture what a great contribution Greta could have made to the cinema art of her day.

The biggest theatrical stars always seem to be born at the very time when their talent shines at its brightest; yet no doubt it is the time itself that creates their particular form of talent. If Garrick or Bernhardt had lived today their performances would certainly have been less flamboyant; they would have fitted themselves to the restraint of the time, but no doubt their contribution would have been just as outstanding. In other professions, and means of creative expression, there are those innovators whose work in early life is too original or advanced to be appreciated; but they live to become accepted as the geniuses they always knew themselves to be; sometimes they survive long enough to be considered back numbers. (The span of a dramatist's talent is the shortest of all, and few playwrights continue to be successful for more than ten years.)

Very early on, Garbo's incandescence was a guiding light for a discriminating Berlin public and her potential as a great actress immediately recognized. But Greta's tragedy was that she left Europe. When she arrived in California, the moving picture industry was going through one of its worst phases. The great inventiveness of the earliest Hollywood film makers had become dissipated, while the days of Hollywood's best commercial potboilers were still to come. At the beginning of her histrionic career Garbo had the highest of ideals. To find herself under contract to appear in a succession of rubbishy screen plays as oversexed, underdressed houris came as a prison sentence. Most of us recover, sooner or later, from some great misfortune: time generally heals the wounds of some surgical operation to even the most nervous system. But those long years Garbo spent making all her silent pictures was a living nightmare that has left an indelible impression. Even when, at the height of her popularity, she prevailed upon Mr. Mayer to give her opportunities to show signs of her true quality and some acting roles of more substance, and the "talkies" certainly gave her greater scope, yet the making of films was, to her, still "a tawdry business."

How different it would have been if there had been a script or a director worthy of her, and she had been surrounded by sympathetic, creative artists! Apart from Lubitsch, she had to rely almost unaided upon her instincts to sustain her through long roles that necessitated every variety of playing. Yet what an infallible instinct she shows! How can she have known so much about the ineffable allure and grandeur of the *cocotte,* Marguerite Gautier, the loneliness of Queen Christina, the desperate quayside toughness of Anna Christie? In all her roles she shows her rare quality of "presence." But if she had come under the wing of some of today's European directors, how her genius would have burgeoned! If only she had been born into a later decade!

During all the years of her youthful beauty the public has never seen her as she should have been shown. Almost all the scenes were shot in the studio (and looked it!) where a gantry above spilled, from every direction, a flood of blinding, unnatural light onto the stars. According to our present standards, every performer was over-made-up, then photographed through a soft-focus lens. If a few scenes were shot on location in the Californian sun, huge reflectors and artificial lights were added to obliterate all shadows. The public has seen nothing of the subtlety of the modulations of Garbo's face; we have had to spell all that we can of her from the white and black mask which has been all that we were allowed to see. Likewise, except for a sitting of a few minutes with Steichen, there were never any still photographs that came near to showing her as she would have been in the natural light of today's realism.

All these relics of Garbo are grotesquely over-retouched: only an artificial façade remains.

It is perhaps not to be wondered at that Greta is not proud of the legacy she has left. Yet, even now, whenever there is mention of a new project, in her mind she harks back to former habits, and of again putting herself in the hands of an old hack director and cameraman. Meanwhile, valuable time is passing. Perhaps, for her, that is not important; she has little respect left for the public taste, and she now thinks more of her personal freedom and liberty.

Telephone—no chance of meeting—she was rusty, in bed and very sorry for herself. She said her face had shrunk and that she looked like a little squirrel. But she is always critical of her appearance and diagnoses it queerly.

She was in her dressing gown on the sofa of her dreary, impersonal, and untidy hotel rooms. She appeared pale and drawn, her hair was curled over her forehead. I told her I had been to see *Ninotchka;* she took a great gulp. "How strange that I got mixed up in that business, but I did!" and she talked quite freely of the experience of working on that particular picture. She had not enjoyed it and was worried that it was vulgar. It did not strike her as being funny until she saw it four years later. Lubitsch was clever: he was so much better as an actor than any of his casts. It was so depressing to see him acting every part well. "I remember, one morning, going in and seeing him, cigar in mouth, with my big leading man, running through a scene on the sofa that I was to do. He was being so funny! But underneath he was a vulgar little man, and he made such a noise on the set, always shouting. One day I said to him in German: 'Please, when you speak to me, please speak more softly,' and he was so surprised that from then on, whenever he looked at me, he became quieter."

Greta had been too ill to see *Ninotchka* the other evening, but might do so as soon as she is well enough—perhaps tomorrow at dusk. But she would feel such a fool going there. She seldom went to see her pictures and was so shy of being seen that she would always leave before the lights went up, with the result that she scarcely ever knew how her films ended.

"You mustn't dally" (she pronounces it "dully"), "I've got to get some rest and become healthy ("helty") again." But it was hard to leave. Greta looked out of her hotel window. "If you walk along the street I can see you from here. I wonder if we can see each other from the Plaza?" I leaned out of the window, but just by a few yards our windows miss being visible to each other. "You walk along that street to that corner and I'll wave to you from here," she suggested. I left. I walked up Park Avenue and, at a given point, looked up at the Tower soaring into the late afternoon sky. Alas, the last rays of sunlight were reflected in the glass pane so I could not see any face at the window. But, suddenly, the minute window opened and a huge white towel fluttered in the air. There she was, waving so gaily. I doffed my hat and bent double with laughter until passers-by stopped and also stared up at the window, which forthwith was shut.

Five minutes later in my hotel she telephoned. "I miss you," she said, "and wasn't it awful of those people to stop and gape! Heaven knows who they were—they might have guessed it was 'Harriet Brown' at the window."

January 13th

I told her the great news that a Frigidaire had been installed in my room and I could now save my precious dollars and have my own meals from the icebox. "You will have unnatural noises in your room, and Mister Attlee will get worried and think you have set the fuse for the atom age." But she also gave me advice about putting in avocados and radishes and cheese and biscuits and fruit. She could not share them with me today, but would be around directly after luncheon. "Well, all right then, at two-thirty." But two-thirty was three, then she telephoned to say she had such bad congestion of the chest that she must remain indoors. I could come and see her. "If you think I look like a witch, don't say so."

She appeared quite extraordinary, hiding in the shadow behind her door, her hair hanging in a most peculiar bell shape. She laughed and croaked and thought maybe she would develop pneumonia. It was her own silly fault, she said, for having washed her hair this morning. She sprawled on the small, uncomfortable sofa and gave a performance of charm, fantasy, and madness. She pulled down her mouth in a grimace and looked in the distance with the most hauntingly beautiful velvet and forget-me-not eyes.

"I'm worried about your birthday present. What can I get you? You're spoiled; you're difficult; you know what things are. You're not like Mister Everley: anything goes for him."

I wanted very much for her to give me a present—something that I can keep always. Suddenly she asked: "Would you go to California if I left here in a week's time?"

"Yes. Could I stay with you?"

"No, because my house isn't organized for that, and it would embarrass and worry me. I live simply, alone with a servant I call 'the Dragon,' and it's just arranged for me there alone."

_____ ***Visit to Tchelitchew***

She was wearing my favorite gray highwayman hat and was in the most dulcet of moods. What a wonderfully intimate manner she has of conversing with a friend! Her attention is completely concentrated and dedicated, her face beautiful in every mood, and even when grimacing she shows those shining big teeth. The French restaurant was so quiet we talked in whispers. A fortune-teller had told her: "You haven't had too good a life, but the latter part will be much better," so she believes. She talked of the dread she felt of having to go to a party tonight: she had made the date long before and now couldn't get out of it. She described fully the boredom and embarrassment she would suffer, but never divulged the names of the hosts. For two weeks now I have tried to take her to see Pavel Tchelitchew, and today that, too, was to come about. She didn't seem averse to the visit until we were already in the elevator when she suddenly became fretful and petulant, so I said: "Then let's leave." We went in.

Pavlik—quiet, serious, shy, and very gentle with huge liquid brown eyes and dry pumice-stone complexion. Before showing us his new drawings he warned us, in his crackling Russian accent, that we'd be shocked by them. He explained, with a great panto-mime of trembling jowls, staccato jerks and starts of his arms, and bursting eyeballs, that he was trying to show the transparencies of the human body: the outer cover alone did not interest him. Greta tactfully and tentatively explained why, indeed, his gouaches were a shock to her. "All these veins and muscles are not seen by us, unless in an accident and under some violent condition." Her simplicity and complete lack of pretense helped create a calm and congenial atmosphere, and she enjoyed Pavlik's highly charged conversation—his brilliant similes and inventive noises where words of any specific nationality failed. Pavlik tried to explain how parsimonious nature was: the butterfly, he said, was the first thing to be designed, and the same design is used over and over again in the muscles of man and in many of nature's phenomena.

Greta admired Pavlik's craftmanship as a painter, but she later confessed she found his pictures ugly, and like many Russians of talent, he was lacking in taste: she would have been thrilled to see something being created that was beautiful. It was sad, she said, that she couldn't be emotionally moved by his work.

Later I asked Pavlik what he thought of Greta. Apropos her reaction to his paintings, Pavlik agreed that in her innate honesty there is a great purity, "but the most important thing about her is that she comes out of the memory as if one had last seen her only a half hour ago." He held forth with galvanized gestures. "Her face is so familiar she's like one of the family—like a cousin—because one has suffered and cried with her. There is no surprise on meeting her, for she is without color—in grays. In real life she is as she is in the films—gray and black and white—and she's like that in dreams, for dreams have no color."

_____ Ideal Husband *Birthday Party*/*January 14th, 1948*

My birthday. A croaking voice on the telephone: "Happy birthday to you!" It ended in a long laugh. "Don't I sound like an elderly woman?" I was touched by the punctuality of the call, which was earlier than any she had before made. We laughed about the awfulness of growing old, and she again quoted Shaw about the unmentionable. "Four-fifteen this afternoon—right."

I hurried back from a photographic session that had involved models of all sorts, children, dogs, and a quantity of elaborate props. Soon my bell rang. Grimacing playfully, I put my head around the door and found myself face to face with an elderly messenger bearing an envelope marked express; it was only an invitation to go to Seattle.

Greta arrived late, but when she appeared she was carrying a chocolate cake with one pink candle on it, and a pink Battersea enamel saucer painted with flowers that we had admired on Third Avenue. We talked of the passing of time. She said she had wasted the best years of her life by being so far removed from life. She had always wanted to make a contribution to the world, but had never dreamt that the film work would turn out the way it had: if she had her life over again she would never touch it. It was a terrible punishment that wherever she went in public she was recognized and given no privacy. Fame of that sort had no compensations. She was hounded everywhere except in her own back yard. All those years, in a huge house on North Rockingham Drive in Hollywood, she had seen no one, had lived only in her bedroom. One day she passed through the dining room, and it was covered in a deep layer of dust. She had run her finger over the surface of the table and left a deep line: the servant would be very surprised. She had a housekeeper and a man driver. He paid no attention to her, wasn't interested in anything she did, and was content to wait for hours. He would motor her, in the rainy season during a storm, to the mountains or to the sea. When the entire shore was deserted, she would walk for miles—for an hour and a half or more— and it was soothing to her. When she came back she felt reborn. But she had missed seeing many delightful people and seen little of life. She wished she had been a painter or a writer: she would have liked the fame of an artist, which was independent of the personality. I said I thought she could be a writer, because she has such a sense of words. She smiled, and told me that a man has asked if she would write her biography; of course she wouldn't do a thing like that. "Nobody wants to be bothered with that nonsense: it's of no interest that as a brat I was dressed up to kill trying to get into the cinema."

We cut the cake, drank, danced, and sang. She clicked her heels together and raised her glass: *"Hoch der Kaiser."* Then she must go now and put on her one afternoon dress and prepare her hair for our birthday evening—a dinner for six at Margaret Case's, to be followed by the viewing of Wilde's *Ideal Husband* which I'd decorated for Korda.

Greta tied her hair back in a bow: it looked strange and audacious. She was in tearing spirits and, on arrival at Margaret's, was effervescent, full of fancies, poking private fun at the others. Of course she was the center of adulation. Margaret provided imaginative food, favorite friends, and a birthday cake inscribed: "Cecil, *An Ideal Husband*." Someone made a short speech about the world having been enriched by my presence, and Greta said that was a wonderful thing to hear someone say, that they are grateful that you were born. Later, at the film, when Wilde was expounding the virtues of bachelorhood, Greta laughed. "Does Miss Case agree?" she asked.

It was a curious sensation sitting next to Greta, watching the result of so much forgotten work being presented on the screen of the vast Roxy Theatre. But Wilde's wit was of little consequence and remote to the unsophisticated audience. The fact that Greta was jubilant because it was my birthday was the only thing that mattered.

Snow was falling in tormented gusts. Greta telephoned in high excitement. "It's like the inferno!" She longed to be out in it now. This battle of the elements against human beings thrilled her and drove her wild. In spite of her cold she would like to come over just as soon as she could be dressed. It meant cancelling most of my day's work, but this I did gladly. Unfortunately the storm had abated, and when the sun came out she waved deprecatingly at the windows saying: "Oh, shucks!" Yet she liked the sun, too, in its season—but she really liked best this snow and storm.

Greta paused by the Frigidaire and asked: "May I make inroads upon the privacy of your icebox?" Miss Cleghorn, who looks like a little white barn owl, had provided us with ham, and Greta brought lightly boiled eggs in an old envelope addressed to "the little man." We had an idyllic morning—Greta lying full length on the sofa, rambling on about her particular fads in cooking. "Never boil vegetables; the water you throw away contains the best of the vegetables, and what you eat is the garbage; therefore steam them." "Never fry with butter—it's animal fat and hits you in the chest—it's indigestible; use peanut oil." She always has sweet butter: "Not that old salt stuff that remains in the shop for months on end." I noticed that she did not eat the white of the picnic eggs. "When you hear something about its not being good for you, you are put off; but it must be shaming for you to see others waste— coming from England where food is still short." Miss Cleghorn's ham was criticized by Greta as being too salty: I was surprised. "But then you don't notice food: you're British," said Greta.

After our picnic I set Greta to work drawing with some colored chalks. She started to do a pot of hyacinths, looked very hard at the flowers, and did a quite skillful representation of them. She was rather self-conscious and excited like a ten-year-old, but soon gave up and perpetrated infantile likenesses of myself with a great number of buttons on my suit. Before throwing the drawing block aside she ruthlessly scratched out her efforts, leaving only a careful drawing of a pink walnut as a relic of her talent.

_____ *February 6th*

"Will you have an icebox lunch with me?" I asked her.

"No, I'm going to do some eggs with Mercedes—you come along."

"But shouldn't I telephone to warn her?"

"No—just turn up. Telephone her, of course, if you want to, but it's not necessary."

Greta, on her own, would not tell Mercedes that I, or anyone else, intended coming to see her. Greta will never even say where she is going: it is a sort of phobia. "Tickets have been got . . . ." "A foreign lady has asked me . . . ." etc.

I arrived at Mercedes's to find pandemonium. The maid had walked out and left her mistress, who is completely hopeless at any housewifery, high and dry. Besides, Greta has a paralyzing effect on her best friend, who becomes tactless and silly in the presence of her high priestess. This is a pity, for Mercedes, at her best, is capable of conversing on a wide range of subjects and about a number of interesting people whom she has known intimately. During the course of her romantic life she has dabbled in Oriental religions and undergone many psychic and occult experiences. But today Mercedes became addlepated; so Greta stage-managed the proceedings with a firm hand, bade Mercedes sit quietly while she laid the table, and brought in the repast: fresh butter, brown hulks of bread crusts, red wine, and eggs fragrant with masses of chives.

We talked about the scents and vegetation of California. Greta told entertainingly of her garden exploits—of her sowing grass seed early in the morning so that the neighbors shouldn't see her "waving her arms about like a fairy."

After lunch there was half an hour to spare before my afternoon's work (a commission to make a drawing of a very "difficult" lady), so Greta and I called upon a Mr. Sam Salz, whose name is one to be conjured with in the world of art-dealing. It was a delight to discover with what professional zest Greta was able to converse about his small, but remarkable, collection of modern paintings; she has a quicker eye and much more profound, though less tutored, appreciation than I have. Mr. Salz showed us a Monet of a water garden—a mass of lilies and roses: it could have been appallingly chocolate-boxy, but the authority of the painting produced a *tour de force*. However, it still remained too pretty-pretty for Greta's taste. But another interior by Vuillard, with an old woman reading by a lamp, was a masterpiece and thrilled both of us. Mr. Salz had a most eminent clientele. He showed us pictures that belonged to Jack Warner and to Horowitz. One Renoir was about to be sent off to Gary Cooper who, when he bought it, remarked: "She's quite a girl."

Greta walked as far as my hotel, then went about making definite plans to leave for California, taking some of her possessions to storage and seeing her travel agent.

Dinner with Mercedes/ February 11th, 1948

Mercedes was determined that I should dine with her. I told Greta of my qualms lest Mercedes's curiosity should prompt her to ask embarrassing questions about our intentions. Greta suggested: "Just say 'Now really, Mercedes, you must be nutsky,' or look her straight in the face and say 'I don't know what you're talking about.'"

But the evening was very different from the one imagined: it was I who did the probing. I asked Mercedes about Maud Adams who, when a great stage star, had much of Greta's love of the elusive about her and is now living in a convent; Marie Doro, Isadora Duncan, and Ghandi, all of whom Mercedes knew intimately. I also asked about her remarkable sister, Rita Lydig, who was renowned for being the most extravagant woman of her day, and travelled abroad with seven servants including masseuse and hairdresser. Mercedes insisted rather that her sister had been openhearted and so generous that her financial downfall had been due to such gestures as giving uncut emeralds as presents to the little woman who fitted her dresses and a priceless Persian rug to a violinist who had played for her.

I had known Mrs. Lydig from her Boldini portraits but only met her once when I first came to America nearly twenty years ago. But by then her health had been undermined by drugs, to which she had become addicted after a careless doctor had caused her terrible suffering. By forgetting to turn off an electric pad placed under her while being given an anaesthetic before an operation, he had inflicted upon her such serious burns that they were never to heal. With her teapot-spout nose and black, shining, satin cushion of hair, her pale lips with the "cat after cream" expression, she had the self-confidence of a slightly unbalanced person, and the vast expanse of plump, pearly breast which she exhibited was, at that time, a little alarming. Her patronage of the arts—with a particular taste for music and encouragement of musicians—resulted in her house's being used at all times for rehearsals or concerts. She had a special penchant for the Renaissance, was an expert on Oriental art, and as innovator of fashion wore the first backless evening dress at the opera. Shoes were also one of her passions, and she possessed literally hundreds of pairs made of Elizabethan lace, rare skins, and *quattrocento* velvet, all buckled, often with jewels, made by the genius Jan Torny, who worked only for women he admired. He did not charge them for every pair—each of a different style—but asked for an initial fee of a thousand pounds. After this, he could afford to have the trees made from wood normally used for making violins. When hard-pressed for money, Mrs. Lydig preferred to fill her house with rare white flowers rather than to eat.

It was not until late into the night that Mercedes switched to the topic of Greta, who, she felt, was in a terrible quandary of indecision and whose life was at the crossroads. "Even at the moment Greta cannot decide whether to go back to California, to sell the house there and put herself under the care of Dr. Kling here, or to stay with you in Europe." This latter information came as a surprise. Greta was without any real interests in life;

yet, if she continued for another two years to dicker away valuable, fleeting time, her professional career irrevocably would be at an end.

Greta had always despised Hollywood motion pictures; even her best films, she felt, were lacking in value or quality. Even when Greta was in a strong enough position to dictate to the management, she was miserably unhappy. (When Mercedes drove her to the studio for the opening day's work on *Marie Waleska,* Greta was in tears all the way to Culver City, crying: "This is prostitution.") She would return from the studio most evenings abysmally unhappy and sit alone locked in the cellar. Every scene she shot must be perfect, yet in her estimation she seldom came up to her own standards. For this reason she would never go to see the rushes: they would disappoint and depress her too much. But she was an actress of great temperament, and for her peace of mind she should continue to cultivate her art; it was madness to damn up this natural fount of energy.

Yet whenever any offer for her to reappear is made, a dread comes over her. Recently offers for radio and television have come in shoals, but Greta never even answers these requests. One telegram she showed to "the little man," who said: "Well, I'm sorry, but this is one thing you can't turn down. It only entails a half-hour appearance, and just look what they're going to pay you. You can't afford to turn it down!" "Oh yes, I can. I don't need the money, and nothing on earth would make me do a thing like that for an advertisement."

"But, if she doesn't work, what is there in store for her? What will happen to her in ten years' time? What is her life now? Hunting around Third Avenue shops for junk, waiting for orders from 'the little man.' She has only a handful of friends, and some of those are pretty suspect." Mercedes said that it seemed fated that Greta, the most suspicious person, should often find herself on friendly terms with those least suited to her by temperament. Terrified of being exploited, she was always being victimized. Gaylord Hauser had used her for publicity purposes for his health food campaign. "And look at Stokowski! When they went to Italy together, Greta discovered that he was sending back reports to the American papers about their forthcoming marriage. When she discovered this, she left in a panic for Sweden to go to her sister-in-law, never to set eyes upon the *maestro* again." Mercedes sighed: "If only she'd marry you!"

——————————————————————————— *Friday, February 13th*

Somehow or other I was incapable of hurrying, and, when I arrived at the Tower after luncheon, I was twenty minutes late. I had imagined we were to embark on our customary walk in the park, but Greta was put out because she had been waiting in the hall in order to hurry out to see a Dostoevsky film. I was abject with apologies for my lapse, and Greta said—half, but only half—jokingly: "Shan't trust you any more." This hurt a lot.

A superstitious Irishman earlier had pointed out that today's date was an unfortunate one. When I repeated this to Greta, she admitted that all morning she, like myself, had been overcome by *angst:* we had both felt depressed for no particular reason. Perhaps if two people share a great emotion, however happy, it produces nervous tension—or maybe the exhaustion comes from merely existing in New York.

Bravely we set off in pouring rain—no taxis—and were soaked on arrival at the movie. We sat with wet clothes piled above and beneath us. Spasmodic waves of tenderness submerged me as I watched Greta watching the screen. She looked like a sprite, her face so white and lilylike under the absurd hat—an inverted toadstool. Gérard Philippe, with his pale star-struck eyes, was the perfect Prince Mischkin, but Greta was even more impressed by Edwige Feuillière. "She is a woman of experience; she wears her costumes with great chic; no one else over here has that authority." Film over. Pile on the clothes: mackintosh over the blue coat, the scarf, the woollen gloves, the umbrella. Now to sally forth into the rain again: it was dark outside.

We walked down the street. Like a flash out of the blue "the little man" appeared. He was ill at ease with me, shook hands, but did not speak a word. He seemed very intimate with Greta; she appeared touched at the sudden sight of him. Greta and he would meet five minutes later. Greta smiled sweetly at him before we continued on our way. "Well, that was a surprise," she said. I felt a sort of belated desperation and wanted to destroy everything. For the first time I was almost pleased that our afternoon together was not continuing. The strain, perhaps on both sides, has been unsuccessfully hidden until recently when it rises more often to the surface. Neither Greta nor I are feeling well; we are both tired and, as she said: "Life is already so complicated, why add to the difficulties?" But since, at the moment, I am one of these difficulties, I must continue to fight to make myself part of her life.

We parted with sad smiles. My cold has made me feel sorry for myself, and I would have liked nothing more than to go to bed for days on end. But not even an early evening was possible; I had arranged to go to a play, so had to drag myself out against my will. When, exhausted, I returned late to my room and was heating up some soup over a chafing dish, the telephone bell rang. Greta was in bed, lying in the dark. "All is black—there is just the light of my cigarette burning." "Mascara off?" I asked. "Yes—and I was just thinking that I'd been rather peckish to you this afternoon and wanted to tell you that . . . but I thought that maybe, since you've a cold, and if you were worried, you wouldn't get well so quickly . . . so I thought I'd better tell you." I was touched. I admitted that I felt sad that she hadn't been as nice to me as before and had noticed a sharp tone in her voice. Now I was comforted by her thoughtfulness. "Maybe I don't give you a chance. It isn't a fair deal you get, and maybe . . . ." But she was not allowed to continue. I interrupted: "We are both tired and depressed and ill; tonight nothing we say is going to be of any help. It's no good discussing difficulties, for there's nothing in the world to prevent my being a good friend of yours."

I told her that Korda had arrived in New York and wanted to see me about further projects and how, although he's a nice enough man and chock-full of charm, the thought of working in film studios still torments me. Greta elaborated upon the dread of being part of an enterprise where everything was so often difficult because, with the technical element uppermost, no one could work entirely on his own or do just what he wanted, and when such vast sums were involved everything had to be cut and dried. "If only the work could be done when one feels like it, and on one's own! If you aren't fond of audiences—and I'm not—it's humiliating to have to show off in front of people. I don't even care to act in front of the electricians, and there is such a lot of noise, even in an emotional scene there are men hammering and spitting everywhere. And you have to be so careful! I used to be véry calm and quiet and never allow myself to get involved. But occasionally you want things to be a little better: when I did *Anna Karenina* I spoke to Gibbons, the art director, and showed him books of the period so that the interiors could look more real. But he was too busy and tired doing too many pictures at pressure. And you have to use the velvet glove gently, and I'm tired of using gloves. It's such a waste of energy not to be able to say: 'I want the thing to be done in this way.' It's gruelling, but after all it's wonderful what you can get on celluloid. It's so much vaster than the stage, with thousands of people seen in one shot, and yet much more intimate. You can show everything on that small strip of film; the rhythm of a whole city can be projected on a few inches of celluloid." Greta said that she had often felt that she'd like to be a director and put on the screen some of the things she had been impressed by: the strange groups that people naturally fall into—not just the conventional line-up that fills the screens today: "Negro feet dancing, trees moving, clouds passing in front of the sun."

Perhaps, after all, Greta will embark on acting in a film, but after eight years it is hard to start again. "But if I could be given a picture like *The Idiot* to do—I'd go back!"

We had dinner in the night club of my hotel. The small orchestra played rhythmically: I asked for "If I Loved You" and "People Will Say We're In Love." I longed to dance. I considered that Greta's woollen clothes would have put to shame the other women in their gaudy glad rags, but I do admit that her galoshes over large boots would have looked curious on the polished floor.

Part of the silence of two years was broken when Greta confessed that she had received flowers from me in Sweden during the time of our "rupture." "Beautiful flowers, they were," she said. This news made me glad. She also let fall the fact that her trip to Sweden had been ruined by the newspapers. "They have assumed the vulgarity of America," she said, "and I had a horrible experience there." But I was not foolish enough to ask what it had been.

Greta was more put out than I was when the waiter rooked me at the end of the evening. By taking my "thank you" as an excuse for not giving me any change from the money I proffered to pay the bill, he pocketed an outrageously oversize tip.

_____ *February, 1948*

Before Korda had time to tell me what he had in mind for me to work on, I suggested he should do Jean Cocteau's play about Elizabeth of Austria, *The Eagle with Two Heads*, with Greta in the role of Elizabeth. He was fired with enthusiasm. "We do it right away in Shepperton in June. We shoot some of it in the Tyrol. We get any director she wants. But I don't want any vagueness. She must sign if I'm going to spend time on the project!" I saw before me a whole new vista with Greta in England.

I telephoned in great excitement to tell her the news. She was very quiet. "All right—I'll have to think about it. I can't think about it now—I'm too tired—but I'll consider it in the morning." Korda telephoned her twice. "Come and see me this afternoon." Greta complied, bringing "the little man" with her. Everything went well. They were more or less decided they would make the picture. Greta would come to England for the studio work. A lot of telephoning back and forth about a director. Such sudden activity that Greta, who was supposed to leave for California, delayed her departure by another week: such excitement that she'd not been able to sleep. However, she was convinced, this time, that the picture would be made. Greta said: "I saw the play in all its wretchedness with Tallulah Bankhead, and I know there's nothing that can't be fixed. I'll do it, but I've got to start preparing, getting fit right away, coaxing my body back in shape, exercising my arms, and if I'm going to wear *décolletage* there's a lot to arrange. Yes, I know I'm going to do this film—I feel it. I've never been as close to anything before."

We sat on the red sofa in my room, eating hard-boiled eggs, toast, and avocado from the refrigerator. Greta asked me questions about how she would live in England. Where was the studio? Could she rent a small house nearby in order to take long walks in the evenings? It was good that in Hollywood, after the searing lights in the studios, you could get out into the clean sunlight and walk and breathe in fresh air. She wouldn't want to live in a town while working. She wouldn't be able to see anyone while on the job; she always gave herself entirely to the project— never saw anyone. We talked of Korda and the possibilities of the cast and crew, and we were suddenly just as matter of fact as two businessmen. Greta telephoned Korda. "It is bad when the Empress tries to work her lover up to kill her by slanging at him like a fishwife. It should be done like an Empress." Greta has been thinking a great deal about the part.

Then she talked of her imminent return to California. "I know I musn't see any human beings for several days when I get back there. I must rest a lot and be alone." However, "the little man" was in all Greta's future plans; he seemed to have proprietary rights over her. It worried me and made me jealous and irritable.

Of all things! Greta was going to a Broadway opening night! Her erstwhile agent, Leland Hayward, had bullied her by saying: "I've always been working for you—now you can do something for me." At the thirteenth hour I was determined also to go to this dreary play about sex-starved sailors in the Pacific called *Mr. Roberts* and to have a bit of fun watching her. I managed to get a single ticket in the third row. For added amusement I took my glasses so that we perhaps could repeat an earlier occasion when, at the film *Cleopatra,* I had put them on as a tease, and she had stared at me across the theatre almost as much as at the screen. It was the only time she had ever seen me wearing glasses and it had intrigued her; two years later she had asked why I had never worn them since.

I looked around the crowded theatre to find the familiar hat that would be hiding the familiar features, but it was nowhere to be seen in the huge mob in the bulk of the stalls. I then remembered she always likes to be very near the stage, and there, sure enough, in the front row, staring basilisklike at me, was her companion, "the little man." When I saw her next to him, my heart stopped. In the intimacy of my room I have become accustomed to the beauty of this face with bedraggled hair, or an old

dark blue hat pulled down low onto her eyes. But this evening
she appeared to me quite different. The onslaught was overwhelming. She had found a sort of skull-cap of black which hid
her hair entirely: over this she wore a medieval hood which
framed her face. I had never seen her appear more striking.
The carving of her head was much more beautiful than it ever
was in her youth, and the expression on her face had such compassion and nobility, yet somehow she retained the unexpected-
ness of fantasy.

With such an apparition in the audience it was impossible to
keep one's eyes directed towards the squalid naval rantings on the
stage. Although to her I must have seemed a needle in a hay-
stack, she spent a great deal of her time looking at me. With my
head cocked at an odd angle so as to give the impression that I
was unable to see her, I spent most of the evening glancing at
her. Occasionally we indulged in the dangerous game of staring
full face at one another. Only when I imagined her companion
might become conscious of this other interest did I hide my face
from his view behind the heads of the people sitting between us.

I came home wondering if she would telephone. I knew she
would be thinking about me—perhaps struggling not to call me.
Then I became truly worried and wondered if perhaps "the
little man," inspired by our chance encounter, had insisted that
she must not go on seeing me. But I put down the darkness of
this passing cloud to exhaustion and ill health. Tonight this
most beautiful creature had once more appeared as a stranger.
Yet, in more lucid moments, I could not but feel proud that her
glances had been for me, and that of all the people in the theatre
I had been the one who was occupying her mind. But the telephone did not ring. After I had fought in vain for over an hour
to lose consciousness I turned on the bedside light.

At one o'clock in the morning, just as I was about to close my
book, the telephone rang. Her sad voice told me: "I've been
lying here in the dark and can't go to sleep. I've had a wretched
time, and I've some very sad news for you." My heart turned
over—my stomach pained me. "But *how* sad? Is it serious for you,
or for me?" She said it was not serious, but she could not talk
about it on the telephone. I surmised that she had had long, unhappy discussions with "the little man," and she said: "I'm afraid

you must not make those arrangements to come to California." My heart sank. "What right has he to monopolize your life? He cannot complain if you have other plans—other friends. He has another life apart from the one with you." "That's not so easy to say to him, but I can't talk over the telephone." "But," I said, "I can't survive your disappearing again—as you did before." She would explain the situation tomorrow: we must meet during the day, and she promised to dine as well. Perhaps she exaggerates the gravity of the situation?

Yet I was most distressed and unable to sleep, imagining her also lying awake in the dark. But the tone of her voice and her endearments comforted me, for she had said, quite simply and honestly, that we loved each other, and that there was nothing to blame me for.

I rang at ten-fifteen in the morning and, alas, woke her from a deep sleep. She had not been able to drop off till so late that now she was breaking all rules by dozing on after 8 A.M. She suggested we meet after lunch for a long walk.

Dirty, smut-dotted snow was still on the ground. We were both sad and silent, our spirits low, and I had the feeling of dread that something violent would happen. But, meanwhile, an effort must be made to be gay. Suddenly we met Mona taking the icy air. She looked forlorn and lonely, I thought, but maybe that is because one is not accustomed to seeing her by herself. Mona shot me a look that conveyed a world of meaning before we marched off in different directions. On returning to the Plaza, past the line of anachronistic hansom cabs, and up the marble steps, we went on the spur of the moment, into the Palm Court. Here we ordered tea. Often when hurrying to my room, probably late and most likely anguished, I had noticed the elderly ladies who, in a manner so untypical of New York, sat listening nostalgically to "Vilia" and "Under the Deodar" played by an old-fashioned string orchestra. Often before I had wished that there had been time and leisure to enjoy this palm-treed oasis. Now, however, our mood was not as serene as the scene around us, for Greta, very sadly and haltingly, tried to tell me about the "tricky subject." It seems that her companion had lately felt that there were all sorts of vibrations and nuances in the air that he cannot quite make out. "What's going on?" he asks. She had answered: "Nothing," but he insists she is bored and restless, and doesn't want to do the things she used to do. Without mentioning me, last night the companion must have made a painful scene. "I don't talk about him," Greta said, "because there are people who talk about things and those who don't, and I belong to the latter category. I wouldn't talk about you either."

"The little man" instinctively feels that there is something more than mere acquaintanceship in our relationship, and it worries him. The fact that Greta never mentions my name makes it worse, but she confesses: "I just can't bring myself to mention your name—it sticks in my throat, and he senses something that is never mentioned." Suddenly she said: "I'm afraid he feels very bitter towards you." I remonstrated. "It's understandable," she said. "You'd be the same. Before you came along I never used to go out anywhere: now he knows I see you and he's worried. He's been such a good friend to me, none better. He's an adorable being if you really get to know him. After four years of devoting his life to me, he has become very unhappy. I hate to make anyone feel sad, but it's difficult—life is difficult."

"But he has made *me* unhappy. You even came to London with him and left without once letting me see you. Then that whole year of silence was a gnawing agony for me."

"But you've made him unhappy too. All during that year, and during the trip to Europe, he sensed there was something there."

This was a revelation to me. I did not realize fully that the war between him and me had been waged for a year and a half. Perhaps I should have read the danger signal when he told Margaret Case that he had made a great mistake in ever letting Greta meet me again, and said: "I can do him great harm."

Greta continued: "If it were to come to a showdown now it would be too bad, but if you like to wait, who knows what might happen? Some day, perhaps, round some corner . . . .? But it's no good forcing any decision, and you mustn't come to Hollywood," she sighed.

"What's to prevent me if I come on legitimate business? If I come to discuss plans with Hitchcock?"

She gave me an Asiatic wink. "Then I couldn't prevent you doing that." And we both smiled and felt much relieved. Suddenly our spirits revived.

Out next morning on my daily business, I realized I had not made my customary telephone call. Returning after lunch a message read: "Mr. Thompson telephoned." An hour later Mr. Thompson called again, a rather sad Mr. Thompson, in bed with a hot water bottle and feeling "downtrodden." We talked of the immediate film projects. "I wondered if perhaps you might like to come and see me tomorrow, and bring with you photographs of the Empress Elizabeth?" I complained of being in a rather dreary mood and said I thought perhaps I might sail back to England with Korda. It was best not to let her know I definitely intended to follow her to Hollywood.

When I rang the bell her door opened two inches and one painted eye appeared. Then, playfully, the door was shut again. Often when I come into a room where I know her to be, she is nowhere; each time she opens her door she secretes herself behind it. Today she had been thinking about her proposed journey to England. What would be the food situation there? Was there still rationing? Could she find fresh butter? And new baked wholemeal bread? She had many qualms.

We looked at engravings of the Empress Elizabeth and, in her liquid voice with its rich, dark tones and the pristine relish of each separate syllable, Greta made observations about the Empress and her clothes. "Look at the line of neck ("naickke")—how straight she holds her head back on the shoulders. You see she wears the necklace short; I don't like them when they hang loose on the chest." "What is lovely is that wide crown—how chic!" ("cheeeacke") Then she put the book down, and mused about her past in the studios.

"I never had a hair stylist, just one girl. We used to do the shapes together; we'd look at pictures and see if they would suit the face. And then I never had anyone touch my face. I did it myself (I wonder if I've forgotten how it should be?)—and no tests, except for lighting—I hate tests. What looks good to the eye looks well on the screen. If a dress doesn't seem right in life, then the screen isn't going to make an ugly duckling into a swan. Then I don't like to work for months on the film before shooting. I don't want to go to the studio except when I'm necessary; I'm not one who must be performing in front of a camera in order to feel good. I don't want to be bored, and the only way I can preserve what I've got to give the screen is to save my energies for my appearance before the cameras ("kahrmerrahs"). There never was a harder worker than I; I never entertained or saw visitors; I never gave any trouble ("trrubble"). I was just there waiting for anybody who wanted me. If I were to write my own dialogue, I'd need more time and experience than I have to give to it, but then I'd have to be on the other side of the camera. As it is, I am the one who is in front of it. The others can make their mistakes, but it is I who am being made a fool of. When I'm working I'm not a nuisance to anybody. But I must work in my own way—if I don't, then I'm sunk. The last film I made was my downfall because I allowed myself to work differently in many ways."

Then, suddenly, Greta became visibly appalled at the idea of making any more pictures. "It never pleased me to act all the time. In fact, I tried to make only one picture every two years so that for months on end I could go to Sweden, or walk in the mountains, and not think about motion pictures." The memory of the fifteen years of anguish overwhelmed her. I knew that if she did come to England, and started to work with Korda, there would be difficulties—and I, for one, would be in for a harrowing time. But it would be worth a great deal if I could help her to give a work of art to the world.

Suddenly the telephone rang—the sound went through us like a pistol shot. It was my rival. He was sorry, but he would have to take his wife to a first night tonight. I, too, was going to the first night with my friend, Leonora Corbett.[1] "Wouldn't you like to come and sit with me while I have my supper at Mercedes's?" This was Greta's preliminary step in a concerted attempt to make me break my theatre date with Leonora. I laughed. "You know it would be impossible to chuck at this late hour. Imagine Leonora's fury!" However, on my way to collect Leonora, I did go to see Greta and Mercedes and found them both in a very giggly mood, indulging in banter and double entendres. By now Greta, by every device possible, was trying to force me to stay and have dinner with them in order to be late for Leonora. Greta pretended that she had never seen me

---

[1] The delightful comedienne, a most witty and entertaining companion, and perhaps one of the last of the *grandes cocottes*.

before in a dinner jacket, that she did not know I had this, or liked that, etc. She kept winking at me and indulging in a pantomime of our being comparative strangers.

I left for Leonora and the theatre. During the first act I thought perhaps Greta would now be feeling lonely back in her hotel rooms, so in the first interval I would telephone. It took some time to find a phone booth, and when I did, I had to wait outside for it was occupied. Why the hell was the occupant in there so long? I nearly banged on the closed door. At last he came out. It was my rival. He had obviously just been telephoning to Greta. We made polite conversation about the play and praised the impeccable charm of Gertie Lawrence. Then I went into the kiosk and, roaring with laughter, put in my nickel. Then more laughter as I explained to her that I had followed "the little man" into the box. She was in good spirits, and, after certain badinage, thanked me for my sweet thought in calling. I wondered if she had said the same to "the little man"? But realizing that he hurries to the telephone on every occasion, as is my wont, and that he has probably done this for years, gives me an indication of how dreadfully devoted he must be; he is something serious to have to contend with.

A really tough battle is on.

_____ *February, 1948*

Reading two biographies of the Empress Elizabeth, I realize how, temperamentally, she and Greta resemble one another in many ways. The Empress and the actress are both abnormally shy and inwardly trembling with nerves. Both invent ways of hiding from the public, travel incognito, and, when cornered, become like wild deer trying to escape. Both are faddists about diet, and paranoid about the approach of middle age (the Empress hiding behind her fan, even in the hunting field, Garbo behind her brimmed hat and dark glasses). Both enjoy exaggerating the seriousness of their ailments. Each lives a part of her life in a world of dreams and fantasies; each has her own eccentricities — so baffling to more ordinary people. Both are at their happiest out-of-doors and enjoy walking in the rain. Both have a love of the simple and the impromptu and an overwhelming charm that puts everyone at ease.

Today the second Empress arrived wearing very tatty old clothes, her hair uncombed, her marble face cold. Ill with a sore throat, I had stayed in bed with a scarf around my neck, but had placed a bottle of iced vodka on the counterpane for my visitor. "You look like the King of Sweden," she said. "Not, I trust, the present King who is eighty or ninety?" "No, the King of Sweden who had a white wig, a taste for everything elegant, and surrounded his court—not with hulking great Swedes—with French people. Eventually he was assassinated in his box at the opera."

Greta leaves on Tuesday for Hollywood, and for three days on the train she will not move out of her compartment. "No, please don't send me a telegram! I'd be terrified: I would have to open the door to the attendant. I don't wish to go back to California, but I must get rid of that house—I don't want it any more. Yet it's rather frightening to think that that is all I possess in the world. I have no belongings, I have no trace of my existence: no papers, no love letters, no relics involving any human beings."

As always, time went by too quickly as we talked, and she was late for dinner with her companion. Painting her lips, she said: "I despair having to put on this war paint and these horrible shoes which distort my toes. Oh, I resent going out to restaurants when I look so tired!" "But you don't look tired!" "I can see—you can't fool me. I know how I look!" she said bitterly.

February, 1948

Monday was like Sunday on account of the Washington's Birthday holiday. Greta leaves tomorrow. She abandoned her packing in order to arrive with a picnic lunch. She had boiled the usual four eggs of which I ate the whites of hers as well as my own share. My icebox provided the et ceteras. She would not be precise about plans, but warned me against coming to California; but, secretly, I am glad she is leaving New York and the present stalemate. "The little man" usurps much of her leisure and always seems to have priority; perhaps his tentacles do not stretch as far as California.

Our good-bye was not sad for it was more an *au revoir.*
Nevertheless, we lingered a long time at the back of the door,
then she waited several seconds for a long, final look at my
hotel rooms before hurrying down the iron stairs marked "Exit,"
her face white with a wide, bright smile and mad, bright eyes.

A moment after I returned from a movie the telephone rang.
"Have you put the light out?" I asked.
"No, not yet."
"Have you still got your mascara on?"
"No, I am scrubbed: I am a clean boy," she said.
I said how happy I had been this winter. My heart broke to
hear her say: "It has been very sweet, hasn't it?"
"There's so much we haven't had time for—to go to that
Chinese restaurant, to pay a call on Mister Molnar and ask him
to tell risqué stories, to pay a visit to the registrar . . . ."
"Stop! Stop! If we go on talking like this, I will think too much
about it and won't be able to sleep."

Next morning typewriter, telephones, "busyness." "Mr. Thomp-
son" on the telephone:
"I just called because I've been out somewhere and thought
maybe you'd called. I just wanted to say good luck, and thank
you."
"But is this the last time? Couldn't I ring this afternoon?
Couldn't you ring me?"
"Well, it would only be to say good luck again and then run."
"It's terribly sad, but maybe it won't be for long—maybe
I'll fly out to the coast to see you."
Laughing: "Oh, no!"
"But if I come vaulting over the garden wall, won't you receive
me?"
"Just once or twice maybe, but you had better not."
"Well, I really ought to see Mr. Hitchcock. . . . Well, thank
you for everything. Be a good girl, and don't bawl out your
neighbors. Good-bye!"

Part 8

CALIFORNIAN FAREWELL
1948

To consolidate my winter's conquest, and perhaps bring it nearer to permanence, I knew I should see her in her own home.
I must be able to spend the days uninterruptedly with her,
staying from morning until bedtime without her looking at
her watch and saying: "Got to go now." It would be best not
to ask her specifically if I should join her in California, for she
did not wish to make the decision or to assume any responsibility.
I sent her vague telegrams. I waited until the last moment to
telephone to gauge whether she really wanted me to take an
airplane; it was obvious that she did. Plans were made in a jiffy.
With what relish I dismantled my expensive hotel rooms, and
packed just one bag for my *embarquement* to Cythera!

   With ticket in my pocket, the old fears at the prospect of
taking flight asserted themselves—a legacy of the air crash
during the war. Eugene, the waiter, did not make matters
easier by saying: "I hate to see people fly—it's so dangerous;
there are many accidents at this time of the year." He looked out
at the stormy skies.

   For long periods during the trip I was afflicted with spasms
of terror; I could not doze. The genteel stewardess came round
smiling like an ogress: "Would you kindly fasten your seat
belts; we are expecting a little turbulence." The palms of my
hands and my scalp were sweating on arrival in Los Angeles,
but I had survived.

   After the shortage in London and Paris it was a happy event
to find a taxi to drive me from the airport and, luckier still, to
find a room available in a bungalow of the Beverly Hills that was
reserved for transients of MGM. It was too late to telephone
Greta so I went immediately to bed. During my sleep I dreamed
that perhaps she would not be as welcoming as I wanted, or that

"the little man" would hear of my departure from New York and come out in hot pursuit.

I awoke early. The Venetian blinds were slatted with diamond brightness. I let in the sun: the sky was brilliantly blue. To be here after the blizzards of New York was almost too great a contrast. I relished the rare treat of a large orange juice and egg and bacon breakfast. I telephoned. A very cheery voice replied: "I've been waiting for you—been up since early and, oh, so busy! I'll fetch you in twenty minutes. I've got to start up the buggy and sometimes she doesn't go. Meet me down by the road where the bus stops outside your hotel."

When, in the thirties, I first came to the capital of the movie world, my dream was to make the acquaintance of its greatest star. I left without as much as a glimpse. On my second visit I did manage—on that evening that will never pale—to meet her. Now, after all these years, I was about to enter her house as an intimate friend and I would see her in a new guise, leading another life from the one we had known together in New York.

Wearing my lightweight flannel suit and feeling very spruce, I waited. I was scrutinizing a palm tree and watching some small, dusty birds high up in its branches when I realized a car had driven up and an intense, rather strained face was leaning forward and bidding me jump in. My heart gave one leap as I recognized the familiar features. Her hair was hanging in thick curls; she wore trousers and a jersey. We were on the way.

She, a little nervous, said: "It's 'the Dragon's' day out, but I don't know if she'll have gone yet, so let's just drive about a bit before we go into the house. But when we *do* go in, you're not to look! Promise to put on blinkers! I'm ashamed: it's awful— so obnoxious, and not as it should be. Now I'm lost—I don't know where we are."

"Well, it's down that way. We turn off here, Benedict Canyon, and it's there." I remembered ferreting out her house that night in her absence.

"Imagine that I've been here six years, and that you have to direct the way!"

The little buggy, champagne or dove-colored, turned an abrupt corner. We drove under a garage roof, and the white secret door was unlocked. Expecting little, I was delighted to find myself in a pretty white-walled garden filled with sun and geraniums, everything neat and orderly: a large sun divan, covered with a white sheet, a huge umbrella, white garden furniture.

"Here, I don't expect you've had orange juice—take this." I was as exultant as when I had been a boy on holiday. "Now, you're not to look inside."

"Not even a peep? I spy a baroque angel hanging on a wall."

"Close your eyes. You see, in a way I'm a perfectionist, and this is far beneath what I would like it to be. But during the war you couldn't get anything done, and now I may sell the place. Everything's unsettled, so I feel—oh heck! let it go—what's the use?"

But I have discovered that always Greta is apt to decry anything merely because it is hers. I found out later that she works in her garden a great deal, and not only does she tend the borders herself, but the Japanese gardener is permitted to work only on the front garden and is not given entrance to this, her hidden sanctum. In fact, she had been mending the fence around her lawn. Often she works at it the whole day, quite naked, but she discovered that people could peer through the fence. She had bought some wood with which to fill the gaps, but it was the wrong kind and had done the job badly!

"It's hot in the sun: I'll get you some bathing shorts."

Greta smoked an Old Gold as she lay back in a pair of tight white trunks and a brassière. We watched the humming birds in the trees and the blue jays, and I relished every detail that was part of this entourage. We lay back, wallowing in sunny happiness. We were both in such a good mood. She was glad I had come.

"So you came all this way to see me—or did you come to see Mister Hitchcock?"

"Nothing in the world would ever induce me to go and see him."

She looked shocked and delighted. "I was determined not to ask you to come," she said, "but when you telephoned I was on the point of sending you a telegram. Suddenly I get so restless." In the brilliant light her beauty was finer and more delicate than one could have imagined: the skin of a polished flawlessness, the eyelashes like a peacock's tail. She looked furtively toward the servants' quarters. "I wonder if 'the Dragon' has gone yet?" She went to a door and listened with an expression of fear on her face. It is obvious that she does not know how to handle servants and that "the Dragon" holds her in terror.

"When may I meet 'the Dragon'? So often I've heard her sad voice on the telephone."

"Not today—tomorrow, maybe, she'll give us dinner."

By degrees, I was allowed to see the house. In the sitting room—a large comfortable place with huge sofas and a lot of color—there were Impressionist paintings, two Renoirs, a Modigliani, a Rouault and, best of all, a most touching, tender, appealing still life by Bonnard of a jug of poppies and meadowsweet. Again Greta deprecated the pictures. "I bought them as investments before I knew anything much about painting. They're rather boring ones, I think." She said she wished the Impressionists had not been so *bourgeois:* the objects they painted were in poor taste and their flowers coarse. Here were her bookshelves, the cupboards with the tennis racquets and the old mackintoshes, the pad with the telephone numbers written in her square, capital lettering. So this was where "the *Divina*" lived.

We walked down a long stone corridor, named by her "the Pullman," to the kitchen. This consisted of two immaculate rooms in which trays were laid out. I was not allowed to take any active part in her preparations for an early lunch of salad, matzoh biscuits and milk. Each brought a tray out into the sun. Blue jays came down from the trees and ate out of Greta's hand. It was enchanting.

Greta enumerated the joys of California. "Living here I have everything. It's an easy life. You'd go mad in California, I know—you'd mind the lack of entertainment—but I like it well enough." A friend of hers considers it unhealthy because the bugs and insects never die. They just lie underground in winter, and go on multiplying, so that soon the whole place will be overrun by them. "See how I've been stung when working among the oleanders!" Her hands were blistered. I told her that, from experience, I knew it was easy to catch a bad cold at sundown, or become stricken with acute laryngitis. "But where today, except in Tahiti, could you lead such a healthy life? And for your work—you're quite undisturbed, and when the day's over in the studio, you can go for long walks in the mountains and by the ocean. There's so much sun, everything grows, and you can be out of doors all the time — I'm never inside."

Here we were absolutely remote from the world, with nothing to disturb us. I basked in drowsy sensuousness, and soon was asleep.

We must go down to the sea. The preparations against the sudden chill of a Californian late afternoon were hilarious as we shared the intimacy of the dressing-room and bathroom. I was rigged out in borrowed corduroy pants, several sweaters, and, on top, a brown windbreaker. Greta was almost similarly dressed. We set off for Santa Monica.

Again I was driving along these familiar landmarks of avenues fringed with palm trees, of suburban mansions with sprinklers whirling over the coarse, too-green grass, past fruit and flower stalls, and whimsical ice-cream parlors, past poor little shacks and enormous advertisement displays. Again I remembered how, on earlier visits, the imperviousness of this woman in the car beside me had managed to transcend this vulgar, venal place. Now that she has retired from the screen and her face is no longer magnified a thousandfold on the hoardings, I felt an extraordinary pride in the fact that this private person, sitting at the wheel, had been the empress of the motion picture industry. She had given the films a luster just as now, by her vivid presence, she warmed our journey with a touch of the sublime.

At last, beyond the hot-dog stands and the bathing shacks, the stretch of shore became deserted, and the "buggy" was parked by a certain white wooden hut where it had been parked many hundreds of times before. We set out along the sand where she had walked many hundreds of times, in all weathers, including the driving downpours of the rainy season. We set off with incredible zest, health, and vitality, climbing over breakwaters and rocks, and running after the seagulls and pelicans, then wrestling with one another, and suddenly going into amorous clinches. We walked for many miles unseen by any eyes and when, at last, we felt the need of a drink we came across a Coca-Cola booth wherein to quench our thirst. Refreshed, we returned to the shore and again started wrestling, to find that a group of delighted roughnecks were watching from the booth.

Greta was very acrobatic and, finding a certain iron framework from a deserted swing, did a number of spectacular exercises. She is in Olympic trim, and goes through an elaborate ritual of training every day. Her body is that of a seventeen-year-old girl—lithe, strong, and supple. It is no doubt the Scandinavian in her that makes her so mindful of health.

Further along the shore there were gatherings of sea birds. As we approached they would take to the air in a dark, hovering cloud. But occasionally one bird would be left behind and, terri-fied, would run from us with a broken wing trailing. Greta was deeply upset by the sight. "Oh, the misery! It knows it is going to die—the others will peck it to death. That is the law of nature—the sick are outcast and doomed—and there is nothing that we can do." We watched a small, dishevelled, black-headed gull on which the cruel birds had started, and it was wretched to see it awaiting its inevitable end. Further along we watched another tragedy of impending death: a bird caught by a wave could not defend itself and was knocked about helplessly. Greta said: "I've seen it so often. We can only try not to frighten it: that is all we could ask if we were in that predicament—but I wish I could give it a fish."

Occasionally on our long walk we would see lovers clasped in each other's arms in their parked cars or lying on the rocks. We noticed one young and respectable couple having a picnic tea. On the return journey we saw a man nearby busily building a sand castle by a breakwater. "What a strange occupation for a grown-up person!" As we watched him he patted his castle with tremendous intensity of purpose. We climbed the breakwater. On the other side we saw the young picnicking couple now flushed and asleep under a rug, and Greta realized in a flash (not I!) that the man had been spying on the couple as they made love. Greta told me of a man she knew whose one pleasure was to stalk lovers.

Nearing the motor she sang boisterously and invented some dialogue as if she were a tough guy making me a proposition. It was done with such realism, and her ear is so exact, that I felt maybe she could have been a dramatist. I was also surprised to discover how many aspects of life she knows about. One would have thought perhaps she was a little remote in her ivory tower, but she is ready to appreciate all types, and this tough guy was utterly realistic and rather frightening.

She sat on some wooden steps scraping the tar, washed up by

the sea, off the soles of my shoes. "If it gets on the carpets it's obnoxious." Then suddenly, as if about to make some profound definition about life, she said: "I can't think quite what to do for dinner — whether to take you out to a little Italian place and look into your eyes, or whether to give you something at home." The latter was happily decided upon.

I watched, spellbound, as if she were performing an act of legerdemain, as Greta prepared lamb chops and vegetables in a steam dish. Outside it was suddenly dark and soon extremely cold: the house became an icebox. "We must have some heating, however much you dislike it," she said. The installation had not previously been turned on this year, so the rooms were filled with a stale smell of burnt metal that was the same as when the old magic-lantern let off its fumes in the nursery. The dinner, however, was good and hot, and was enjoyed sitting on a cedar-colored sofa under the Bonnard.

A noise of dry leaves scraping together was heard from outside in the alley. Like a frightened animal Greta was on the alert, then in a flash was peering through the slats of the blinds. This was a most pathetic sight, for she spends hours at the windows trying to see if anyone is about. Ever since her house was burgled, her nerve has gone, and she is in a bad state of restlessness. We went through the empty rooms to see that no one was hiding in them. Now I was allowed to see the series of rooms that are unfurnished, the store room, dining room, drawing room, the suites of vacant rooms. Yes, the house is much too large for her. Having peered in all nooks and crannies I convinced her that all was well.

It was still quite early, according to most people's timetable, when Greta said good night to me at her front door. I waved to her in the dark. Walking around her garden walls on my way home, I looked up to see her peering from her bedroom window through the Venetian blinds.

_____ *March 4th*

Early morning was again brilliant in her garden, and she said: "You've no idea how lucky you are — you brought the sun with you." Now, exhausted, she relaxes on the sofa with a cigarette and describes the chores that she has done since dawn, when she has been clearing up the undergrowth and digging strenuously in her garden. "Once I cut down an enormous bougainvillea that covered the entire wall. It lay all over the lawn, and I had to cut it up in small pieces and cart it away, and it took days to tidy up afterwards. Sometimes when there are rough jobs to do, like sawing, and there's a big branch on that tree that is so tempting—oh my, my!—I get up before anyone is awake. I once took a ladder out into the alleyway at five o'clock in the morning. I had on no mascara, and the most wild-looking clothes imaginable, and I started to saw away a huge tree, and as I was at the job a man came along with a dog. I trembled—oh, I trembled!—in case he would come up and talk to me. But I kept right on, and mercifully he continued down the alley, but I noticed he turned round to stare and I dare say he had anxieties about my sanity. I am always busy here, there's always such a lot to do. I work like a slave, and it's so hard keeping in trim and getting limbered up."

She then demonstrated some Yoga exercises that she had taught herself from a book, and which left her quite sweating and exhausted. Again she lay down and relaxed and talked about restarting her film career, and of Mrs. Viertel's[1] contribution to her former pictures. "If there was ever any argument about a script I always had this woman to fight for me. She was indefatigable and worked on them to saturation point and always found something good that others would not bother about. If only I could have her around on *The Eagle* I should feel so much more secure! (I shall try to arrange it.) And please send a cable to Korda asking for the script." We discussed the conditions of working on screenplays in England, and I minimized the difficulties. I was pleased and excited to see how strongly G. was convinced that she would be making the picture.

As we lay basking in the sun I watched the contours of her face and noticed that the little lump at the bridge of her nose, which I had seen in her photographs, is of cartilage and not bone: she had never known that it was there. I asked why she had always worn this heavy eye make-up, and she answered: "Because I am an

---

[1] Salka Viertel, scenario writer for many Hollywood films and wife of the film director.

Oriental." She explained that only in the last six years had she worn lipstick: "Because my lips became so thin and pale, but I despise lipstick—it's messy and degrading! But oh, what's the use—I look so pinched and pale! I couldn't sleep very well last night. I kept hearing noises in the alleyway as if someone were working there. I tried in vain to see anyone, but the noises went on all night, and I thought 'He can't be working all night.' It was a sound as if someone was dumping some metal objects on the ground." Even as we lay in the sun I could, from time to time, hear this metal clinking. I could not imagine at all what it might be, but I must discover. It's hard that Greta should be kept awake when sleep is so rare and precious to her.

We decided to go to the Farmers' Market. Greta, adding to her mascara and looking sadly into the mirror, said "Oh, I look so ugly!"

On the way she told me of her difficulty in driving the car: she is scared of parking and, since she finds it hard to choose a suitable place, drives around and around. Once she was in a great predicament. Having run out of paint while painting her garage, she stepped into the buggy in her filthy shorts to buy some more tins. When she parked the car it was in an isolated spot, but on returning to it with the paint cans, other cars had parked close, both front and back, to hers. She was appalled. She tried to get out, but in vain. Her heart beat, she panicked. She jumped out of the car and started to walk for miles. Should she call Harry Crocker and get him to help her? At that moment her friends, the Reginald Gardiners, appeared. "How are you?" they asked conversationally. "Oh, I'm in terrible trouble." "No, not really? How bad?" When she told them, they roared with laughter and came to her rescue.

Greta knows her way about Hollywood only sketchily, and is in a constant state of anxiety about being nabbed by the police or submitted to the public gaze. But the Farmers' Market is one of the places that she feels she can find—though not without difficulties, as it turned out. However, we were both in such good spirits that a few reversals were quite comic, and with me to ask the way of passers-by, she eventually managed to find our goal. At the market Greta showed an interest in the kitchen utensils and stainless steel but, as usual, preferred to look rather than buy. She hates to be hurried into a purchase and will return many times to make her decision before getting landed. For myself it is just the opposite, so that I have respect for her conscientiousness. The stalls of fragrant fruit, the preserved fruits and sweets looking like mounds of precious stones, the inviting cooked-food stalls, were all highly-colored and appetizing. There was one particular Spanish counter that made the juices run, but we had already eaten our lunch under an umbrella, and jolly good it was too, of mixed salad and prawns and chicken. Suddenly we were confronted by an English spinster—none other than the redoubtable Phillis Wilbourn, Constance Collier's saintlike companion, secretary, and "Man Friday." Phillis pointed to where her beloved mistress was sitting, an imposing Roman empress in yellow, musing under a sunshade. When Greta stole up and kissed Constance Collier from behind, Constance exclaimed: "I thought I must be mad!" Constance remembered a time when I had told her how unhappy I was that Greta and I were no longer friends. Now she saw us together again and she was delighted; to Greta's intense surprise she said: "Why don't you two settle down?" In reply Greta ruined my reputation by saying: "But you don't think he's that sort of man, do you?" Phillis led the laughter. Greta asked questions about postwar conditions in England, and Constance said all the wrong things but one: "I came away ill from undernourishment, and life is very hard there, but, nevertheless, it's life, it's vital, and I want to go back. It's ruined me for this place—this," waving her sunshade, "is stagnation."

We pottered about the market until it was time for our planned walk in the mountains. While Greta again changed her clothes in the dressing room, I went out onto the balcony of her bedroom determined to discover the noise that had kept her awake. I could still hear, from time to time, the metal click that reverberated against the walls of the house. It was quite loud even in daylight, but at night time it must seem doubly so. I listened. There it goes—this time a double click of metal. By degrees I realized that the noise came from Sunset Boulevard, and happened whenever a car passed. Perhaps it was a ramp in the road. Suddenly I spied a large, angular bar of steel lying on the tarmac. Each time a car ran over it, it jumped. That was it. I drove out and picked up the object which had caused such pangs of anxiety and nervous exhaustion.

After motoring through a high winding path into the mountains we got out near the summit to walk. The afternoon sun was still hot, but quickly the day was coming to an end and, in the distance, the mountains were the blue-purple of Greta's eyes. This is one of the times when I want most to remember her, for now her beauty is at its zenith. Her fine skin has the sheen of a magnolia, her hair falls in smooth, lank bosses, her figure is lithe and thin with flat haunches, flat stomach. She is in high spirits and starts reciting poetry, singing old songs, and being the most companionable of human beings. When she wishes she has the capacity to talk by the hour, and her brain is alert and quick. She recounts how she used to walk alone for miles in the mountains. She would talk to herself, and shout and sing, and "go to the little boys' room," thinking she was all alone and free of the world to do anything. But one day she saw a photograph of herself walking in the mountains, miles away from anyone, and she recognized the spot. It must have been taken by someone hiding in some bushes. "When I saw it I got such a fright. I though maybe I'd be followed and attacked—anything might happen and since the burglary I'm afraid to be alone. I never used to be like that—but I am now!" In that house down that mountainside a friend of hers, now dead, had lived. Once he had become drunk and pointed a revolver at her, and she had fled out into the night and gone into some stranger's house and said: "I find I'm without a car." They had been nice people and, although they must have realized something was very wrong, they had not talked and the story had never reached the newspapers.[1] She reminisced a great deal about attacks in the papers on her, of how Louella Parsons had written—merely, perhaps, because she had refused to appear at some publicity benefit—that she should be deported. As we walked we approached an isolated house, which Greta had watched the inhabitants building with their own hands. A number of alarming dogs ran out to greet her, and she was ecstatically happy patting them and playing with them, although some were so large that they jumped up to her shoulders. Greta said, after fondling a pet donkey: "These must be nice people who live here, so close to nature. People can exist like this in California if they want to—oblivious of the movies and Miss Parsons."

---

[1] Perhaps this was an allusion to her friendship with John Gilbert.

The sky grew dim and in the distance lay the twinkling carpet of Los Angeles glittering in millions of lights. We talked a bit about the terror of another war and the preparations for deadlier weapons that are being made and of the horrors that would result. Greta told me that she was still a Swedish subject, that she had not bothered to fill in the last forms to become an American citizen and that her application had therefore lapsed, so that if Russia took Sweden, then all her money could be blocked. I was quite exercised about this and said that we must bestir ourselves and ask the Mendls,[1] or some such influential people out here, to help, for without money she could not maintain her present independence. It gave me quite a shock to think that this could possibly happen. It would be the final disaster if she were again to become poor when it might be too late to continue making moving pictures.

We drove down the hill. We were to dine in her house, and I was to have my first glimpse of "the Dragon" who was preparing a dinner that was to be a surprise. The room was filled with the pink and scarlet carnations which I had bought in armfuls at a roadside stall. The central heating was turned on, and the table was set with candles and mats we had bought at the Farmers' Market. "The Dragon" turned out to be a most refined German woman of middle age: she obviously looked after Greta like a mother. Fortunately Gertrude, as she is named, does not mind being alone much of the time. The "surprise" was Irish stew, and very well prepared it was. Greta talked about her inability to cope with servants. When she had had a chauffeur she never knew what to do with him in between pictures. She felt self-conscious when he was hanging about doing nothing, so sometimes she would get into the car and tell him to drive to Arrowhead, sixty to seventy miles away. Here she would go on the lake in a canoe and read a book, and later she would telephone for the chauffeur to come all the way back to fetch her. Often she would be driven to Santa Barbara, nearly a hundred miles away. There she would go into a tea shop and, after ten minutes, return to the car and be driven all the way back—a five-hour journey for that one cup of tea. "What a waste of the best years of my life—always alone—it was so stupid

---

[1] Sir Charles Mendl, British diplomat, married to Elsie de Wolfe, interior decorator.

not being able to partake more. Now I'm just a gipsy, living a life apart, but I know my ways and I must not see people. Generally Gertrude serves me my dinner at six-thirty in bed, and three-quarters of an hour later I'm asleep."

_____ *March 5th*

I am obsessed by Greta. The moment I wake in the morning I start to think about her, and so it goes on all day and then in my dreams at night. I telephone early. "Come over as soon as you can." However, Greta was today tired and out of sorts; she again had not slept well and was awake at dawn. She had several items of news. "Black and white" Mercedes had wired to say she was coming to California, and that would make for complications as Mercedes could be very proprietary. Crocker had put a special delivery letter in her box. She had guessed he was around, and so had closed the curtains last night. "My instinct is so strong. He gossips too much, but he can't help it. They're all like children out here: they can never keep anything to themselves. But I never let them know or see anything if I can help it. Once I was out with Cukor[1] and Miss Akins[2] and they wanted to see where I lived. I said they could look at my garden. So on the journey home we drove miles out of their way and I let them look at my pool, and Zoë Akins said: 'It's like being inside of the Vatican,' and I said: 'Well, that's all you can see. You've got to go now.'"

We lay back on the patio sofa in the sun, and Greta brought out her carefully annotated French grammar, and together we went through a Maupassant story. She knows more French than she realizes and her accent is true. She is an apt pupil and has powers of concentration when she wishes, but before the end of the story she became *distraite*, eventually getting up to do some strenuous exercises; then she went to a corner of the lawn to hose herself before lunch. We had the usual salad, and the birds came for their tidbits. We rested. Later we went into Beverly Hills to buy a big basket, for gathering fallen leaves, and more lamb chops for dinner. Greta's appearance caused quite a small commotion in this

_____

[1] George Cukor, film director.
[2] The late Zoë Akins, dramatist and writer of countless film scenarios.

village where everyone is so film-star conscious, but I laughed when, coming out of one shop, there was a most ferocious bulldog who collected a big crowd and created a counterattraction. Greta is really completely immune to the stares of the public and never behaves in a self-conscious way although the attention is very disagreeable to her.

We went to many shops and, as usual, bought nothing. "We are just looking today: we'll come back some other time," she explained. We then motored to another mountain top from which we hiked for hours. Greta sang like a troubadour and appeared irrepressibly youthful. With her long hair and downbeat trousers and sweater she strode along with infinite zest and grace.

_____ *Sunday*

But for a telegram arriving from the Condé Nast publications, asking me to remain on a few extra days to take photographs for them, this would have been my last day here. I was determined that it should remain free: all connections with the outside world were cut. Being Sunday, "the Dragon" was out for the day, and so in her privacy Greta was able to go around as she wished. She did strenuous exercises, she hosed herself, and put on a shirt for preparation of lunch. She hurried around the kitchen with professional efficiency. She showed me how to cut the celery and carrots for the salad. Expertly she tended the stoves, opened and shut the right cupboards, and stacked trays. A sort of devil possesses her under these conditions, and she becomes almost inhuman with little time for pleasantries and remote from affection. When the lunch is prepared, then she can relax and become human again. Greta said: "I can work hard—harder than anyone. Afterwards I can lie down in the sun almost forever: I have an infinite capacity for relaxation."

While lying in the sun, I noticed that Greta appeared tired and drained of sparkle. Early in the morning she had been particularly beautiful but, as the day advanced, her face became pinched. She realized this, but did not let it make any difference. No one has less airs and pretenses to beauty, and if ever her beauty should leave her, she would shrug her shoulders: "It's too bad, but there are compensations. Life is full of interests—I really love life," she keeps repeating. Nevertheless, today we both felt tired and had vitality for nothing. The climate here is treacherous, and I have been stricken with a virus that has attacked my throat.

With an effort we tore ourselves from lazy indolence and dressed for a mountain walk: being a Sunday there would be too many people on the beach. But Greta took a path that was already in the shade, ar ' the cold, damp air affected my throat so that soon I was unable to speak. The night fell abruptly. Back at her house we turned on the heating and pulled the curtains, and after I had drunk a bumper of whisky my voice returned to a croak. Greta put artic! okes and celery in the steamer and broiled veal chops. After the meal, my throat was recovered enough for me to smoke a cigar as I lay on the cedar-colored sofa.

Greta said: "When I went back to Sweden after working in pictures I was a novelty. You see, I was a poor child, and I didn't know any rich aspects of life until I returned and stayed with some friends of mine, and they had an English nannie and I adored that little old woman. Once, when there was a party, I took her in my arms and she looked up into my eyes like a lover, and we danced together until she became dizzy and had to stop. She was so sweet, and that was the first time I began to realize how much I like English people and what they stand for. Now tell me what happens when you go home."

I lay looking up at the ceiling and extemporized about my return. After docking at Southampton, Hare, the faithful driver from the village, would doubtless meet me with the tinny blue car. Along the familiar roads he would give me the local news. At Reddish House with my mother showing me the improvements in the garden: "Here, you see, the terrace has been widened"— "These are the new standard roses"—and my sisters asking if I didn't think the new greenhouse was far too big, I rambled on as if in a trance about Maud, my secretary, until suddenly Greta said: "That's enough of that. I see perfectly that you are hag-ridden."

—————————————————————————————— *Monday*

She said: "I've been digging so hard and putting so much fertilizer into the ground that I'm exhausted, and I shouldn't do that—I look very badly." When I remarked, rather pompously, that, after the all-out war effort in England, it was strange to see men watering lawns here as if there were nothing more important in the world to do, she said: "There is nothing more important."

We started preparations to go out to dinner with the Mendls, who will help with her citizenship papers. Greta put on a blue dress—an event—and a silk scarf of mushroom color. It was dark when we started off on foot: a nice walk, and we arrived in high spirits for our first Hollywood party together. It was fascinating to watch her mesmeric appeal at work. She is like a magnet in attracting crowds, little children and all sorts, to herself. The vast cinema-screen picks up this quality so that the enlarged picture is not just an expanse of emptiness (as is the case with most other actresses in close-up), but has something that draws all the audience to her. It is something she can summon at will, but can never entirely discard, so that when least she wants it she will be surrounded by admirers. It is something that cannot fade, that will always be with her. Tonight this magnetism was turned on at full strength: Greta much lauded as *La Divina*—a lot of pleasantries, flirtations, jokes and badinage. Greta assumed the role of great seductress, then said: "No, Sir Charles, I have no glands." A doctor present took her remarks seriously and they went into a long serious huddle, but Greta laughed about it to me later. The food consisted of a thirty-two year old lobster and a chicken in its heyday—cooked by the Mendls' French chef. Elsie Mendl cried: "We may live in California, but we eat every night in France!" In spite of all the paeans of praise lavished on her, Greta never for a moment lost her realistic approach or her sense of humor, which is always based on reality. With lowered eyelids she laughs and all the men and women become sycophants, but the Scandinavian peasant in her never loses touch.

The evening came to an end without anything helpful being said about the citizenship papers. We walked home and Greta said: "Oh, why did we waste our time like this? How senseless—where does it get you? It's no credit that some people are born without certain social exuberance or curiosity, but somehow it just has never impressed me to meet the king and queen of England or of Sweden. I'm interested in less material things—but that doesn't mean I don't understand people who aren't. I'm sure Elsie Mendl has a full life, and as soon as she wakes in the morning says: 'Well, now, let's make some contacts!'"

When I arrived this morning I found Greta's buggy had disappeared; I guessed she had gone out shopping for more fertilizer. Gertrude admitted me to the holy precincts, and in five minutes my surmise was proved right. Greta, in dirty blue shorts, had hurried off in wild excitement to buy six more sacks of manure. We carted the bags from the car and dragged them to a spot where I noticed the ivy was killing a nearby jasmine. I suggested that an orange tree should be planted in the hole left where another large ivy had recently been dug up. No, she did not accept the suggestion forthwith, and thought perhaps a fig tree would be more suitable. "Perhaps I love fig trees because they are so near to the Bible. But then they're quite bare in winter." Later I found the orange tree idea had been accepted, and she spent the whole day cutting down all the neighboring ivy.

By now my complete retreat from the world was over: I must continue to earn my living. First, I must go and visit my agent; Greta insisted on taking me in her buggy. Just as I was entering his office building, I looked back to wave and saw that the engine of the car had stalled. Frantically she was pulling or stepping on every gadget, in a panic lest she should be discovered. Eventually, with much backfiring, a neck-breaking jerk of the head and terror in her eyes, she drove off.

When, after doing an uninspiring and uninspired job photographing with the local Condé Nast people, I returned to the white-walled enclosure in the garden, I found her feeling very satisfied with her work: she had earned a rest and a "pipe."[1] Once more she appeared to me quite different—less exotic, more vulnerable and human. I kept thinking of her as a pathetic little waif, and she had something of the aquiline, birdlike, appealing quality of my dear Aunt Cada.

We did not know where to dine: all restaurants by this hour would be full. We took our chance on an English roadhouse. Hey presto! a table for two, and the most colossal portions of food you could ever imagine. Greta talked of a walk alone in Sweden: "The ground was shining with stones like diamonds. Suddenly I realized they were part of me: our bodies are all

---

[1] Greta's manner of referring to a cigarette.

particles of a bigger unit. The sudden knowledge of it made me feel so happy, for I felt if we die we become part of the earth again: our ashes are thrown to the seas and they all come back —you can't waste anything in nature. And I love nature, and it was good to realize that we're all part of this entity of which nothing can be destroyed."

After our dinner, we looked in the illuminated windows of antique shops. They were filled with clever, fashionable trash: in her present earthy mood Greta had no feeling for any of it. She behaved like a rustic urchin and whistled and sang "That New Look, That New Look Like a Chicken" in imitation of the comedienne Nancy Walker. I felt rather remote from this hearty little fellow, but the mood was extremely appealing to watch and admire. We went back to her house where, in the hall, she sat listing the number of her empty rooms. I told her that, with her short coat, tight trousers, lanky hair, and pathetic urchin face, she looked like Oliver Twist. It was a picture that I shall never forget—her eyes filled with sympathy and sadness, down-cornered mouth, sensitive nose, and parchment skin. (This last page written while fighting sleep in the train—very hot and claustrophobic. A pity because I would like to try and describe this mood and appearance of Greta, one of the most appealing I had known: she became like a tired fifteen-year-old and more seriously beautiful than I had ever known her.)

_____ *Wednesday*

Greta telephoned early to say she wanted me to make a date with someone else this evening: she must go to bed with a tray at six o'clock and rest. "I feel so depleted—I don't know what's the matter with me."

Arrangements had been made for me to go on a long day's photographing for *Vogue* at Palos Verdes. The expedition was slow in starting, and I telephoned later to tell her I'd just received a telegram from Korda. "Is it bad news?" I read the message that he was unable to make *The Eagle* owing to previous commitments with Eileen Herlie, the actress who had made such a success in the Haymarket Theatre London stage production. But would Garbo like to do *The Cherry Orchard* in September? Greta sighed. "We'll talk this evening when you return."

I got back late. It had been an exasperating day, trying to make photographic masterpieces out of ordinary fashion models in more than ordinary beach clothes. Greta answered the front door wearing a white towel on her head, pajamas, and a dressing gown. She felt and looked "*verwahrlost.*" I noticed her stockings had fallen around her ankles. "Well, it seems the Almighty doesn't want me to do a picture: every time I think I'm going to start again, something goes wrong." If bad luck had not intervened, she would have come to England at the beginning of the war to film *St. Joan.* She had been all set to travel on a Portuguese boat at the time of the bombing of London; but, at the last moment, Gabriel Pascal's plans with Shaw fell through. "That was the first serious disappointment in my career—a hefty blow—after that nothing has happened. I really thought this time we would be doing *Elizabeth. Oy veh!* But somehow I'm never surprised by the most unexpected things; often people may be amazed—I'm not. Although I may never have imagined such things, when they happen they don't seem strange. If they're bad things, then I'm sad but seldom surprised or disappointed. I'm sure I'm a reincarnation."

"But what do you think of the Chekov?" I asked.

"It's not exciting—it's not for me."

"Must I write that in a telegram?"

"No, let's wait. Don't let's discuss it any more."

She then informed me that Harry Crocker had prevailed upon her to dine again this evening with the Mendls in order to meet a Judge O'Connor who might help her with her nationalization papers. So, against her will, she was going but in no mood to enjoy herself. She explained how she would be quite blunt and plain of speech throughout the evening. "It clears the air and people respect it, and it's so much better than adding to the artificiality of a gathering." I left to dine with the Garson Kanins—the only evening I was away from her during this whole full week.

_____ *Thursday*

Greta was in a bad mood: she had been out too late. In spite of her desire to be home by ten-thirty, it had been after midnight before she was able to escape the judge, Sir Charles, Mary Pickford, and all the others who had made her evening exhaust-

ing. Today she was exasperated and her tonsils were hurting her;
she was trying to ward off a cold. She hurried about the house and
garden in a businesslike way. Her hair, hanging in straight folds,
was parted at the nape of her neck. Her neck appeared tall and
thin, her eyes were lowered, her eyebrows twitched high; her
hands looked thin, and her legs long and wiry as she bent down
to get things out of a cupboard or reached for something off a
rack in the immaculate kitchen. I watched but spoke little: I
knew I must use great tact and restraint not to annoy her. I did
not offer to help in the preparation of the lunch (again, it was
Gertrude's day out) as I knew she did not approve of that. As
she hurried into the garden with the trays and plates and swept
up leaves with a broom, it struck me again how unlike every other
film star she is. Her tastes have remained essentially and irrevocably simple, and this domesticity is really what she cares for.
What a true picture of Joan of Arc she would have given, and
what a loss it was that that film was never made.

After our lunch, when lying under the fur rug in the garden,
we discussed *The Cherry Orchard.* Apart from my own selfish
wish to have Greta come to England and to work with her
(for I would insist upon designing her costumes and setting),
this is without a doubt my most loved play, and I would give
almost anything to see Greta as Madame Ranevska—a role that
in many aspects resembles her (the indecision, the incapability
to face facts now). But Greta felt it would not be a public success and that people would put her in another category, as a less
important star. In some ways she has the urge to do more interesting plays, to be experimental in production, and yet she harks
back to the safety of old-time directors and her former cameraman. By degrees, like Madame Ranevska, she arrived at no
decision, changed the subject and talked about last night's
party.

"I was sitting next to a young actress, and I suddenly saw
myself reflected in a mirror and looking lined and wrinkled. I
appeared so old, and I realized how quickly youth has gone—
it has gone in a flash." She then talked of death, and of the
terror that old people must feel when they knew of its approach.
Even for someone as ebullient as Elsie Mendl, who now must
be nearing the ninety mark and suffers a great deal of pain with

a dislocated spine, it must be terrible to know that her bodily existence would soon be taken from her. That knowledge was one of Christ's torments in the garden: He did not wish to die and, like everyone else human, had a terror of the nails and the tomb. It was a frightful prospect for the old to have to face the unknown, to start life again on a new plane, when perhaps they would wish to revert to childhood. She wondered if life would not be easier if we started as old, wise people, and gradually lived to attain an innocent happiness.

Then, apropos of nothing, Greta, relaxing under the sun-umbrella and smoking her "pipe," reminisced about her days at the Theatre School in Stockholm, when she demoralized all the pupils by being inattentive and never learning anything, so that the others too did not bother to make an effort; how she had a friend who was rich, and told of her house in the country and of life in the big cities abroad, and the two often would sit up late at night smoking—and it was all thrilling, enchanting! Now she never more could feel that exuberance.

I persuaded Greta to go into Beverly Hills to buy *The Cherry Orchard* so that we could read the play together. Yes—and more important still—she wanted to buy some more sacks of manure. This is really the one thing that thrills her, and she works frenetically, getting out of bed at screech of dawn to spread the stuff over the front lawn before the neighbors are awake to watch her.

On the way back from the bookshop, I insisted that she should go to the local Museum of Modern Art recently opened here. "Why?" "Because you're interested in contemporary painting, and it's up to you to be a supporter." "Oh, shucks!" Once there, she waxed enthusiastic—in fact, her earlier mood disappeared into one of gaiety and happiness. But, unfortunately, as we left, two silly girls on the sidewalk stared at her. I could not help but be amused at Greta's expression of pained sadness as she drove past them—her eyebrows so high, her mouth turned down, super-sullen, in contrast to the impertinent tilt of her nose.

We were to dine with dear old Winifred (Clemence) Dane, the English novelist and playwright, at the suggestion of Constance Collier who, with the saintlike Phillis at the wheel of her car, would lead the way to the faraway Palisades. I enjoyed the adventure of motoring through the darkness with Greta, who

was somewhat alarmed at having to follow the leading car at
such speed. "It's only thirty-four miles an hour, but at night it
seems so fast." At one point she recklessly waggled the wheel
of the car, which created a very funny "dodgem" effect, and a
bit later a sexily-booted police officer appeared alongside on a
motorcycle and bawled out: "You're going pretty fast, young
lady!" Greta's eyes popped, and she clutched her heart.

Winifred is a huge, ebullient, adorable human being, bursting
with heart and talent, always good company, intelligent and
kind, and habitually surrounded by delightful devotees. Tonight
there were many writers and painters, enormous platters of
Biblical-looking food and, of course, the evening was sympathetic and entertaining. No one tells a story better than Charlie
Chaplin. Tonight he described his fascination for Elinor Glyn,
the scarlet-haired, white-faced, romantic novelist who wrote
Three Weeks and looked like one of her own heroines. Reputedly
Mrs. Glyn brought good taste as well as sex to Hollywood. One
day Chaplin saw her watching a scene from one of her pictures
being played on the movie set. The lights in the early silent
days were incandescent and made everyone appear as if dead.
Elinor Glyn, powdered with thick paint, became bright green
while her teeth, which were false, seemed mauve. Mrs. Glyn
was amused by the scene she was witnessing and laughed widely,
the mauve enamel teeth fully exposed. Suddenly she spied
Chaplin scrutinizing her, and at once she tried to assume her
usual expression of enigmatic mystery but the lips, stretched
wide, would not readily close over the large, dry expanse of
ratelier. At last, with an all-out determined twitch, she finally
managed to cover the dentures and resume her role as sphinx.

Chaplin told another somewhat macabre tale of an eleven-
year-old boy who, when taken out to lunch in a restaurant by
his aunt, was obsessed watching opposite him a man eating alone
who periodically went off into hysterical facial jerks and giggles.
The boy was told not to stare as the poor man had some paralysis.
Chaplin gave generously of his large repertoire of imitations,
including a wry, but excruciatingly funny, ballet of Christian
Scientists who, overcoming the fact that they were the lame and
the halt, leapt into the air with terrible limps and in the most
grotesque, but dreadfully comic, manner, performed their

arabesques and *fouettées.* Greta also did imitations with an ease of manner that took me by surprise: I sometimes forget how professional an artist she is.

One particularly funny vignette she improvised was of how ridiculous Michael Duff and I had appeared when one day we took her out to luncheon in New York. I had put on some weight, and my suit was so tight for me that it revealed *la forma divina:* I wore a sombrero. Michael Duff, in equally old and tight clothes, wore a small green pea as a hat. Blissfully ignorant of the spectacle we created, we spluttered and stuttered about the British Empire as we waited for the street lights to turn green. Then, stiff as ninepins, we strode very quickly in formation, saluting acquaintances on our way down Fifty-Seventh Street. To me, Greta's would-be English accents were not recognizable as such, but the pantomime was brilliant and received the applause it deserved.

But the evening cost Greta a great effort. When we drove home again she had little vitality and said: "It's awful to be bored, but really for once I was. If I saw these people every day I'd perish."

When, in her hall, I tenderly bade her goodnight she said: "I haven't been very nice to you today. If I'd felt well, I would have been much more loving." This warmed and comforted me, and made me love her more dearly. We waved in the lantern light, and by the time I had walked to Sunset Boulevard she had reached her bedroom window and was silhouetted against the light, and again we waved at each other. Later she told me all she could recognize was my shadow in the lights of passing cars. Each evening this pantomime takes place; it is a delightful ritual and sends me to bed feeling content.

Friday

Greta had, of course, been up early to distribute the sacks of fertilizer over the lawns: she was still hard at work. I had an elaborate schedule of business dates that would occupy me until after lunch time, but I would then call for her to go with my agent, Carlton Allsop, who had arranged for me to see Greta's old picture, *Anna Karenina,* in a private room at MGM Studios.

It would be almost an uncanny experience to watch this great epic in the presence of *La Divina*. I had told Allsop that I would like to bring a friend to join us. "Fine—I'll call for you." When Greta, with scarves flying, came rushing out and I introduced her, Allsop's face went scarlet with astonishment. Greta at once became inevitably, irrevocably, and so easily and honestly the seductress that Allsop was completely bewitched.

"Well, well, it takes Beaton to get me to the studios for the first time in six years!" As we approached Metro, she became quite a bit flustered. It was an emotional experience for her. The studios, which one might almost say she had partly created, had been also for so long her prison; she had been unhappy there, but she owed them a lot, too, and to return after such an interval made her feel self-conscious. She did not know the men at the gate any more, none of the faces were familiar; nobody moving along corridors and alleyways recognized her and, as usual, she was adept at concealing herself.

We were shown to a drab little projection room—not at all important but quite private—and the lights went out. The titles were flashed on the screen, the lion roared, the rather *schmalzy* orchestra blared Tchaikowsky, and Greta, next to me, lit an Old Gold.

During the running of the film, Greta would interject: "Those were real Russians"—"That's very well done"—"Those were feathers" (apropos snowstorm)—"A woman's crowning glory—or is it a fuzz?" (apropos her hairdo in the ballroom sequence). The telling of the story was done in a straightforward, clear way; the scenes were suitably chosen and full of vigor. The background to the lives of the main characters was well established, so that one realized why the romance was impossible and disaster overtook Anna. Although we have condemned Hollywood for such widespread vulgarization of the classics, this popular epic possessed a great deal of the bare bones of the Tolstoy tragedy, and the superficial shortcomings were merely in the trimmings. Even more than her physical beauty it was Greta's voice that struck a note of such warmth and humanity: deep and melodious with such tenderness and such strength, with so many varying lights and shades, it comes across the sound track exactly as it is in life. Many of the sentiments expressed might have been said by her any day; the effect was uncanny.

Greta was pleased how little the picture had dated; she gave Salka Viertel much credit for getting such authenticity onto the screen. "When I read the script it was the first time that I was a little thrilled." Carlton Allsop behaved with tact and charm. "Mister Mayer would die of delight if he knew you had been to his studio today. You have become his goddess—you're a living legend." "Thank you—thank you." As we emerged from the little theatre, and the operator saw to whom he had been running the reels, he tottered as if about to fall. Greta, behind her hair, slouched out of the studio, and once back in the car felt relieved and safe. But she had been pleased to see the picture and delighted that it was something of which she need never be anything but rather proud.

_____   _____ *Saturday*

Gray skies—the first time I had not awakened to brilliant sun in the orange tree outside my window. It was cold and blustery. I wondered what Greta would be doing in her garden. When I went round, Gertrude shook her head and said: "She has been doing much heavy work, cutting away the branches to keep warm." Greta was now sweeping leaves with a fan-shaped broom. "Oh, no other woman would do it!" She lit her "pipe" and relaxed, but she did not appear to be in a loving mood. This morning we became two professionals discussing her business, her film scripts. Having read *The Cherry Orchard,* she did not consider Ranevska a suitable role. "But aren't you touched by the pathos and amused by the absurdity of human nature? There are laughs as well as tears of regret." No: she had no enthusiasm for any of it. "And its particular theme is so pertinent today." "No-ow!" she snapped. I saw the chances of our life together in England were becoming smaller. Oh, hell! What to concoct as a reply to Korda? "Let's leave it another day."

As we sheltered, under rugs, on the garden sofa, the front doorbell rang—an unusual event. Soon Gertrude appeared, bearing a novel that Allsop had submitted to Greta as the basis for a possible moving picture: the book was tied up with orchids and tulle. Greta looked wonderingly at the orchids: they were pale mauve, fleshy, and with yellow centers. "I must say I've never seen more beautiful specimens; but what a pity Hollywood has ruined these flowers!" By the time she had unwired them she was quite exasperated.

Suddenly the rain came down in twenty-five-cent drops. A scramble to clear up. Everything placed under cover. Then the rain stopped. "What shall we do? Remain here? Have our lunch trays here?" I knew Greta frets at being indoors whenever she can be in the fresh air, so we braved the elements swathed in scarves. She told me of how, in the rainy season, she would sit under the garden umbrella, dressed in mackintosh and hat and overcoats galore, wrapped in a tarpaulin rug, having her lunch on a tray while the rain poured cats and dogs around her. After her lunch, she would remain in the torrent with a book, delighted not to be indoors.

Later, the rain did come down pretty violently, so we decided to go shopping; more fertilizer was needed. We also visited a nursery garden where, in the pouring rain, we walked for miles to choose the much-discussed orange tree. Greta enjoyed pottering in the downpour, but the rain became tropical and the gardeners thought us mad to be here. Our shop assistant slipped off a greasy plank and fell headlong into the mud. After more shopping in Beverly we bought tomorrow's newspaper. "It's to look at, at night, to make me feel I'm in a hurry to go to sleep —otherwise I stay awake. If I could have a nap in the daytime, all my troubles would be over. But ever since I was a child I've had difficulty in sleeping. In the old days it didn't matter much, but now I feel, oh, depleted, and I look so pale!"

We are being very social, for we have one engagement each day. This evening we arranged to go to Clifton Webb, the actor, and a mutual friend. Long ago, Greta had told me of some man who had said: "We're not getting any younger. Why don't we go our own ways, but preserve something for our old age by getting married?" Now I discovered Clifton was the person, but his remark was only made on the spur of the moment, and on another spur from Greta, dismissed. We felt obligated to see his new house, a rambling bungaloid affair of no originality or interest. Neither he nor his indefatigable octogenarian mother, Mabel, who wore satin pajamas, spared us a detail of the interior wrought-iron work and pebble-dash walls, hung liberally with signed, glossy, publicity photographs of the film elite.

I enjoyed listening to Greta's reactions to Clifton's tart anecdotes. In some cases she knew a lot about the topic in question,
but it suited her to feign ignorance. I noticed how careful she
was not to give any information that might be taken in evidence
against her. She plays quite a game with her fellow beings.

Clifton gave a horrifying description of Marion Davies at the
recent public dinner party given to celebrate the "somethingth"
anniversary of the gossip-writer Louella Parsons. "Crazed by
drink" soon after the soup, Marion was led from the hall. Later
Greta said: "It would be so much nicer if everyone behaved
well and didn't remark upon these things. If no one talked, no
one would know—it's *that* simple!"

We returned late for Gertrude's dinner at the card table, but
Gertrude was not worried. After a meal of veal chops we sprawled
on the drawing room sofa, and talked about much that had to be
said before I return to New York, London, and the indefinite
future. It is impossible to bind Greta. She is a virtuoso at delaying
tactics, shelving decisions and leaving a situation in the air.
That Mr. Mayer was ever able to make her sign a contract
earns him my full admiration. I was not successful this evening.

As I trailed my weary body home, I wondered if I had made
any advance towards an arrangement for a moving picture or a
trip to England, and I had to admit to myself that I had not.

Sunday, March 14th

When I rang the front doorbell, there was a long delay before
it was answered. I was about to explore the garden when she
shouted: "Beaton?" and poked her head out of a ground-floor
window. She had not been able to see if it was I who rang and
daren't open the door to a stranger. We linked arms and went
into the garden. A tragedy—the orange tree we had bought
had thorns! She did not want to plant an orange tree with thorns;
she was much perturbed about it. We asked everyone we saw
whether oranges do have thorns, and I suspect that she will
take back this five-dollar tree and exchange it for another.

We started to discuss the telegram that I must send in reply
to Korda. "Put 'G.' instead of my name. They even get news here
from telegrams, and the gossip columns write 'So-and-so is long-

distancing so-and-so.' Always be careful, and if anyone asks you anything, just say 'I don't know.' It doesn't demean you, and it makes it quite simple."

In spite of yesterday's deluge the drought is serious and, in an effort to save water, all clocks had today been advanced an hour. Before one expected it, lunch time had arrived. So Greta, delighted at the chance of a delay, suggested: "Let's talk about the telegram after lunch."

Greta was less efficient than usual, for she burned the matzohs, and the tomato soup wasn't hot enough. After coffee we composed a sad message to Korda, rejecting *The Cherry Orchard*, and Greta concluded: "I know if I don't do a picture this year, I never will again."

"But won't you please come to England in any case? A freighter could take you straight from California to England."

"I don't know. I must stay put a bit and rest."

That means she will remain within these walls, doing the jobs of a handyman, exercising, gardening, and sunning herself. A happy enough existence, and more or less peaceful, but sad that the world does not benefit by her unique quality. However, she would answer: "What is one film more or less?"

I felt restless. I had long wanted to do a drawing of her, and this was my last opportunity, but she would not remain still for a moment. It would have been good, too, to have some snapshot mementos of her in the intimacy of her secluded garden, but when I produced my Rolleiflex, she put on a discontented pout and I knew the pictures could not be successful. Her hair suddenly became fluffy and messy, and she looked more like a film star than herself. I was appalled to realize how much her appearance sways my affections. I became rather sad. Later, when she went upstairs to dress in "mad clothes" for an outing and wrapped a shawl around her head, I adored her again and my heart became like pulp.

Then suddenly she asked: "Are your sisters smaller than I am?" I could not understand her interest, until later when she produced an overcoat which she said she would like to give to one of them, as she knew clothes rationing was still in force at home. It is interesting to discover along what subterranean channels her brain works. If one waits patiently, one will solve any mystery; but she will not be precipitated into committing herself until she has made the necessary preparations in her mind.

We set off in the car to pay two visits. First, to the eccentric, scarlet-haired old Baroness d'Erlanger who, undoubtedly, is one of the most remarkable human beings now unaccountably living in an ordinary suburban little villa in this tight little community. She was a prewar figure of artistic tastes and a banker's fortune, whose original flair for entertaining was a part of London and Venetian life. As a widow unable to look after her money affairs she migrated to the sun of California. Since I had first glimpsed her in Venice, in a magenta dressing gown and painting a pumpkin gold, Catherine had become an early supporter of mine, and she always proved a loyal friend. She helped to bring back to life the Tiepolo-frescoed Malcontenta, the beautiful villa built by Palladio on the Brenta; she created an Aladdin's cave out of a fisherman's house in Venice. She could be relied upon always to be doing something startling and original in the way of decoration. I felt a glimpse of her might stimulate and entertain Greta, and certainly Catherine would appreciate Garbo's visit—especially as the film colony here have completely ignored her.

In her days of grandeur Catherine lived in Byron's house in Piccadilly, but now her money has been "frozen," and her emeralds stolen from their hiding place (sewn in a cushion) by one of the "naughty boys" she likes to have around her. Greta was, at first, somewhat aghast at the litter, salvaged from the past, of broken Venetian glass and shells, the cluttered mess of eighteenth-century scraps, witchballs, metal fringes and brocades, and the vast collection of Catherine's own paintings of her friends, all looking like waxworks. Whereas Catherine could find delightful rubbish in the markets of Venice, Paris, or London, here she must rely upon the stalls onto which the worst Hollywood junk was thrown out of studio "prop" departments. Catherine had lost her eye for this kind of thing, and the mess was interspersed with cans and cartons of patent foods. However, Catherine was delighted with her new home. "Come and admire my swimming pool with its walls of 'cabochon emeralds.'" The "cabochons" turned out to be beer bottles—thousands of them

placed one on top of the other; Catherine saw the effect as beautiful. Two naked young men appeared. "These are my Greek gods,"
Catherine said, by way of introduction. She showed us her
latest scrapbooks made of clippings from tawdry magazines,
which she intended to sell at vast sums to the research department of Columbia Pictures. Greta responded to Catherine's
enjoyment of her present existence, with no regrets for the
past or the onslaught of old age.

After such mess and litter, Greta was impressed by the anti-
septic antidote provided by George Platt Lynes's essentially
modern house. Greta appreciated the restraint of having a room
that possesses only a table, a chair and a picture. George, a
photographer with a pristine talent very much his own, who was
one of my earliest New York friends, until recently lived in
New York in a mossy oasis of green plush, and a Forest of Arden
of flowering plants. His emigration here has not yet benefited
his work. In fact, his friends are worried; the move from the
east to west may prove a disaster.[1] George, unlike Catherine,
did not seem at peace in this new environment, but he was
being comforted by the presence of his old friend, Katherine
Anne Porter.

I was pleased to hear Greta asking these friends about me.
"How long have you known him?" "Where was that—in Venice?
In Connecticut?" When, having met with her usual effortless
success, Greta was about to leave, and remarked to Katherine
Anne Porter that she didn't know when they'd meet again,
Mrs. Porter, somewhat surprisingly, replied: "Oh, don't worry
—the world is such a small place today."

Later, Greta decided it would do us good to walk to our dinner
at a spaghetti restaurant. So, in the dusk, down an avenue of
royal palms, we strode like Grenadiers. It is unusual for the
inhabitants of Beverly Hills to go for a hike, and a pedestrian
is likely to be arrested by roving police in cars on suspicion of
loitering with intent of theft. However, we were unmolested
and enjoyed being able to see into the lighted windows of the
houses each side of the road: in many of them a Sunday cocktail

---

[1] George's photographic work was in fact too realistic to be appreciated by the film studios.
He became disillusioned, ill, and died at an early age.

party was in progress. How thankful we were not to be there in any of them!

At Peppino's, sitting at a small table in a corner, her face lit from below by a flickering candle, Greta held forth as if we had never before had an opportunity to talk.

She discussed food, and her dislikes and likes. "The English know nothing of food. I used to eat quite a large lunch when I was first working in the studio: all sorts of mixed things—a dill pickle, an apple tart, pastry, meat—and I felt so heavy and ill. Then I learned about food and just brought my own—a basket with sour cream and fruit—and I would feel so light and easy. You see, I can't mix foods—I don't feel well; I like just one thing." (It always amuses, and sometimes embarrasses me when, at even the best restaurants, Greta takes her knife and fork, looks around nervously to see if the waiter is looking in her direction, then dips them in her tumbler of water before surreptitiously wiping them on her napkin.)

She talked about her youth, and how unhappy she was. When I interjected: "But you've always told me you were such a tomboy and had so much fun leading the other children into mischief." She replied: "Cecil Beaton, how can you say such things! There are three hundred and sixty-five days in the year!" She talked of the first time she had seen an animal killed. She was a city child, living in Stockholm, but once, in the country, she saw some men take a knife to a sheep, hit it on its head, cut it open, and pour its blood into a basin. She still could see the scene vividly, and with such horror, although she was only twelve at the time. She had stood there, rooted to the spot, with mouth wide open, incapable of moving, aghast that such things could happen. "Oh, how awful life is!" she kept saying.

There are things and people she still doesn't wish to discuss: Maurice Stiller, who was her Pygmalion, is never mentioned except by implication, or as "someone I have great devotion for— and always will." She continued: "But people have so often used me—have hurt me by doing things that have surprised me. I have known crooks and they've treated me so brutally, and although I have been shocked I still don't believe they're bad. I know there's good in each person, and it's quite simple to bring out the best. If the other unimportant people want to harm you, how can they? They haven't got the power like the more fortunate of us; the others can't give. We can offer little things that can be of great importance, but none of us are important really. By a miracle we have become privileged people, and we can afford to tell the truth. But if you tell many people the truth they'll recoil and are shocked, embarrassed or afraid." She rambled on: "I love life—it's really thrilling," and she looked ecstatic. "Existence is so full of surprises and vitality and goodness."

Greta later said that, in her youth, she was "ready very early for life," but that since then she had not advanced or developed. Suddenly she found herself no longer a promising youngster. She said so sweetly: "I can never think of myself as being of advanced years. I don't feel any different, but it worries me that I don't know where the years have gone." She still behaves, and moves, and thinks like a young girl. And if, on some days, her face is pale and drawn, she always possesses the unspoiled quality of a child, and the passing years have only made her beauty more sensitive and delicate.

I realize how clumsy it is of me to force conversation with her, to try and make her be serious when she is not in the mood. The moments of communication come on their own. It was following an allusion to her one visit to Italy—to the Villa Cimbrone in Ravello[1]—that we progressed to the tricky subject of the press. For it was here that reporters hounded her to such an extent that she could never leave the precincts of the villa: even the garden was within range of telescopic lenses. After a few days the "English woman" (whoever she may have been) living next door, became exasperated and asked Greta point blank: "And if you hate the press so much, why did you join the ranks and become a film star?" Greta was baffled and said: "When one enters a new life one does not know where it will lead. One thinks of the magic, not of the disadvantages, and often the magic turns into something quite different."

Maybe I was in a truculent mood, but I wanted to know just at what point the press became so exasperating to her. "Would it not save you a lot of trouble, whenever you take a trip abroad, if instead of running with them in hot pursuit you posed for one picture?"

---

[1] In the company of Leopold Stokowski.

"They are never satisfied: they will never let you go. Besides, one gets mad with them." Greta branched off: "You've no idea of the power of the press! You can have no privacy at all unless you lock yourself in your back yard, and even there you're not safe." Once on a visit to New York, she said, Walter Winchell had bribed a maid in her hotel, during her absence, to let him into her bedroom in order to report on anything of interest he could discover. "If the editor says: 'Go and get that story—or else . . .' then the reporters become desperate; they'll do anything. Those people can wreck your life—look what they did to Lindbergh!"

"But surely some film stars cannot have enough of it? Someone like Lana Turner enjoys it!"

"Cecil Beaton, how can you say such things! Even Lana Turner comes to a point when she can't stand it. Suppose she's in love with a man, and the rumor floats around. Then the press gets hold of it, and as she's on her way to see him, they photograph her." Greta became quite exasperated by my stupidity. She felt I had been flippant, that altogether I was not a very serious-minded person.

"Oh, you know, it's only serious people who can afford to be really frivolous," I said in a desperate attempt to be Wildean.

Greta considered that I was fortunate in that I had not suffered much in life. I wondered if one can estimate the relative amount of misery that goes into a lifetime? Certainly I have had a comparatively sheltered life. But does that necessarily mean that I have endured less pain than others who have had to face violence and tragedy? Yes, I have known suffering, but I have learned to live with my troubles. Is it not as well if I give the impression of going through life with wings? Few people want to hear about the plight of others.

When the talk turned towards loneliness, Greta said what a dangerous responsibility it was to become attached to any particular person. Again I disagreed. "It's so cruel when things change," she said. "When you no longer love someone, and he continues to feel just the same about you." I knew to whom she was referring and, wishing to further my own cause, I suggested: "But one cannot just resign oneself to negativism and holding back emotions. In any case, you've done that too long."

"I should be Christlike and be all things to all men."

I was determined not to allow her to be her usual evasive

self: she must listen to me. Doggedly I expounded on the possibilities of what we could make of a life together. We would
add to each other's interests and activities, we would fire each
other's enthusiasms. On a more prosaic level, the idea that we
might have a child and could have also just those things that
others have in the course of their, perhaps rather ordinary,
lives, might prove to us to be more fantastic and exciting than
anything that had happened. No, she could never undertake
the terrifying responsibility of having a child. If she had one,
she would "behead it." I was shocked at her joke.

In her hallway we lingered: then the elaborate pantomime of
the waving from door and window. As I trudged up the steep
asphalt drive to my bungalow for the last time I realized that,
having done little for the past few months but devote myself to
Greta, I would be going back tomorrow to an existence without
her. It would be like starting life over again.

_____ ***Departure**/ Monday, March 15th, 1948*

Brilliant sun to speed me, a turquoise sky through the orange
blossoms. An anxious telephone call from Greta: she could not
quite find words. "What—what are you doing? Shall I fetch you?"
I hopped into a taxi to my favorite flower stall and bought her
an armful of mixed flowers, all colors, ranunculi, stocks, gardenias,
roses, orchids, hyacinths, freesias. I rushed to take them to her.
Gertrude said in quite a shocked voice: "She takes on the heaviest work!" Greta was in gray shorts, digging out the last vestiges
of the root of the ivy from a deep hole where she intends planting
our orange tree. I left the flowers and ran to my room, to return
as soon as possible with my baggage. By the time I got back to
her, there was only half-an-hour to spend together before I must
leave for the long train journey to New York.

We sat in the sun, and I felt rather as if I were about to under-
go an amputation. I could hear that my voice was very clear and
cold. We talked about nothing in particular, and then Greta
asked from what station I leave? "Los Angeles," I answered.

"Why not go to Pasadena? The train arrives there half an
hour later. I'll motor you there."

"No, please, it'll mean your driving all the way back, an
hour's journey—alone."

"That I don't mind, but I've been doing such hard work, and I don't know if my arms will stand the effort. Look, they're trembling now." She stood up and held her arms out as if she were a water diviner and they trembled violently as if a spring had been discovered.

"Darling, I'm accustomed to traveling alone."

"But it's so cold and lonely not to have anyone wave good-bye. Why didn't I think of it before? I want to go to Pasadena."

Again she stood up and looked down at her quivering arms. On the ground was a huge basketful of root she had hacked away for two or three hours—hard, solid, rocklike. I took the spade and saw how difficult it was even to chip off a small fragment—little wonder her arms felt as if they would drop off. For ten minutes she battled with herself. "I want to go to Pasadena, but I'm so indecisive. I don't know if I can. Are you ever indecisive? I don't believe you are." It would be half-past four by the time she returned here without having had any lunch. I suggested: "Better to make a clean break now. I'll ask Gertrude to get me a taxi, and go straight to Los Angeles." She pouted and again held onto an invisible steering wheel. "But I want to go to Pasadena."

"Just take me for a last tour of the garden and show me what you're planning to do."

With arms linked, we walked a few paces, and then a very unexpected thing happened. I was feeling quite matter-of-fact and hardheaded when, suddenly, I realized that there was to be a break from someone who had been important to me for a long time: my cheeks became wet. My whole chest shook and quivered convulsively. I was completely jellylike and incapable of holding back my feelings. It had never struck me quite how much I would mind this parting. I have never felt more sorry for myself, or so much alone. Life held no immediate prospects, and I hated having to carry on with little more than courage and trumped-up confidence. I knew that, in some ways, I had scored a victory over Greta: I knew that I had made her love me. Yet I had failed to give her the strength to act, to have the ability to take a more positive stand with herself. In spite of our closeness, I realized that there was nothing more concrete about our future. I had no hold over her. She had for so long designed her life to protect herself—locked up in her walled garden, with "the little man" on duty as Cerberus to keep reality at bay—that even I could get no closer than before. I had won the battle, but the main campaign had been lost. Greta had conquered again by sheer stasis. This, after many victories over frustration, was the crux of my agony.

We clasped one another. Greta looked utterly miserable, but my lack of restraint had given her an incentive to be stoic; yet her face contained a world of sympathy and sadness. She comforted me: "You see how difficult and neurotic I am—I'm impossible to get along with."

"Oh, no," I moaned, "I really do want you—I love you so much," and once again I trembled. After a moment I blurted: "It's just that we've had too little time—we've tried to crowd so much into these days. But I *can* compete."

We stood still on the small patch of lawn, our arms still entwined. "I'm ashamed of myself; I shouldn't let myself go." Greta replied: "I expect I shall do the same in a few minutes when I realize that Cecil has gone."

My sorrow was cut short by Gertrude coming out to announce the arrival of the taxi.

"Oh, if only I'd thought earlier about going to Pasadena we could have been together another hour!"

I shook hands with Gertrude and turned to clutch at Greta once again. My face was hot and red and my eyes swollen and still a stream poured down each side of my nose. Greta stood, half hiding around her front door, a timid child with a hand up to her mouth, her eyes wide and full of pity.

I got into the Yellow Cab, and pulled down one window and waved. The child waved back. The taxi moved forward and turned in a semicircle. I pulled down the other window and waved. I could hardly see the blurred figure. The driver put his foot down on the accelerator, and we were off.

The driver then started a conversation about his having been to England—he'd fought in England. Did I know Kid Berg? The driver had been a heavyweight champion of the world himself. He'd retired now, but he'd still got his health—that was the most important thing, wasn't it?. . . . I did not answer. But he continued. I did not hear what he was saying. It was as well that he did not notice in his mirror that he was in charge of a middle-aged crackpot who was convulsed with sobs.

Garbo by Beaton

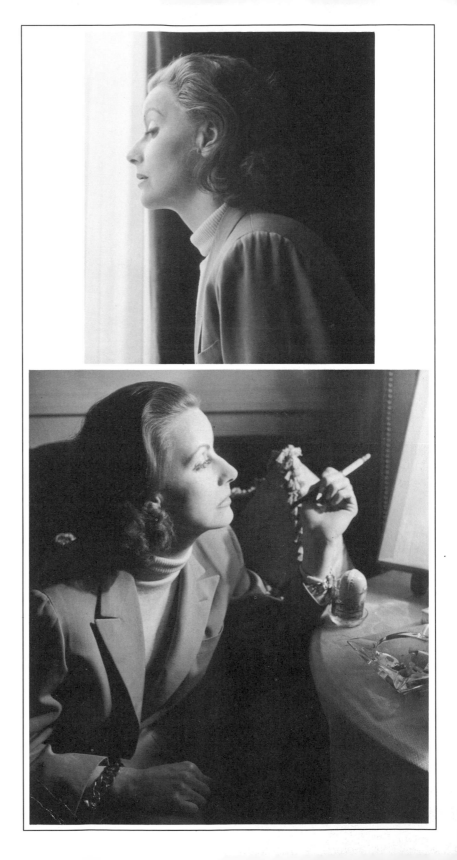

index